The Cambridge Introduction to
Narrative

The Cambridge Introduction to Narrative is designed to help readers
understand what narrative is, how it is constructed, how it acts upon us,
how we act upon it, how it is transmitted, and how it changes when the
medium or the cultural context change. Porter Abbott emphasizes that
narrative is found not just in the arts but everywhere in the ordinary
course of people's lives. Abbott grounds his treatment of narrative by
introducing it as a human phenomenon that is not restricted to literature,
film, and theatre, but is found in all activities that involve the
representation of events in time. At the same time, he honors the fact
that out of this common capability have come rich and meaningful
narratives that we come back to and reflect on repeatedly in our lives. An
indispensable tool for students and teachers alike, this book will guide
readers through the fundamental aspects of narrative.

H. Porter Abbott is Professor in the Department of English at the
University of California, Santa Barbara. He is the author of *The Fiction of
Samuel Beckett: Form and Effect, Diary Fiction: Writing as Action, Beckett
Writing Beckett: the Author in the Autograph,* and editor of *On the Origin of
Fictions: Interdisciplinary Perspectives,* a special issue of the journal *SubStance.*

The Cambridge Introduction to
Narrative

H. PORTER ABBOTT

CAMBRIDGE
UNIVERSITY PRESS

PUBLISHED BY THE PRESS SYNDICATE OF THE UNIVERSITY OF CAMBRIDGE
The Pitt Building, Trumpington Street, Cambridge, United Kingdom

CAMBRIDGE UNIVERSITY PRESS
The Edinburgh Building, Cambridge CB2 2RU, UK
40 West 20th Street, New York NY 10011-4211, USA
477 Williamstown Road, Port Melbourne, VIC 3207, Australia
Ruiz de Alarcón 13, 28014 Madrid, Spain
Dock House, The Waterfront, Cape Town 8001, South Africa

http://www.cambridge.org

First published 2002
Fifth printing 2004

Printed in the United Kingdom at the University Press, Cambridge

Typeface Bembo 11/12.5 pt.   *System* LaTeX 2_ε [TB]

A catalogue record for this book is available from the British Library.

ISBN 0 521 65033 X hardback
ISBN 0 521 65969 8 paperback

For Jason and Byram

Contents

Illustrations

The author and publisher are grateful to be able to include the following illustrations.

Preface

The purpose of this book is to help readers understand what narrative is, how it is constructed, how it acts upon us, how we act upon it, how it is transmitted, how it changes when the medium or the cultural context changes, and how it is found not just in the arts but everywhere in the ordinary course of people's lives, many times a day. This last point is especially important. We are all narrators, though we may rarely be aware of it. A statement as simple as "I took the car to work" qualifies as narrative. As we seek to communicate more detail about events in time, we become involved in increasingly complex acts of narration. We are also the constant recipients of narrative: from newspapers and television, from books and films, and from friends and relatives telling us, among other things, that they took the car to work. Therefore, though much of this book is devoted to narrative in literature, film, and drama, it grounds its treatment of narrative by introducing it as a human phenomenon that is not restricted to literature, film, and theater, but is found in all activities that involve the representation of events in time. In its early chapters, the book moves back and forth between the arts and the everyday. At the same time, the book honors the fact that out of this common capability have come rich and meaningful narratives that we come back to and reflect on repeatedly in our lives.

This book is descriptive rather than prescriptive; it seeks to describe what happens when we encounter narrative, rather than to prescribe what should happen. All along the way questions arise that are very much alive in current work on narrative. These are often tough issues, and, with a few important exceptions (as for example the definition of narrative that I employ), I try to keep these issues open. In organization, the book introduces the subject of narrative by moving outward from simplicity to complexity, from the component parts of narrative in Chapters Two and Three to its numerous effects, including its extraordinary rhetorical power and the importance of the concept of "closure," in Chapters Four and Five. Chapter Six deals with narration and the key role of the narrator.

Chapters Seven and Eight, in taking up issues connected with the interpretation of narrative, shift the focus from the power of narrative to the power of readers and audiences. In this sense, narrative is always a two-way street. Without our collaboration, there is no narrative to begin with. And if it is true that we allow ourselves to be manipulated by narrative, it is also true that we do manipulating of our own. These chapters take up this interplay of audiences and narratives in the process of interpretation and culminate in Chapter Eight's treatment of three fundamentally different ways of reading that we all engage in: intentional, symptomatic, and adaptive. The differences between them are important and bring in their wake different understandings of what we mean by meaning in narrative.

Chapter Nine turns to the differences that different media make in narrative and to what happens when you move a story from one medium to narrate it in another. Chapter Ten opens out the subject of character, both as a function of narrative and as intimately connected with what we loosely call "the self" in autobiography. In the final two chapters, we return to the broad subject of narrative's role in culture and society. Much of politics and the law is a contest of narratives. Chapter Eleven looks at the ways in which these conflicts of narrative play out, particularly in the law. And in Chapter Twelve, I look at the ways in which narrative can also be an instrument by which storytellers and readers seek to negotiate the claims of competing and often intractable conflicts. Stories, for example, that are told over and over again (cultural masterplots) are often efforts to settle conflicts which are deeply embedded in a culture.

In this book, I have endeavored to avoid writing another anatomy of narrative, of which there are fine examples available in print (Genette, 1980; Prince, 1987). Instead, I have sought at all times to restrict focus to the most useful concepts and terminology. The field of narratology has produced a great arsenal of distinctions and terms. I have kept my selection of these to a minimum, using only those that are indispensable. These key terms will be found throughout the book and are featured in boldface in the Glossary. As such, this is a foundational book. The tools and distinctions it supplies can be employed across the whole range of nameable interpretive approaches.

Nonetheless, by selecting the terms I do and by treating them the way I do, I have written a study that is bound to be controversial. The simple reason for this is that all studies of narrative are controversial. Despite a burst of energetic and highly intelligent research over the last thirty years and the genuine progress that has been made, there is not yet a consensus on any of the key issues in the study of narrative. If, like language, narrative is an inevitable human capability that we deploy every day without conscious effort, it is also, like language, a complex and fascinating field that often seems to defy our best analytical efforts at exactitude. Therefore, and above all else, I have aimed at clarity in this introduction to narrative. I have also been highly selective in recommending, at the ends of Chapters Two through Twelve, secondary texts that seem at this date to have stood the test of time (though for some areas, like hypertext narrative, the works have only barely been tested). At the same time, it is important to acknowledge here the assistance I have received from the work on narrative by many brilliant scholars, among them: M. M. Bakhtin, Mieke Bal, Ann Banfield, Roland Barthes, Emile Benveniste, Wayne Booth, David Bordwell, Edward Branigan, Claude Bremond, Peter Brooks, Ross Chambers, Seymour Chatman, Dorrit Cohn, Jonathan Culler, Jacques Derrida, Umberto Eco, Monika Fludernik, Gérard Genette, A. J. Greimas, David Herman, Paul Hernadi, Wolfgang Iser, Roman Jakobson, Fredric Jameson, Robert Kellogg, Frank Kermode, George P. Landow, Claude Lévi-Strauss, Wallace Martin, Scott McCloud, J. Hillis Miller, Bill Nichols, Roy Pascal, Gerald Prince, Vladimir Propp, Peter J. Rabinowitz, Eric Rabkin, David Richter, Paul Ricoeur, Brian Richardson, Robert Scholes, Shlomith Rimmon-Kenan, Marie-Laure Ryan, Saint Augustine, Victor Shklovsky, Franz Stanzel, Tzvetan Todorov, Boris Tomashevsky, Hayden White, and Trevor Whittock.

I want to give special thanks for hands-on assistance to Josie Dixon who caught on to the idea of this book right away and never failed in her encouragement. Her successor at Cambridge University Press, Ray Ryan, together with Rachel De Wachter, gave helpful guidance during the later stages. Derek Attridge read at least two versions of the manuscript for Cambridge and made some sharp suggestions which I incorporated. Fiona Goodchild, Jon Robert Pearce, Paul Hernadi, and Anita Abbott all read it through (the latter more than once!). I am thankful to them for their many shrewd and helpful comments. To my teaching assistants and many students over the years in a course called "The Art of Narrative," I send my thanks for their ability and (more important) their willingness to pose wonderful questions I never would have thought to ask. Finally, thanks are long overdue to my former colleague Hugh Kenner, whose ability to make revelatory connections, and to do so with an efficiency that always surprises, is to my mind unsurpassed.

Acknowledgments

The author and publisher are grateful for permission to quote from the following texts.

"A Common Confusion," by Franz Kafka, from Willa and Edwin Muir (trans.), *The Great Wall of China*, copyright © 1936, 1937 by Heinr. Mercy Sohn, Prague. Copyright © 1946 and renewed 1974 by Shocken Books, Inc. Reprinted by permission of Schocken Books, distributed by Pantheon Books, a division of Random House, Inc.

"Bedtime Story," by Jeffrey Whitmore reprinted with permission from *The World's Shortest Stories* edited by Steve Moss, copyright © 1998, 1995 by Steve Moss, published by Running Press, Philadelphia and London.

"Taboo," by Enrique Anderson Ibert, from Isabel Reade (trans.), *The Other Side of the Mirror*, copyright © 1966 by Southern Illinois University Press.

Chapter 1

Narrative and life

The universality of narrative

When we think of narrative, we usually think of it as art, however modest. We think of it as novels or sagas or folk tales or, at the least, as anecdotes. We speak of a gift for telling stories. But as true as it is that narrative can be an art and that art thrives on narrative, narrative is also something we all engage in, artists and non-artists alike. We make narratives many times a day, every day of our lives. And we start doing so almost from the moment we begin putting words together. As soon as we follow a subject with a verb, there is a good chance we are engaged in narrative discourse. "I fell down," the child cries, and in the process tells her mother a little narrative, just as I have told in this still unfinished sentence a different, somewhat longer narrative that includes the action of the child's telling (" 'I fell down,' the child cries").

Given the presence of narrative in almost all human discourse, there is little wonder that there are theorists who place it next to language itself as *the* distinctive human trait. Fredric Jameson, for example, writes about the "all-informing process of *narrative*," which he describes as "the central function or instance of the human mind."[1] Jean-François Lyotard calls narration "the quintessential form of customary knowledge."[2] Whether or not such assertions stand up under scrutiny, it is still the case that we engage in narrative so often and with such unconscious ease that the gift for it would seem to be everyone's birthright. Perhaps the fullest statement regarding the universality of narrative among humans is the opening to Roland Barthes's landmark essay on narrative (1966). It is worth quoting at length:

> The narratives of the world are numberless. Narrative is first and foremost a prodigious variety of genres, themselves distributed amongst different substances – as though any material were fit to receive man's stories. Able to be carried by articulated language, spoken or written, fixed or moving images, gestures, and the ordered mixture of all these substances; narrative is present in myth, legend, fable, tale, novella, epic, history, tragedy, drama, comedy, mime, painting (think of Carpaccio's *Saint Ursula*), stained-glass windows, cinema, comics, news items, conversation. Moreover, under this almost infinite diversity of forms,

1

> narrative is present in every age, in every place, in every society; it begins
> with the very history of mankind and there nowhere is nor has been a
> people without narrative. All classes, all human groups, have their
> narratives, enjoyment of which is very often shared by men with different,
> even opposing, cultural backgrounds. Caring nothing for the division
> between good and bad literature, narrative is international,
> transhistorical, transcultural: it is simply there, like life itself.[3]

Barthes is right. There are, of course, narrative *genres* (literary kinds) –
the novel, the epic poem, the short story, the saga, the tragedy, the comedy,
the farce, the ballad, the western, and so on – in which narrative provides the
overall structure. We call them narratives and expect them to tell a story.
But if you look at any of the so-called non-narrative genres, like, say, the
lyric poem, which is frequently featured as pre-eminently a static form –
that is, dominated not by a story line but by a single feeling – you will still
find narrative. "Drink to me, onely, with thine eyes," wrote Ben Jonson in
the first line of his "Song: To Celia," and already we have a micro-narrative
brewing – "look at me" – overlaid by another micro-narrative which acts
as a metaphor – "drink to me."

> Drink to me, onely, with thine eyes,
>   And I will pledge with mine;
> Or leave a kisse but in the cup,
>   And Ile not looke for wine.
> The thirst, that from the soule doth rise,
>   Doth aske a drinke divine:
> But might I of JOVE'S *Nectar* sup,
>   I would not change for thine.
> I sent thee, late, a rosie wreath,
>   Not so much honoring thee,
> As giving it a hope, that there
>   It could not withered bee.
> But thou thereon didst onely breath,
>   And sent'st it backe to mee:
> Since when it growes, and smells, I sweare,
>   Not of itself, but thee.

Here you have a poem dedicated to the expression of a powerful feeling,
erotic love (threaded with irony and good humor), but the poem as a whole is
structured by two narrative situations. The first is a series of micro-narratives,
in the conditional mode, involving looking, kissing, and drinking. The second, beginning midway through, tells a more elaborate story of flowers that
were sent, breathed on, returned, and now flourish, smelling of his beloved.

Narrative capability shows up in infants some time in their third or fourth
year, when they start putting verbs together with nouns.[4] Its appearance
coincides, roughly, with the first memories that are retained by adults of

their infancy, a conjunction that has led some to propose that memory itself is dependent on the capacity for narrative. In other words, we do not have any mental record of who we are until narrative is present as a kind of armature, giving shape to that record. If this is so, then "[o]ur very definition as human beings," as Peter Brooks has written, "is very much bound up with the stories we tell about our own lives and the world in which we live. We cannot, in our dreams, our daydreams, our ambitious fantasies, avoid the imaginative imposition of form on life."[5] The gift of narrative is so pervasive and universal that there are those who strongly suggest that narrative is a "deep structure," a human capacity genetically hard-wired into our minds in the same way as our capacity for grammar (according to some linguists) is something we are born with.[6] The novelist Paul Auster once wrote that "A child's need for stories is as fundamental as his need for food."[7] For anyone who has read to a child or taken a child to the movies and watched her rapt attention, it is hard to believe that the appetite for narrative is something we learn rather than something that is built into us through our genes.

Narrative and time

Whatever the final word may be regarding the source of this gift for narrative — whether from nature or from nurture or from some complex combination of the two — the question remains: what does narrative do for us? And the first answer is that it does many things for us, some of which we will go into in later chapters. But if we had to choose one answer above all others, the likeliest is that *narrative is the principal way in which our species organizes its understanding of time.* This would seem to be the fundamental gift of narrative with the greatest range of benefits. And it certainly makes evolutionary sense. As we are the only species on earth with both language and a conscious awareness of the passage of time, it stands to reason that we would have a mechanism for expressing this awareness.

Of course, there are other ways to organize time and to express it. In our own age, the commonest of these is the mechanical timepiece: the clock or watch. But mechanical clocks have been around only since the Middle Ages. Before that, the measurement of time was more proximate than exact. Still, there were then (as there are now and always will be) dependable non-narrative ways of organizing time: the passage of the sun, the phases of the moon, the succession of seasons, and the season cycles that we call years. Like the clock, these modes of organizing time are abstract in the sense that they provide a grid of regular intervals within which we can locate events. Narrative, by contrast, turns this process inside out, *allowing events themselves to create the order of time.* "I fell down," cries the child and in so doing gives shape to what in clock time would be roughly a second. In effect, the child carves out a piece of time, spanning her collapse and fall to the ground. This is the way time, to quote Paul Ricoeur, becomes "human time": "Time becomes human time to the extent that it is organized after the manner of a narrative; narrative, in turn, is meaningful to the extent that it portrays the features of temporal existence."[8]

If we extend our example just a bit, we can show how much we rely on the free exercise of narrative to shape time according to human priorities:

> The child fell down. After a while she got up and ran, until at last, seeing her mother, she burst into tears: "I fell down," she cried. "There, there," said her mother. "That must have hurt."

Here time is comprised of a succession of events that appear as links in a chain: the fall, the getting up, the running, the seeing of her mother, the bursting into tears, what she said, and what her mother said. If one tries to imagine this sequence underscored by integers of clock time (--), one might come up with something like this:

The Child fell down.

After a while she got up and ran,

----

                                                until at last, seeing her

----

mother, she burst into tears: "I fell down," she cried.   "There,

----

there," said her mother. "That must have hurt."

The juxtaposition of the two kinds of time makes the difference clear. Clock time, like other forms of abstract or regular time, always relates to itself, so that one speaks in terms of numbers of seconds or their multiples (minutes, hours) and fractions (nanoseconds). Narrative time, in contrast, relates to events or incidents. And while clock time is necessarily marked off by regular intervals of a certain length, narrative time is not necessarily any length at all. In the short narrative above, for example, we could slow this whole sequence down simply by adding details, and in the process, we would have expanded time.

> The child fell down. She sat where she had fallen, her eyes frightened, her lower lip trembling. She rubbed her knee. Was it bleeding? No, but the skin was scraped. Where was her mother? Carefully, she got to her feet and started running . . .

We have not added clock time to what happened. But we have added narrative time. We have added time in the sense that we have added greater complexity of narrative shape to its passage. This complexity is a matter of the accumulation of incident. It is as if we went inside the phrase "After a while she got up and ran" and lingered there to observe a fabric of micro-events. Conversely, we can make narrative time go like the wind:

> "There, there," said her mother, "that must have hurt." In the following months, the child fell often. But slowly she acquired confidence and eventually stopped falling altogether. Indeed, as a young woman, the assurance of her gait would command attention whenever she entered a roomful of people – people who would have found it hard to imagine that this was once a little girl who fell down all the time.

Here a new narrative structure comes into place, stretching over years. Time becomes a sequential reduction of falls and the acquirement of balanced poise, while all the numerous incidents that must have marked the daily life of this child/woman are screened from view. With a few broad strokes time is now structured as the history of an acquired capability.

This gives some idea of how fluid narrative time is. Of course, it is important to acknowledge that this way of expressing time, though in a way the opposite of the many modes of regular, or abstract, time, is rarely kept in strict isolation from regular time. Notice, in the example above, that I used the phrase "In the following months," invoking the thirty-day interval with which we are all familiar. In narrative, then, though it is the incidents that give shape and that dominate our sense of time, the regularity of abstract time, which is also an integral part of all our lives, unavoidably adds its own counterpoint to the time structured by incidents.

Both of these kinds of time have been with us as far back as history can trace. We have always been aware of the recurring cycles of the sun, moon, and seasons, and at the same time we have always been shaping and reshaping time as a succession of events, that is, as narrative.

Narrative perception

Narrative is so much a part of the way we apprehend the world in time that it is virtually built in to the way we see. Filmmaker Brian De Palma put this idea even more strongly: "People don't see the world before their eyes until it's put in a narrative mode."[9] Even when we look at something as static and completely spatial as a picture, narrative consciousness comes into play. Is it possible, when "reading" the following picture, to resist some kind of narrative structuring?

We may not see a full, clear story in abundant detail (a storm arises, a ship founders and runs aground). But we do see more than a ship; we see a ship *wreck*. In other words, included in the present time of the picture is a shadowy sense of time preceding it, and specifically of narrative time – that is, time comprised of a succession of necessary events that leads up to, and accounts for, what we see.

This human tendency to insert narrative time into static, immobile scenes seems almost automatic, like a reflex action. We want to know not just what is there, but also what happened. Artists have often capitalized on this tendency. In the renaissance, it was common to depict a moment in a well-known story from mythology or the Bible. In the painting on page 7 by Rembrandt, we see action in progress. The painting draws on the Old Testament story of Belshazzar's feast, told in the Book of Daniel (Chapter 5). Belshazzar, the last king of Babylon, arranged a great feast and ordered that the golden vessels that his father, Nebuchadnezzar, had plundered from the temple in Jerusalem be set out and filled with wine. At the height of the feast, when his princes and wives and concubines were drinking from the holy vessels, a divine hand suddenly appeared and wrote on the wall mysterious words in Hebrew ("Mene mene tekel upharsin"). Belshazzar was struck with fear. Eventually, Daniel was called for to interpret the words, which he did: "Thou art weighed in the balance, and found wanting." That very night, Babylon fell to Darius, and Belshazzar was slain. In his painting, Rembrandt has caught the climax of the narrative: the moment when Belshazzar, with less than twenty-four hours to live, sees the handwriting on the wall. Everything appears to be in motion, from Belshazzar's horrified gaze to the wine pouring from the golden vessels as his concubines also gape at the words. We grasp it all in the context of a story in progress.

Rembrandt, *Belshazzar's Feast*. National Gallery, London.

But even when we don't already know the specific story depicted in a painting, we can still be tempted to look for a story. We have many narrative templates in our minds and, knowing this, an artist can activate one or another. Looking at the painting below by Michel Garnier, is it even necessary to prompt ourselves to ask what is happening? It would appear, in fact, that we begin right away, in the act of perception itself, to answer this question. We may never know who is being depicted or what specific story they may be a part of. But we do, nonetheless, have narrative formulas stored in our memory that quickly fill in certain elements of the story so far. That the young woman was playing her instrument is indicated by the fact that she still holds the bow in her right hand. Indeed, that she still holds it tells us that things are happening fast. And we have a very good sense of how the young man, now pulling hard on her dress and looking imploringly, must have been feeling a few moments ago during her performance. We also have an expectation of how the story will develop. But here we have a range of possibilities, just as we do in the middle of any good story. She could successfully fend him off. She might even hit him with her bow and he, ashamed, come to his senses. Then again, she might succumb, either willingly or unwillingly. It is this uncertainty that in part gives the painting so much of its energy.

Michel Garnier, *La douce résistance* (1793). Private collection.

It is also this propensity to narrativize what we see that allows painters to achieve some of their most amusing and most troubling effects. Part (if not all) of the impact of Andrew Wyeth's "Dr. Syn" depends on our immediate effort to situate what we see not just in space but in time as well. Can you put together a narrative here that sufficiently accounts for the picture's anomalies? What, for example, happened to the figure's socks and his trousers? There are no vestiges of them on the floor. Was he not fully

dressed when he sat down? And if not, why not? Or are we dealing with
an entity that never went through the process of decay? Is this, rather, the
picture of an animated skeleton? And who is Dr. Syn? Certainly much of
the effect of this painting lies in the way it arouses and then refuses to satisfy
our narrative perceptions. You might call this "narrative jamming."

Andrew Wyeth *Dr. Syn* (1981) tempera on panel. Collection of
Andrew and Betsy Wyeth © Andrew Wyeth.

More disturbing in the way they jam our narrative response are paintings
like Francis Bacon's "Three Studies for Figures at the Base of a Crucifixion" (1944). If we explore how our minds react as we look at these, one
of the things we become aware of is the way certain narrative questions
arise without leading to any clear understanding of what is going on. There
are, for example, clear signs of great pain, but no clear indication of the

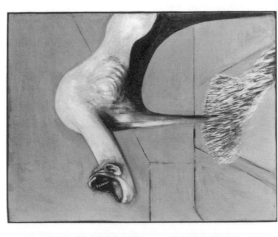

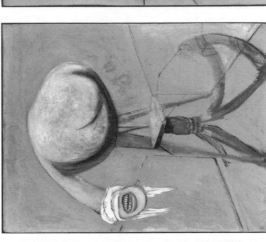

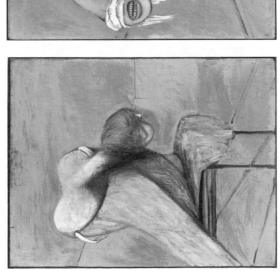

Francis Bacon, *Three Studies for Figures at the Base of a Crucifixion* (1944). Courtesy of the Tate Gallery and Art Resources, New York.

causes of the pain or the reasons for it. What tortures are in progress? Are these people (and are they people?) being punished? What did they do? And what are the tables being used for? What is the function of the cloth? Is it a bandage or a blindfold? However shocking the truth may be, we still want to know what on earth is going on. We reflexively try to comprehend the scene by fitting it within a narrative in progress. At the same time, part of the great power of the painting comes from its refusal to satisfy the narrative desire that it arouses. The experience of indeterminacy, of wanting to know and not being allowed to know, is itself a kind of pain and dimly echoes the terrible pain that the pictures express.

To sum up, wherever we look in this world, we seek to grasp what we see not just in space but in time as well. Narrative gives us this understanding; it gives us what could be called the shape of time. Accordingly, our narrative perception stands ready to be activated in order to give us a frame or context for even the most static and uneventful scenes. And without understanding the narrative, we often feel we don't understand what we see. We cannot find the meaning. Meaning and narrative understanding are very closely connected, a point that is paradoxically driven home by both the Wyeth and the Bacon paintings. By jamming our narrative response, they frustrate our desire to get to the meaning of the pictures.

But the connections between narrative and meaning are many, and they will occupy us frequently during the course of this book. Hayden White pointed out in his book *The Content of the Form* that the word "narrative" goes back to the ancient Sanskrit "gna," a root term that means "know," and that it comes down to us through Latin words for both "knowing" ("gnarus") and "telling" ("narro").[10] This etymology catches the two sides of narrative. It is a universal tool for knowing as well as telling, for absorbing knowledge as well as expressing it. This knowledge, moreover, is not necessarily static. Narrative can be, and often is, an instrument that provokes active thinking and helps us work through problems, even as we tell about them or hear them being told. But, finally, it is also important to note that narrative can be used to deliver false information; it can be used to keep us in darkness and even encourage us to do things we should not do. This too must be kept in mind.

Chapter 2

Defining narrative

The bare minimum

Simply put, narrative is *the representation of an event or a series of events*. "Event" is the key word here, though some people prefer the word "action." Without an event or an action, you may have a "description," an "exposition," an "argument," a "lyric," some combination of these or something else altogether, but you won't have a narrative. "My dog has fleas" is a description of my dog, but it is not a narrative because nothing happens. "My dog was bitten by a flea" is a narrative. It tells of an event. The event is a very small one – the bite of a flea – but that is enough to make it a narrative.

Few, if any, scholars would dispute the necessity of at least one event for there to be narrative, but there are a number who require more than this. Some require at least two events, one after the other (Barthes, Rimmon-Kenan). And more than a few go even further, requiring that the events be causally related (Bal, Bordwell, Richardson). To both of these camps, my examples of narrative above would appear too impoverished to qualify. In my own view and that of still others (Genette, Smith[1]), the field of narrative is so rich that it would be a mistake to become invested in a more restrictive definition that requires either more than one event or the sense of causal connection between events. Both of the latter are more complex versions of narrative, and in their form and the need that brings them into being they are well worth study in their own right. But in my view the capacity to represent an event, either in words or in some other way, is the key gift and it produces the building blocks out of which all the more complex forms are built.

That said, it is important to note that most of us – scholars, readers, viewers – find it difficult sometimes to call some longer, more complex works narratives, even though they contain numerous examples of these little, and sometimes not so little, narrative building blocks. This is one of the reasons why there has been such a debate about what deserves the title of narrative. John Bunyan's *Grace Abounding* (1666), T. S. Eliot's *The Waste Land* (1922), Samuel Beckett's *The Unnamable* (1953), and Tom McHarg's *The Late-Nite Maneuvers of the Ultramundane* (1993) are full of narratives and micro-narratives, yet many would hesitate to call the works as a whole

12

narratives. They just don't seem to have the cumulative effect of narrative. I will return to this subject in the next chapter.

The definition of narrative that I have chosen is controversial in yet another way, since there are a number of scholars who would also dispute my other term – "representation" – as much too broad. Here, for example, is part of a definition of narrative by a well-respected scholar in the field who would have trouble with the unqualified word "representation":

> The recounting . . . of one or more real or fictitious EVENTS communicated by one, two, or several (more or less overt) NARRATORS to one, two, or several (more or less overt) NARRATEES . . . . [A] dramatic performance representing (many fascinating) events does not constitute a narrative . . ., since these events, rather than being recounted, occur directly on stage. On the other hand, even such possibly uninteresting texts as "The man opened the door," "The goldfish died," and "The glass fell on the floor" are narratives, according to this definition.[2]

For this scholar (Prince) and others, a narrative requires a *narrator*. Films and plays, because they only rarely use narrators and rely instead on acting and other elements to communicate the story, fall outside their definition of narrative. But for many other scholars, requiring a narrator is a needless constraint. For them, the narrator is one of a number of instruments – among them actors and cameras – that can be used in the narrative process of representing events. As we noted in the first chapter, even fixed, silent instruments like paintings can convey the events of narrative. In this book, I accept this larger definition of narrative. I do so in part because it allows us to look at the full range of the most interesting and vital aspect of the field: the complex transaction that involves events, their manner of representation (whether it be by narrator, actor, paint or some other means), and the audience. The difference between events and their representation is the difference between *story* (the event or sequence of events) and *narrative discourse* (how the story is conveyed). The distinction is immensely important.

Representation or presentation?

Representation is a vexed term in other ways as well. Those who favor Aristotelian distinctions, sometimes use the word *presentation* for stories that are acted and representation (re-presentation) for stories that are told or written. The difference highlights the idea that in theater we experience the story as immediately present while we do not when it is conveyed through a narrator. My own view is that both forms of narrative are mediated stories and therefore involved in re-presentation, conveying a story that at least *seems* to pre-exist the vehicle of conveyance. A good counter-argument to my position asks:

Where is this story before it is realized in words or on stage? The answer, so the argument goes, is: Nowhere. If that is the case, then all renderings of stories, on the stage or on the page, are *presentations* not representations. The extent to which stories are at the mercy of the way they are rendered is an important issue, and I will return to it in this chapter and later in this book. But for my definition, I will stick to the term "representation." I do this in part because the word is so commonly used in the way I am using it and in part because it describes at least the feeling that we often have that the story somehow pre-exists the narrative, even though this may be an illusion.

Story and narrative discourse

The difference between story and narrative discourse is, to begin with, a difference between two kinds of time and two kinds of order. It gives rise to what Seymour Chatman has called the "chrono-logic" of narrative:

> What makes narrative unique among text-types is its "chrono-logic," its doubly temporal logic. Narrative entails movement through time not only "externally" (the duration of the presentation of the novel, film, play) but also "internally" (the duration of the sequence of events that constitute the plot). The first operates in that dimension of narrative called Discourse . . . , the second in that called Story . . . .
>
> Non-narrative text-types do not have an internal time sequence, even though, obviously, they take time to read, view, or hear. Their underlying structures are static or atemporal.[3]

In other words, when we read a "non-narrative text-type" like an essay, the only time involved is the time it takes to read, and the only order is that of the structure of the essay. But when we read a narrative, we are aware of, on the one hand, the time of reading and the order in which things are read, and, on the other hand, the time the story events are supposed to take and the order in which they are supposed to occur. When you think about it, it is remarkable that we have this gift that allows us to hear or say things in one way and to understand them in another. We can squeeze a day's worth of events into one sentence:

> When I woke up, I packed two loaded guns and a ski mask, drove to the bank, robbed it, and was back in time for dinner.

Perhaps even more interestingly we can tell the same story backwards and still convey both the timing and the chronological sequence of events:

I was back in time for dinner, having robbed the bank to which I had driven with a ski mask and two loaded guns just after my nap.

We can also make many other changes in the narrative discourse and still deal with the same story. We can, for example, change the point of view (from first to third person) and expand the narrative discourse to dwell on a moment in the middle of this series of actions and still communicate with fidelity the same order of events:

> He loved that old familiar, yet always strangely new, sensation of being someone else inside his ski mask, a pistol in each hand, watching the frightened teller count out a cool million. Nothing like it to wake a guy up. Nothing like it to give him a good appetite.

As we noted in Chapter One, narrative discourse is infinitely malleable. It can expand and contract, leap backward and forward, but as we take in information from the discourse we sort it out in our minds, reconstructing an order of events that we call the story. The story can take a day, a minute, a lifetime, or eons. It can be true or false, historical or fictional. But insofar as it is a story, it has its own length of time and an order of events that proceeds chronologically from the earliest to the latest. The order of events and the length of time they are understood to take in the story are often quite different from the time and order of events in the narrative discourse.

The exceptions to this general rule are found most frequently in drama, where the time and order of events in the story are often the same as the actions and dialogue of actors in "real" time. Aristotle saw this "unity" of time as a virtue in theatrical work. In the renaissance when his unities were revived and codified, dramatists like Corneille and Racine often adhered strictly to this "rule." More recently, filmmakers like Jean-Luc Goddard, John Cassavetes, and Andy Warhol, in their very different ways have capitalized on film's capacity to document the moment-by-moment flow of life. But even with the difference between action time and viewing time eliminated, we are almost always called upon to sort out a story from the narrative discourse. This is because people on stage or in films talk, and as they talk we learn about events in which they are involved and which extend way beyond the boundaries of what we see on stage. In *Oedipus Tyrannus*, for example, a play that adheres strictly to Aristotle's rule, Oedipus must reconstruct his entire life. And the audience joins him in his effort, slowly piecing together a long, terrible story in which Oedipus, without knowing it, has been the central player.

Problems for English speakers: story, discourse, plot, fabula, and sjuzet

Most speakers of English grow up using **story** to mean what we are referring to here as **narrative**. When in casual conversation, English speakers say they've heard a "good story," they usually aren't thinking of the story as separate from the telling of it. When a child wants you to read her favorite story, she often means by that every word on every page. Leave a word out and you are not reading the whole story. But as I hope will become clear as we go on, the distinction between story and narrative discourse is vital for an understanding of how narrative works.

There is a parallel problem with the term **narrative discourse**, especially if we take narrative to mean all modes of conveying stories. It is a little awkward in English to apply the term "discourse" to elements like *montage* or camera work in films, or design in painting. And yet it is true that these things are a kind of language or discourse that we understand and can read, and out of which we can reconstruct a story.

A number of scholars prefer to use the distinction **fabula** and **sjuzet**, rather than story and narrative discourse. But as it usually refers to the way events are ordered in the narrative, sjuzet is a less inclusive term than narrative discourse. Other words for sjuzet are Aristotle's **muthos** or **mythos** as well as the familiar **plot**. Unfortunately, for English speakers "plot" is pretty well disabled, since we so commonly use it not to refer to the order of events in the narrative but to its opposite, story (as Chatman does in one of the quotes above). I will be drawing on this traditional English understanding of the word "plot" in Chapter Four when I introduce the concept of the *masterplot*. But the point of this brief discussion is to let you know that there are alternative terms, should you want to use them. My own position is that the distinction of "story" and "narrative discourse" is now widely enough used in the discussion of narrative to serve us well.

So far we have established three distinctions: **narrative** is the representation of events, consisting of *story* and *narrative discourse*, **story** is an *event* or sequence of events (the *action*), and **narrative discourse** is those events as represented. Can we break this down any further? Are there other identifiable parts of narrative that recur in *all or most narrative situations*? There have been efforts to subdivide narrative discourse into: 1) the order in which events are recounted (*plot* or *sjuzet*) and 2) "style" or "discourse," but I find that these distinctions tend to blend into each other. Nor can I think of other elements that are necessary to, or defining qualities of, narrative discourse. This is especially the case given the breadth of our approach to this dimension of narrative. Stories, in other words, can be conveyed in a variety of media, with a variety of devices, none of which, including the device of a narrator, will *necessarily* be present in any particular narrative.

On the other hand, the concept of story can be further subdivided at least once. There are two components to every story: the *events* and the *entities* involved in the events. Indeed, without entities, there would be no events. What are events but the actions or reactions of entities? (Note that the reverse is not true, since there can be entities without events.) As a term, "entity" seems cold and abstract, especially when applied to "characters" (entities that act and react more or less like human beings). Most stories do involve characters. Even when the stories are about animals or extraterrestrial creatures or animated objects (Ronald the light bulb), "character" seems the appropriate term. But if the narrative concerns the story of an atom, say, or an experiment involving the interaction of chemical elements, or the history of shifting landmasses, or the evolution of planetary systems, it would seem strained to continue to speak of characters. So, for better or worse, we'll stick with "entities" as the necessary element in all stories and "characters" as those entities with human qualities.

One other common ingredient in stories is the "setting." But common as it is, it is still optional, unlike events and entities. "I fell down" is a story entirely without setting. Were we to elaborate this narrative, setting would most likely emerge, but it does not have to emerge for the story to remain a perfectly valid story.

The mediation (construction) of story

One important point that the distinction between story and discourse brings out is that we never see a story directly, but instead always pick it up *through* the narrative discourse. The story is always mediated – by a voice, a style of writing, camera angles, actors' interpretations – so that what we call the story is really something that we construct. We put it together from what we read or see, often by inference.

But wait a minute: what really comes first, the story or the discourse?

It may look like there is a story out there that pre-exists the narrative discourse and therefore is "mediated" by it. But isn't this an illusion? After all, as we noticed above, the story only comes to life when it is narrativized. For Jonathan Culler, there is at bottom an ambiguity here which will never be resolved. He calls it the "double logic" of narrative, since at one and the same time story appears both to precede *and* to come after narrative discourse. On the one hand, a story does seem to have a separate existence, lying out in some virtual realm while the narrative discourse endeavors to communicate it. This effect is especially powerful in stories that are narrated in the past tense, since the narration seems to start at a point after the completion of the story. On the other hand, before the narrative discourse is expressed, there is no story.[4] Tolstoy, for example, recounted that when he was writing *Anna Karenina*, he found that, after Vronsky and Anna had finally made love and Vronsky had returned to his lodging, he, Tolstoy, discovered to his amazement that Vronsky was preparing to commit suicide. He wrote on, always in the past tense, but faster and faster, to see how the story would turn out.[5] In other words, without first creating the narrative discourse, he would never know the story.

One thing that strengthens the sense that stories are always mediated is that they can be adapted. Cinderella, for example, or the Faust story are not bound by any particular discourse but can travel from one set of actors or film or prose rendition to another, and yet still remain recognizably the same story. As Claude Bremond puts it, a story is "neither words, nor images, nor gestures, but the events, situations, and behaviors signified by the words, images, and gestures."[6]

But then what exactly is this story that travels? If we never know it except as it is mediated in one way or another, how can we say for sure that a story is a particular story and not some other story? We've all seen the Cinderella story in many different versions. A diligent scholar in the nineteenth century dug up roughly 1100 versions of Cinderella (and that was long before Disney's 1950 animated feature film). Leaving a film, I might say: "That was a Cinderella story," and people might agree. But what if they disagree? How would we settle the dispute? Leaving a production of *King Lear*, I might say: "That was a Cinderella story" and find that some people strenuously disagree. I would then point out how it features a beautiful, honest, virtuous sister (Cordelia) who, because of her wicked, selfish, dishonest sisters (Goneril and Regan), is neglected and cut off from the family fortune. My opponents, though, would point out quite rightly all the differences: that Cordelia is not forced to work as a scullery maid, that there is no fairy godmother, no coach, no ball, no glass slipper, and for that matter no happy ending. Moreover, most of our attention is devoted to events involving other people, like Lear and Gloucester. I would probably lose the argument, but in the process we would have raised an interesting question. What is necessary for the story of Cinderella to be the story of Cinderella? Between the traditional fairy tale and *King Lear*, when does the story of Cinderella stop being Cinderella and start being something else? Is a magical transformation of Cinderella necessary? Is the ball necessary? Is the Prince's search for Cinderella necessary? Is the happy ending necessary?

This is a question that can never be answered with precision, in part because each of us reads differently. But for that reason, the pursuit of the issue can still be interesting, if only to explore these differences. In the dispute above, it may be that the Cordelia story dominates my perceptions of *Lear*, and for that reason I am more inclined to see the framework of a Cinderella variant in this tragedy than others. And the reasons for this perceptual bias of mine might be interesting (at least for people who are interested in me). But the enabling condition that permits this kind of slippage in figuring out when a story has mutated into some other story is found in what we observed at the outset of this section: *story is always mediated (constructed) by narrative discourse.* We are always called upon to be active participants in narrative, because receiving the story depends on how we construct it from the discourse. Are stories, then, at the mercy of the reader and how diligently he or she reads? To a certain degree this is true. But most stories, if they succeed – that is, if they enjoy an audience or readership – do so because they successfully control the process of story construction. Where differences between readings become fraught with significance is in the area of interpretation, or the assignment of meaning.

Can stories be real?

The constructed nature of stories led Jean-Paul Sartre famously to announce that there are no true stories. In this view, all of our non-fictional understandings, from the smallest anecdote to histories, biographies, cosmologies, even stories told by science, do not refer to the "real world," which is utterly disorganized or at least utterly unknowable. On this raw flux, we impose the stories that give our lives meaning. Variations on this idea have gained wide currency since Sartre's 1938 novel, *Nausea*. But opponents point out that there is something very like a story in the cycles of life and death, since these have the beginnings, middles, and ends that stories usually have. They also point out that our lives depend on the stories scientists tell us about the way our bodies work. Once you start thinking along this line, more examples come to mind. In other words, though stories are always constructed and always involve our willing collaboration for their completion, that does not mean that they are necessarily false.

> But the healthy side of this suspicion of stories is the way it has
> allowed us to see how easily and in how many ways stories that have
> very little truth can pass for the truth. Whatever your view of this
> philosophical issue, it is surely the case that we live much of our lives
> in and among stories. This is one way in which stories are quite real
> and it makes the subject of narrative well worth trying to understand.

Constituent and supplementary events

The question concerning when retellings of a story like Cinderella can no
longer claim the name of Cinderella leads us to another, broader issue: that
of the relative importance of the events in a story. Both Roland Barthes and
Seymour Chatman argue for a distinction between constituent and supplementary events. Barthes uses the terms "nuclei" (*noyeaux*) and "catalyzers"
(*catalyses*) for this distinction, and Chatman uses the terms "kernels" and
"satellites."[7] In this analysis, the *constituent events* ("nuclei," "kernels") are
necessary for the story to be the story it is. They are the turning points,
the events that drive the story forward and that lead to other events. The
supplementary events ("catalyzers," "satellites") are not necessary for the story.
They don't lead anywhere. They can be removed and the story will still be
recognizably the story that it is.

On the face of it, this distinction would appear to create a hierarchy in
which constituent events are rated more highly than supplementary events.
But here we need to be careful. Constituent events are only necessarily
more important than supplementary events *insofar as we are concerned with
the sequence of events that constitute the story itself.* But supplementary events
can be very important for the meaning and overall impact of the narrative.
Barthes puts this well: "A nucleus [constituent event] cannot be deleted
without altering the story, but neither can a catalyzer [supplementary event]
without altering the discourse."[8] In short, there is more to narrative than
story. And in that "more" can be much that gives a work its power and
significance.

In James Whale's 1931 film adaptation of Mary Shelley's 1818 novel,
Frankenstein, the events surrounding the creation of the monster are greatly
elaborated beyond what Shelley gave us. In Shelley's novel very little attention is paid to how the monster is put together, but in Whale's version we
are given a host of supplementary micro-events involving 1930s high-tech
instrumentation. The thickening of narrative texture at this point expresses
a shift in cultural attention toward the technology of production – a shift
that had evolved during the 113 years since Mary Shelley first published her

novel. With this particular enlargement of supplementary business, Whale could load up Shelley's nineteenth-century story about the consequences of scientific over-reaching with twentieth-century anxieties about our relationship with technology.

To take another example, a key event of the story in Jean Renoir's 1938 film classic, *Grand Illusion*, is the downing of a plane in World War I. The French officers Captain Boeldieu and Lieutenant Marechal are shot down behind the German lines and captured by troops under the command of General von Rauffenstein (played by Erich von Stroheim). Yet this major constituent event of the story is not shown in the film. At the outset, we see the French officers, preparing to depart. We then find ourselves in the German encampment, where shortly the two officers are brought in through the door. The only visual trace of the first major event of the story is the sling in which Lieutenant Marechal's arm gracefully reposes. What we are invited to dwell on during the long opening stretch of the narrative discourse is a series of micro-events – a round of dining and conversation in the German general's headquarters – none of which is necessary for the *story*. But these events do a great deal to establish the ambiance of a world on the verge of extinction, marked by aristocratic courtesy and camaraderie among men of breeding, even though they may be at war.

Briefly, to review, **constituent events** are events that are necessary for the story, driving it forward. **Supplementary events** are events that do not drive the story forward and without which the story would still remain intact. Naturally, a great deal of the energy, moral significance and revelatory power of a story are released during its constituent events. Lear's division of his kingdom, Macbeth's murder of the king – these constituent events are moments when we see what the protagonist is made of. They are also the moments in which the future is determined. In these regards, the importance of constituent events should not be underrated. But as I have shown above, supplementary events invariably have their own impact and can carry a considerable amount of the narrative's burden of meaning. They also raise an interesting question that constituent events do not: Why were they included? Since they are not necessary to the story, why did the author feel compelled to put them into the narrative? Asking these questions is often a very profitable thing to do in the interpretation of narrative.

Just as a language always changes as long as it is alive, so stories are constantly changing in not only their constituent and supplementary events, but their characters, settings, and a whole range of finer and finer details of form and content. In the ancient German *Faustbuch*, in the two versions of Marlowe's play *Doctor Faustus* (1604 and 1616), in Goethe's long, barely performable two-part drama, *Faust* (1808 and 1831), in Thomas Mann's

1947 novel, *Doctor Faustus* – in all four of these immensely different works we recognize the bone structure of the same story about a man who made a pact with the devil for powers far beyond those of other mortals. We call it the Faust story. Yet almost everything in the story is open to revision, including the name of the central character, whether he falls in love, whether he has children, what craft he practices, whether he is punished for his sins, even whether he lives or dies. Almost all of the narratives of Shakespeare and Chaucer are patchworks of such revisions. The nature of art and culture seems to require this constancy of change. And yet, at the same time, we recognize the persistence of a story as it shows up in different literary incarnations. So if change is inevitable, so too is recurrence. Elements of the story persist even as they are subject to change.

Narrativity

There is one more topic, narrativity, that needs some mention in this chapter on the definition of narrative. From time to time so far, I have been using as examples tiny narratives like "I fell down" and "She drove the car to work" to illustrate how narrative works. And you may have understood in the abstract how the terms "narrative" and "story" apply to these strings of words. But given the way we customarily use these terms, it somehow does not feel right to apply them in these cases. One way to put this is that these narratives lack "narrativity." We don't have the sense of someone "telling a story," of a performance, of narrative "for its own sake." Narrativity is a vexed issue, and as with many issues in the study of narrative there is no definitive test that can tell us to what degree narrativity is present. Do we, for example, need more than one event for there to be narrativity?

> She ate lunch. Then she drove the car to work.

In this instance, the additional event does not help a great deal. In other words, the increase in narrativity is fractional at best. Yet we don't necessarily need to pile on elements like development, rising action, setting, or a recognizable narrative voice to shift this modest narrative into a higher register of narrativity. Narrativity is a matter of degree that does not correlate to the number of devices, qualities or, for that matter, words that are employed in the narrative.

> Brooding, she ate lunch. Then she drove the car to work.

The addition of that one simple word, "brooding," does much to augment narrativity – that is, the feeling that now we are reading a story. And this may simply be because the word itself is more common to narrative than it is to ordinary discourse. Or it may be because the word gives depth to the character (she has a mind and there is something troubling it). Whatever the cause, I bring up the subject of narrativity first to acknowledge an objection you may have had while reading how narrative is defined. But I also bring it up to show that there are, and will always be, gray areas in a field like narrative that has so much to do with subjective human response. I'll be producing more gray areas for you in the next chapter.

Selected secondary resources

Two excellent sources for useful definitions and distinctions in the field are Gérard Genette's *Narrative Discourse* and Gerald Prince's *A Dictionary of Narratology*. A good overview of the specific issue of defining narrative can be found in the third chapter of Brian Richardson's *Unlikely Stories*. Richardson arrives at a position quite opposed to my own. Two very accessible texts that expand the scope of analysis to include film as well as prose fiction are Seymour Chatman's *Story and Discourse* and his *Coming to Terms: The Rhetoric of Narrative in Fiction and Film*. Before any of these texts, there was Roland Barthes's "Introduction to the Structural Analysis of Narratives," which remains one of the best and most compact introductions to the functioning of narrative. Jean-Paul Sartre's several attacks on the idea of a "true story" can be found in his novel *Nausea* (1938), the collection of essays *What is Literature?* (1947), and also in his autobiography, *The Words* (1964). The ninth chapter of Jonathan Culler's *The Pursuit of Signs* ("Story and Discourse in the Analysis of Narrative") develops the apparent paradox of the "double-logic of narrative," whereby neither story nor narrative discourse can be seen as clearly preceding the other. For a thoroughgoing treatment of the concept of narrativity that goes far beyond what I have presented here, see Philip J. M. Sturgess's *Narrativity: Theory and Practice*.

Additional primary texts

Of narratives that put a strain on the relationship between narrative discourse and story, the most commonly cited is not an experimental twentieth-century novel but the extraordinarily enjoyable eighteenth-century comic novel, *Life and Opinions of Tristram Shandy* (1759-67), by Laurence Sterne. There are numerous examples of modernist works that place considerable demands on the reader's quest for story, among them, Virginia Woolf's *Jacob's Room* (1922),

James Joyce's *Finnegans Wake* (1940), Samuel Beckett's *The Unnamable* (1952), Alain Robbe-Grillet's *In the Labyrinth* (1959), William Burrough's *Naked Lunch* (1959), Thomas Pynchon's *The Crying of Lot 49* (1966), and J. M. Ballard's *The Atrocity Exhibition* (1970). Two fascinating borderline cases of narrative with hypertext are Carolyn Guyer's *Quibbling* (1993) and Shelley Jackson's *Patchwork Girl* (1995).

Chapter 3

The borders of narrative

Framing narratives

As you move to the outer edges of a narrative, you may find that it is embedded in another narrative. The containing narrative is what is called a "framing narrative." Classic examples of framing narratives, or frame-tales, are Boccaccio's *Decameron* (1351–53), Chaucer's *Canterbury Tales* (1387–1400), and *A Thousand and One Nights* (c. 1450), in which an embracing narrative acts as a framework within which a multitude of tales are told. In *The Thousand and One Nights*, for example, the sultan Schahriah in his bitterness against women, resolves to marry a new woman every day and to strangle her each morning before sunrise to insure that she will never be unfaithful to him. Scheherazade marries him anyway but escapes execution through the strategy of telling the sultan a story every night and breaking off just before the climax each morning at sunrise. The sultan is hooked, and Scheherazade winds up telling a thousand and one stories. This framing story has its own conclusion, which I won't give away here, but it also works as a way of collecting together a multitude of quite different stories.

There are numerous examples of framing stories that are much more modest than these in that they only frame a single narrative, either a short story, or a novel, or a film, or whatever. Yet such framing narratives can play critically important roles in the interpretation of the narratives they frame. Henry James's novella *The Turn of the Screw* (1898), for example, is a bizarre and horrifying ghost tale conveyed through a manuscript written by the tale's central figure, a governess who is either a courageous heroine or a pathological, power-obsessed hallucinator. The narrative appears to support both readings (and others) of her character. But there is a framing narrative of about eight pages in length that begins the novella and that gives an account of how the governess's manuscript was found. It is here that proponents of the "heroic governess" reading draw key support for their interpretation of her character. The narrator of the framing narrative, to whom the manuscript was entrusted by the governess, tells us that some time after the events in the tale she had later become his sister's governess and that "She was the most agreeable woman I have ever known in her position; she would have been worthy of any whatever."[1] Needless to say, this evidence has been strongly countered in the continuing debate over this amazing short novel. But for my purpose in this chapter, the important point is that framing narratives can, and often do, play a vital role in the narratives they frame. The connection of the framing narrative to the narrative it contains is another one of those gray areas where you find, on the one hand, *embedded narratives* that can easily stand alone, like those in *The Decameron* and *The Thousand and One Nights*, and, on the other hand, embedded narratives like that of the governess that would change considerably were they torn from the framing narrative in which they are embedded.

Frames and framing

The term "frame" is currently used in many different ways in the discussion of narrative. One scholar has isolated at least ten.[2] So I emphasize here the compound term "framing narrative," a concept about which there is some consensus. A promising, but quite different, use of the term "frame" is the adaptation to narrative of "frame theory," as first developed by the sociologist Erving Goffman in his book *Frame Analysis* (1974). This general approach examines the interaction between audience and text in terms of the models of understanding, or frames of reference, that audiences bring with them. It examines the ways in which narrative texts gratify, frustrate, or in other ways play with these cognitive structures by which we make sense of our world.

Paratexts

Where does narrative end and the "real world" begin? In one sense, this is an easy question to answer. The narrative begins at its beginning and ends at its end. But the division between narrative and world is not quite so neat. Narratives usually come packaged in additional words and sometimes even pictures – chapter headings, running heads, tables of content, prefaces, afterwards, illustrations, book jackets (often with blurbs). Dramas often come with program notes, posters, and marquees. In addition, authors give interviews, or a novel is second in a series of novels, or the author's correspondence reveals that she was thinking of a certain person when she created a certain character. All of this tangential material can inflect our experience of the narrative, sometimes subtly, sometimes deeply. So in this sense all of this material *is* part of the narrative.

Gérard Genette invented the word "paratexts" for this material that lies somehow on the threshold of the narrative. Talking about the impact of a narrative, we can easily overlook the contributions of paratexts. We get into the habit of assuming that the narrative is identical with the story we read or see. Of course, the influence of some paratexts, like the kind of paper a novel is printed on, or the texture of its binding, may have very little influence on how we experience a narrative. (Though even here one can find exceptions. Wilde's Dorian Gray purchased "nine large-paper copies" of his favorite novel "and had them bound in different colours so that they might suit his various moods."[3]) But a strong recommendation on the book jacket might predispose us to read a narrative with a favorable mindset or, conversely, to be doubly disappointed when the narrative fails to match the expectations created by the blurb. Or an ad, perhaps for commercial reasons, may lead us to expect one kind of play or film, when the work is quite something else. The American premier of Samuel Beckett's *Waiting for Godot* – a stark, static, darkly humored representation of the human condition – was advertised as "the laugh sensation of two continents." As a result, the production played to, if not the wrong audience, the wrong set of expectations. On opening night, the upper-middle-class Miami audience, lured by the prospect of light comedy, left the theater in droves before the end of the first act.

The influence of paratexts can not only be profound but sometimes can permanently affect the reception of a narrative. When in 1919 readers first read W. N. P. Barbellion's life story, *The Journal of a Disappointed Man*, they were deeply moved by its account of a gifted young naturalist's doomed struggle with muscular sclerosis. The last words of the text were: "Barbellion died on December 31 [1917]." The book was immensely popular, going through five printings in the space of a few months. But when readers later learned that Barbellion had not died on 31 December 1917, but had in fact continued to live long enough to read the reviews of his life story, the feeling of betrayal was as deep as it was widespread, and the book fell into an obscurity from which it has rarely emerged. So here is a case in which a piece of paratextual information outside a narrative transformed the narrative without, at the same time, changing a single word of it. In fact, paratexts in general work this way. The phenomenon is a vivid reminder that, though we may call things like texts, books, or films "narratives," where the narratives actually *happen* is in the mind.

The outer limits of narrative

When does narrative become something else? What are its outer limits? Questions like these have come up frequently in connection with modernist and postmodernist experimental fiction, and more recently with hypertext fiction, including *hypertext narrative*, a form of writing which underwent an explosive proliferation in the 1990s. The first thing to make clear is that, to make sense, this question of when something ceases to be narrative must be applied at the level of the work itself, or its overall effect, rather than at the level of its parts. As I noted in Chapter One, narrative occurs almost everywhere in human communication, including almost all the kinds of written, scripted, and visual art. A lyric poem may not be called a narrative – that is, it may not have the impact or felt quality of a narrative – yet almost invariably it will include all kinds of narrative bits and pieces. These bits can even have a high degree of narrativity, yet still the effect of the whole is not that of narrative. Regarding modernist, postmodernist and hypertext fiction, like James Joyce's *Ulysses* (1922) and Virginia Woolf's *The Waves* (1925), William Burroughs's *Naked Lunch* (1959) and Thomas Pynchon's *Gravity's Rainbow* (1973), Michael Joyce's *Afternoon* (1987/1993) and C. D. Coverly's *Califia* (1999), they all may push at the outer limits of narrative experimentation and yet they are at the same time packed with narrative. So the key question is: When do we say that, despite the fact that a work may include much narrative, the whole thing is really something other than narrative? Is there some kind of line that is crossed?

Electronic narrative and hypertext narrative

"Electronic narrative" has proliferated exponentially with advances in desktop software and especially since the invention of the Web in 1993. In this short time, it has achieved a great range of effects by capitalizing on the electronic capability of breaking up the text and including pictures, graphics, and sound. But combining pictures and sound with narrative are ancient capabilities that have been realized in other, non-electronic, media. Likewise, though electronic narrative can also lend itself to the collaborative authorship of narrative, it only does perhaps more quickly and efficiently what has frequently been done in the past in other media.

The *unique* narrative experience that late twentieth-century electronic resources have enabled is, I think, a direct consequence specifically of the hypertext function. "Hypertext narrative" is that subset of electronic narrative that makes use of this capability. It uses the linking function to allow readers to link to other virtual spaces in which almost anything can be found (though these things have been placed there, in most current instances, by the author). George Landow in his *Hypertext 2.0* uses Roland Barthes's term *lexia* to refer to prose links – supplemental narrative discourse, alternate continuations of the story, fragments of still other narratives – but links can also consist of footnote material, definitions, pictures, poems, music, and so on. As links, they allow readers to switch instantaneously out of any particular passage and link up with something else and, perhaps even more significant, they give readers the option of either choosing or not choosing to exercise any particular link. Even in this regard there have been anticipations of this capability in other media. Julio Cortazar's novel *Hopscotch* (1963) invites the reader to read the chapters in two different orders. The novelist Marc Saporta went even further when he published *Composition no. 1* (1962), which was marketed as a box of unnumbered and unbound pages to be read in any order the reader chooses. But there have always been readers who like to skip around as they read. Is this a comparable experience? And then there is the very natural experience that most of us have of recalling earlier parts of a narrative as we read, or imagining what might come next.

Broad generalizations have been made about the radical departure inherent in electronic narrative, but it is important to bear in mind that far and away the majority of electronic narratives are transcriptions or imitations of hard copy. In these numerous cases, the only difference is reading off a screen rather than a page. Where radical innovation has occurred has been in the work of small groups of dedicated artists who have capitalized on the resources of the electronic medium, especially hypertext linking. But even in these works, whether or not they go beyond what we would call a narrative (and there are a number that do), depends not on the mere presence of hypertext linking, but on how that linking is deployed. Are these links, in other words, deployed in such a way that we continue to look for, and occasionally find, the thread of a story? Or do they so disburse attention from the story line that we see the whole thing as something other than narrative: an extended prose poem, for example, or a meditation, or an "anatomy," or any one of a number of non-narrative genres?

Some discussion of the unique departure of hypertext and other kinds of experimental fiction has turned on the way it undermines narrative *linearity*, where linearity has meant following in a line from earlier events to later ones. Given the multitude of *lexia* in hypertext fiction and the freedom of the reader to order these scraps of narrative as she or he pleases, such narratives defy the notion of any single narrative order, much less one that starts at the beginning and moves forward to the end. But here again we have to recall that narrative has always had two components: *story* and *narrative discourse*. And as we noted above, narrative discourse can go forward or backward or inside out. So, in this sense, non-linearity has been common to narrative discourse from the earliest recorded instances of story telling. Ancient epics commonly began "in the middle of things" (*in medias res*) and then recovered earlier parts of the story as the narrative proceeded. In contrast, *story* by definition is linear. It can only go forward in the one direction that time moves. Strictly speaking, then, hypertext lexia are simply a new twist on an old narrative condition. That they permit readers to some degree to arrange the narrative discourse, and to distribute its parts differently in different readings, does not in itself violate the essential narrative condition, *so long as there is a story to be recovered.* In a hypertext novel like Michael Joyce's *Afternoon, a Story*, which makes extensive use of hypertext possibilities, the experience of many, reading it for the first time, has been that they are every bit as much in quest of the story as readers of Faulkner's modernist "hard copy" novel *Absalom! Absalom!* (1936).

Can a story go backward ?

In 1991, Martin Amis published a novel, *Time's Arrow*, in which everything goes backwards:

> First I stack the clean plates in the dishwasher.... So far so good. Then you select a soiled dish, collect some scraps from the garbage, and settle down for a short wait. Various items get gulped up into my mouth, and after skillful massage with tongue and teeth I transfer them to the plate for additional sculpture with knife and fork and spoon.... Next you face the laborious business of cooling, of reassembly, of storage, before the return of these foodstuffs to the Superette, where, admittedly, I am promptly and generously reimbursed for my pains. Then you tool down the aisles, with trolley or basket, returning each can and packet to its rightful place.[4]

But even here, I would argue that the backward representation of events is an extreme version of Chatman's "chrono-logic," or a kind of deranged narrative discourse (indeed, it baffles even the *first-person* narrator of this novel). Notice how, in reading, your mind automatically sorts out the forward motion of the story. In fact, much of the curious appeal of this writing depends on this automatic reconstruction. And this reconstruction of the story is required, too, for the overall effect of this novel. As we go further along in our reading – that is, further backward in the life of the central figure – we become aware of early events and actions that cast a devastating moral light on his later opinions and behavior. I won't give away what we learn, but the point is that the novel depends for its full effect on our reconstructing the true temporal order of events.

To sum up the discussion so far, just as the presence of narrative within a text does not qualify a text as a whole as narrative, so the radical departure of narrative discourse from the linearity of story does not by itself *dis*qualify a text as narrative. Rather the key element in answering this question is *whether story predominates*. Nelson Goodman argued that if you twist up the narrative discourse sufficiently, a text can pass from being a narrative to being either a "study" or a "symphony," arousing respectively either a state of meditation or a state of pure aesthetic enjoyment.[5] Here is one of those gray areas I promised at the end of the last chapter. It's gray because determining when the twisting is enough is a subjective judgment call. People also use the term "poetry" to describe a predominating impact different from that of narrative. In Jonson's "Song: To Celia," the stories we teased out of the poem do not dominate but serve as metaphorical expressions of the lover-poet's state of mind. In the opening lines, the micro-narratives of looking and drinking combine in a witty and complex metaphor of erotic yearning. So, too, in similar ways, Robert Kendall's hypertext *A Life Set for Two* (1996) and Michael Joyce's hypertext *Reach* (2000) generate a more poetic than story-oriented frame of mind. Attention in these texts is focussed not so much on figuring out the story (though some of the narrative fragments are certainly tantalizing) as enjoying the way the lexia play off against each other. George Landow goes so far as to argue that the hypertext link itself enables poetic effect: "the link, the element that hypertext adds to writing, bridges gaps between text – bits of text – and thereby produces effects similar to analogy, metaphor, and other forms of thought, other figures, that we take to define poetry and poetic thought."[6]

Is it narrative or is it life itself?

From the point of view of narrative theory, a fascinating hybrid activity is the role-playing game. With the extraordinary success of *Dungeons and Dragons* since it was first published in 1974, role-playing games have proliferated among "gamers," a small but not insignificant game-addicted subset of the global population. The players enter into the game with their characters, but underlying each game is a kind of skeletal story, with critical "plot points," all under the control and the devising of the "Game Master." Here is something that appears to be narrative but that is so free that characters, while they are involved in trying to understand the larger story, have (within a wide range of limits, depending on the game) the capability of introducing events on their own. So the whole thing is a kind of collaborative enterprise in which players and Game Master produce what none of them could have intended at the outset. It appears, then, to be narrative that to a degree invents itself.

In this it is like theater improv. Since the late 1970s, role-playing games have transited to personal computers, CDs, the Internet, and the Web. One of the more ambitious of these (at this writing!) is *Asheron's Call*, an MMORPG or "Massive Multi-user Online Role-Playing Game." Evolving month by month with new elements of the master story and new plot points to uncover, *Asheron's Call* has some 45,000 subscribers, of whom at any one time at least 2,000 are actively playing on any one of the game's nine servers. They are busy looking for plot-points, trying to uncover the key characters and events that have been loaded into the various servers by non-players who run the whole operation. But at the same time they are meeting together, conversing, and even engaging in pretty extensive *subsidiary events*. It is not uncommon, for example, for players (that is, the players' characters) to get married, complete with a ceremony and celebration that others join in.

But is this narrative? If things are happening right now for the first time, do we call it narrative? Do we refer to our lives, for example, as narratives? Do we say things like: I wonder what is going to happen next in my narrative? We might do so, but it sounds strange. Also it raises a definitional problem. If there is no difference between narrative and life itself, are we not in danger of exhausting the usefulness of the term "narrative" by making it include so much? And how, then, do we distinguish between life and what we have been referring to as narrative? Do we need yet another term or can we think this through and preserve a more restricted, and therefore useful, meaning of the term "narrative"?

To sort this out, we might start by going back to the distinction between story and narrative. Story, you will remember, is something that is delivered by narrative but seems (important word) to pre-exist it. Narrative, by the same token, is something that always seems (again, an important word) to come after, to be a *re*-presentation. Narrative, in other words, *conveys* story, and even if Culler and others are right that the story doesn't really exist until it is conveyed, we still have the sense of story's pre-existence of the narrative that conveys it. If we hold to this useful distinction between story and narrative, then neither life nor role-playing games qualify as narrative, since there is no pre-existing story. In this sense, role-playing games, like theater improv, are like life itself. As in life, we are aware of something happening that has not been planned or written or scripted in advance – something making itself up as it goes along.

But then, if life and role-playing games are not narrative, are they story? This is a tougher question to answer. Given what I have just been arguing, one might first say, no. The logic here is that just as our lives and role-playing games are not narrative, so they are not stories re-presented through narrative. Still, if people don't come up to you and ask "What's your narrative?", they do sometimes ask "What's your story?" as if you already had a story, or were involved in one. One way to make sense of this would be to say that they are asking you to cast your eye over your day, or month, or year, or life, and pick out what's important, that is, its *constituent events*. Story, as I wrote in Chapter One, is our way of organizing time according to what is important for us. So, if life and role-playing games are not the same thing as stories, we might call them the seed-ground of stories – stories that then can be rendered in narrative, the way I might narrate a short story about two players who got married during the game of *Asheron's Call*.

The problem with this solution is that it still goes against usage. For we do say "Hey, what's the story?" with the same meaning as "Hey, what's happening?" And when historians try to get at the truth of events, they will often say they are trying to expose the real story. In the same way, detectives working on a crime might say they are trying to get at the story of what happened, and cosmologists are trying to reveal the story of the universe. In every case, what is being said is that *events really happened*, somebody was murdered, the universe evolved in a certain way, Washington crossed the Delaware. In other words, Sartre wasn't right after all. There are true stories. A limb falls from a tree and knocks a love-letter from a lover's hand. The letter blows across the field. Later it is discovered by a young woman who secretly adores this man whom she now learns loves another. In despair, she throws herself in the millrace and drowns. These things happen every day. Life is jammed with events. But call them what you will – stories, latent stories, virtual stories, untold stories – what we are interested in in this book is what happens when they are told, or re-told, or staged, or filmed, or mediated in whatever way. In other words, we are interested in *narrative*, the first rule of which is that it leaves its mark on the stories it tells. So if things are really happening in the world, we nonetheless cannot pick them up with our words, or scripts, or film, or paint without adding, framing, coloring, and generally inflecting those events in a multitude of ways. This is the narrative difference.

Ergodics and intrigue

Espen J. Aarseth, in his book *Cybertext* came up with an interesting solution to the role-playing conundrum that you may find useful, or at least provocative. In a game, like a football game, for example, Aarseth argued that you have a sequence of actions but not a story. The actions, then, are not narrative actions, but "ergodic," that is, "a situation in which a chain of events... has been produced by nontrivial efforts of one or more individuals or mechanisms." In "adventure" or role-playing games, the "user" (not reader) to a degree creates by her or his own actions the ergodic chain of events, but only within the constraints of something that seems like a hidden story. Aarseth uses the term "intrigue" for this plot-like element that the user can only find out by making moves, that is creating events through action. Instead of a fixed story with its linear course, there are multiple possibilities, and that series that happens is recorded in the manner of a log: "Instead of a narrative constituted of a story or plot, we get an intrigue-oriented ergodic log."[7]

In this chapter and the last, I have stuck closely to what is essential in defining narrative so that we know what it is we are dealing with when we move on to focus on the dynamic interaction between ourselves and stories. There are a great many other features of narrative, formal and affective, that have been named and classified over the years. And there are terms like "mimesis" and "diegesis," "heterodiegetic narrators" and "homodiegetic narrators," "focalization," "prolepsis," "analepsis," "topos," and "type." In this book, I have sought to limit my focus to the most vital and useful of these many terms. They will come up in various appropriate places in the chapters that follow, and many more are included in the Glossary.

Selected secondary resources

Katherine S. Gittes's *Framing the Canterbury Tales: Chaucer and the Medieval Frame Narrative Tradition* (New York: Greenwood, 1991) is a solid introduction to the historical genre of framing narratives. In this chapter, however, I wanted especially to feature the less generic but much more various and broadly distributed device of framing a central narrative with a narrative fragment that provides its own unique rhetorical impact. There are few studies of the device described as such. Gérard Genette's *Paratexts* covers the subject in its title. As for narrative's interesting new life in electronic media, there are three important texts worth recommending, George Landow's *Hypertext 2.0: the Convergence of Contemporary Critical Theory and Technology*, his edited volume, *Hyper/Text/Theory* (Baltimore: Johns Hopkins University Press, 1994), and Espen Aarseth's *Cybertext* (Baltimore: Johns Hopkins University Press, 1997).

Additional primary texts

The history of literature abounds in examples of framing narratives. Many, as in *The Turn of the Screw*, are devoted to the initial situation of the telling of a story, or the finding of the manuscript that tells a story, or the recovery of an ancient book that tells a story, and so on.

The story that is then told is almost always in the first person. A classic example is Conrad's *Heart of Darkness* (1899), whose initial narrative of the story's telling plays a critical role in most interpretations of the work. One of the more complex examples of the use of framing and embedded narratives is Mary Shelley's *Frankenstein* (1831 edition). In this novel, readers make their way in and then out of a succession of at least seven different narratives, each with its own narrator. These narratives are layered within each other like Chinese boxes. In the 1831 edition, the outermost layer is actually a paratext, an introduction written by the author, narrating the circumstances under which the novel was originally conceived. Another powerful example of an embedded narrative is Mikhail Lermontov's *A Hero of Our Time* (1840).

As for stories that go from end to beginning, few are so thoroughgoing at the molecular level in the manner of Martin Amis's *Time's Arrow* (mentioned above). One that comes close is the short story "Journey to the Source" (1944) by the Cuban novelist Alejo Carpentier. Don DeLillo's *Underworld* (1997) moves backward in time through a succession of large stretches of (forward-moving) narrative. Harold Pinter's play *Betrayal* (1978) similarly moves backward scene by scene, and on 20 November 1997, the American sitcom, *Seinfeld*, screened its own version of Pinter's backward narration in an episode titled "The Betrayal" (coyly underscoring the theft by naming Elaine's boyfriend "Pinter"). A fascinating final example is Christopher Nolan's "backward thriller," *Memento* (2001), which is premised on the neurological condition of "anterograde memory loss."

Chapter 4

The rhetoric of narrative

The rhetoric of narrative

The rhetoric of narrative is its power. It has to do with all those elements of the text that produce the many strong or subtle combinations of feeling and thought we experience as we read. These include those elements that inflect how we interpret the narrative: that is, how we find meanings in it. Arguably, *everything* in the text contributes to its impact and our interpretation of it, and so everything has some rhetorical function. Change one thing, and the effect of the whole changes, if only subtly. As Barthes says, "everything in [the text] signifies. . . . Even were a detail to appear irretrievably insignificant, resistant to all functionality, it would nonetheless end up with precisely the meaning of absurdity or uselessness" ("Structural Analysis," 261).

> ### Who is exercising this power?
>
> Note that when Barthes says that "everything has a meaning" he is not saying that the author of the text is necessarily in control of, or even aware of, the meaning of everything in the text. This is not to denigrate authors or to demean their often extraordinary gifts, but to acknowledge that interpreting texts is a complex transaction that invariably has to do with more than what the author consciously intended. The issue of meaning and its relation to the author is as important as it is vexed. I will return to this issue in Chapters Seven and Eight. But it is important to establish before we get too far along that the impact of a narrative, including its meaning, is not something that is securely under the author's control.

It is no exaggeration, then, to call narrative an instrument of power, and in fact many exceptionally powerful narratives reflect upon this power. Richard Wright, who became a story-teller of great power in his own right, described the impact of hearing the story of Bluebeard as a poor black child in the South: "As she spoke, reality changed, the look of things altered, and the world became peopled with magical presences. My sense of life deepened and the feel of things was different, somehow. Enchanted and enthralled, I stopped her constantly to ask for details. My imagination blazed. The sensations the story aroused in me were never to leave me."[1] This chapter and the next are devoted to some of the major rhetorical effects of narrative and some of the devices that produce them. In this chapter, I will start out with two closely related effects that are more mundane than what Wright was describing, but no less important for that – the sense of *causation* and (more broadly) *normalization*. Then I will turn to a major rhetorical device, the *masterplot*. Chapter Four is devoted entirely to the issue of *closure*, which is both an effect and a device in narrative's rhetorical arsenal.

Causation

We are made in such a way that we continually look for the causes of things. The inevitable linearity of story makes narrative a powerful means of gratifying this need (whether accurately or not is another issue, which we will come to shortly). No wonder, then, that many of the greatest narratives (the Babylonian *War of the Gods*, the Book of Genesis in the Bible, the *Aeneid*, *Paradise Lost*) are narratives of causation on the largest scale. Epics like the *Aeneid* traditionally tell of the origin of a nation. Some, like Genesis and the *War of the Gods*, tell us about the origin of life itself. Sometimes these two – the origin of the nation and the origin of life on earth – are the same:

> You know, everything had to begin, and this is how it was: the Kiowas came one by one into the world through a hollow log. They were many more than now, but not all of them got out. There was a woman whose body was swollen up with child, and she got stuck in the log. After that, no one could get through, and that is why the Kiowas are a small tribe in number. They looked all around and saw the world. It made them glad to see so many things. They called themselves *Kwuda*, "coming out."[2]

N. Scott Momaday's rendering of the Kiowa myth of origin not only tells how the Kiowa people came into being, but it also answers other questions of causation: Why are there so few of us? Why do we love the world so much? How were we named? Myths and epics are kinds of narrative that, among other things, explain the world for us in terms of cause.

But the issue of reading causation in narrative is not restricted to myths and epics. Narrative itself, simply by the way it distributes events in an orderly, consecutive fashion, very often gives the impression of a sequence of cause and effect.

"Please," he implored, "give me one more chance!"
Suddenly she felt a headache coming on.

Reading these two lines of narrative in succession, one automatically connects *her* headache with *his* emotional outburst. In the real world, the headache could arise from any number of causes: hypoglycemia, a stroke, migraine, barometric pressure. But given the information we have, and the narrative form in which we have it, we will read a causal connection whereby what comes after (her headache) is triggered by what went before (his pleading). Some might contend that we need more than this to allocate cause. In a classic study of the novel, E. M. Forster argued that there is a major difference between a narrative like "The king died and then the queen died" and one like "The king died and then the queen died of grief." The difference, he argued, is that the latter shows causation.[3] Nevertheless, as Chatman argues, the sequencing of narrative works on us so suggestively, that we often don't need the explicit assignment of cause to be encouraged to think causally.

> [T]he interesting thing is that our minds inveterately seek structure, and they will provide it if necessary. Unless otherwise instructed, readers will tend to assume that even "The king died and the queen died" presents a causal link, that the king's death has something to do with the queen's. We do so in the same spirit in which we seek coherence in the visual field, that is, we are inherently disposed to turn raw sensation into perception. (*Story and Discourse*, 45–6)

Must narratives show cause?

As I noted in Chapter Two, there are narratologists who require a clear causal sequence as an essential defining feature of narrative, though in this book, I (along with others) am casting my net more broadly, defining narrative as "the representation of events," whether bound together by a clear sequence of causation or not. A quest story, for example, can include many events that come one after another without causal connection (first the knight sinks into a bog, then he is set upon by wild rodents, then his pants catch on fire . . .), yet it would be difficult on that score alone to say that it is not a narrative. Here is an instance where the term **narrativity** may help. For, if the sense of causation is not a defining feature of narrative, it is so commonly a feature that we can say that its presence increases narrativity.

Narrative by its arrangement of events gratifies our need for order, of which perhaps the commonest is the kind of order we have just been discussing, the perception of cause. If this can make narrative a gratifying experience, it can also make it a treacherous one, since it implicitly draws on an ancient fallacy that things that follow other things are caused by those things. The Latin phrase for this fallacy is *"post hoc ergo propter hoc"* (literally: "after this, therefore because of this"). Barthes goes so far as to call this fallacy "the mainspring of narrative.... the confusion of consecution and consequence, what comes *after* being read in narrative as what is *caused by*" ("Structural Analysis," 266). Bad social science frequently exploits the force of this narrative illusion. "Teen Crime Rate Drops 18% after Uniforms Introduced in Local Schools." Such a headline, in effect, is a short narrative, trading on the seductive force of this common confusion whereby mere consecution (one thing following another) is taken to suggest cause.

Another way of putting the *propter hoc* fallacy is the rule that scientists cut their teeth on: a correlation does not establish a cause and effect relationship. The author of this book had a grandmother whose narrative consciousness in this regard was quite strong. For example, she found that our visits to her house invariably correlated with heavier-than-usual sunspot activity. I am not entirely sure what she was getting at, but my assumption is that she was making a causal connection between the occurrence of sunspots and our visits. It is easy to laugh at my grandmother's sense of causation because the two events (sunspots and our visits) are separated by so great a distance. But for millennia, astrologers have been invoking the same narrative logic over distances extending from events on earth to stars that are many light years beyond the sun. In less obvious (and therefore more insidious) forms, this same narrative sleight-of-hand thrives on a daily basis in political speeches, sermons, advertising, legal disputes, and many other forms of public discourse. Often, of course, these narratives draw their power from what we want to be the case ("Use these breath mints and, we guarantee, your loneliness will be at an end"). Desire, wedded to the suggestiveness of narrative succession, is an awfully powerful combination.

But it isn't just our human desire, plus illusion, that makes us suckers for this logic. We fall for it in part because so often during our lives we have actually experienced stories (true ones) in which *post hoc ergo propter hoc* seems to be vividly confirmed. First we lean back in the chair, then we fall over backward. After all, cause and effect work sequentially, just as stories do. In the Newtonian universe, which is the universe we grow up in, effects always follow causes. So there is a good empirical basis to explain why, when reading narratives, we should be tempted to apply this paradigm more quickly than we ought to. The error lies in passing from the valid assumption that all effects follow their causes to the false one that to follow something is to be an effect of that thing. A cause can in fact be any number of things, or any combination of things, that precede an effect, not necessarily the thing the narrative draws to our attention. Conversely, we could say that scientists, conducting their experiments, are trying to write narratives that are so uncluttered by competing elements that cause and effect are genuinely demonstrable in the stories they tell.

> ### Which comes first, cause or effect?
>
> This may sound like an odd question to ask, but Jonathan Culler draws on an insight developed by Nietzsche to argue that what we assume to be plain common sense may be a mental operation that runs in the opposite direction.
>
> > [F]irst, there is cause; then, there is effect; first a mosquito bites one's arm, then one feels pain. But, says Nietzsche, this sequence is not given; it is constructed by a rhetorical operation. What happens may be, for example, that we feel a pain and then look around for some factor we can treat as a cause. The "real" causal sequence may be: first pain, then mosquito. It is the effect that causes us to produce a cause; a tropological operation then reorders the sequence pain-mosquito as mosquito-pain. This latter sequence is the product of discursive forces, but we treat it as a given, as the true order.[4]

Normalization

The impression of causation that we have been examining is one of the ways – a powerful one – of suggesting normality. But we can extend the rhetorical leverage of normalizing to many other features of narrativity. In this sense, narrative could be called a kind of "rhetoric of the real" in that it accounts for things. You could in fact argue, and people have, that our need for narrative form is so strong that we don't really believe something is true unless we can see it as a story. Bringing a collection of events into narrative coherence can be described as a way of *normalizing* or *naturalizing* those events. It renders them plausible, allowing one to see how they all "belong." This is a constant theme in the work of historian Hayden White:

> The very distinction between real and imaginary events that is basic to modern discussions of both history and fiction presupposes a notion of reality in which "the true" is identified with "the real" only insofar as it can be shown to possess the character of narrativity.[5]

This is also a condition that the Austrian novelist Robert Musil examined at the personal level in his long unfinished work, *The Man Without Qualities*

(1930, 1932): "Most people relate to themselves as storytellers. . . . they love the orderly sequence of facts because it has the look of necessity, and the impression that their life has a 'course' is somehow their refuge from chaos." Ulrich, the protagonist of the novel, finds to his dismay that the illusion no longer works: "he had lost this elementary, narrative mode of thought to which private life still clings, even though everything in public life has already ceased to be narrative and no longer following a thread, but instead spreads out as an infinitely interwoven surface."[6]

> "Nothing in Government occurs by accident. If it occurs, know that it was planned that way."
>
> – Patriot militia member

The unwillingness to tolerate the condition of **un**knowing in which we all live may lie behind the ancient and persistent tendency to believe that some powerful force controls all aspects of our lives – a power, in other words, writing a story that will eventually become clear. Some apply this at the political level to sinister forces, like the government or international conspiracies. But in fact this has long been, and continues to be, a very common way of viewing the universe itself. In his 1979 study of the interpretation of narrative, Frank Kermode puts this point strongly:

> If there is one belief (however the facts resist it) that unites us all, from the evangelists to those who argue away inconvenient portions of their texts, and those who spin large plots to accommodate the discrepancies and dissonances into some larger scheme, it is this conviction that somehow, in some occult fashion, if we could only detect it, everything will be found to hang together. (*Genesis of Secrecy*, 72)

Certainly we can all think of examples where the attraction of narrative coherence has overridden both reason and the evidence of the senses. The mass suicide in California of cult members dedicated to the idea that they will be rescued from this life by a spaceship hidden behind comet Hale-Bopp was an event that required suppressing awareness of a host of contradictions between the story and the facts of the empirical world. But given the urgency of their need, cult members found in this scenario a story in which they could place themselves and which (if true) would rescue them from the trials of their mortality. Bizarre as it seems, the incident demonstrates the enormous persuasive power of narrative coherence when wedded to human desire.

But here again there is need for caution in our generalizing. We are also well aware of narratives that purport to be true but which, precisely because of their *narrativity*, fail to persuade. "Oh, don't believe in that," we say, "it's just a story." So it is not narrativity in itself that persuades us that a story is true, but some subset of the qualities that convey narrativity. Two possible candidates are the qualities of "continuity" and "narrative coherence." If it "hangs together," as Kermode writes, it responds to a bias that favors order over chaos. But then there are numerous fairy tales that have wonderful continuity and coherence that we would never mistake for reality. The issue gets more complicated still. For some, the very qualities that make a narrative convincing are for others qualities that invalidate it. Qualities of the tale that lured the cult members referred to above are qualities that for others make it "just a story." For a more powerful example of how differently different people read narrative, we need go no further than the divided public reaction to the verdict in the first trial of O. J. Simpson.

In the summer of 1994, the black American athlete and media celebrity O. J. Simpson was charged with the brutal slaying of his wife, Nicole Simpson, and Ronald Goldman, both of whom were white. The sensational trial that followed lasted a year and concluded with Simpson's acquittal. The Simpson trial, like any trial, was a contest of narratives involving two parties, each seeking to bring the facts (or what could be adduced as facts) into conformity with a coherent narrative that favored its conception of the accused. It is important to stress at this point that people can actually be "persuaded by the evidence," just as it is true that someone (or ones) definitely did kill Nicole Simpson and Ron Goldman, and that O. J. Simpson either is or is not guilty of these crimes. The truth, as the expression goes, is out there. But the intensity with which people adhere to one narrative explanation or the other often has less to do with raw evidence and more to do with a potent instrument of narrative, which we can call the masterplot.

Masterplots

There are stories that we tell over and over in myriad forms and that connect vitally with our deepest values, wishes, and fears. Cinderella is one of them. Its variants can be found frequently in European and American cultures. Its constituent events elaborate a thread of neglect, injustice, rebirth, and reward that responds to deeply held anxieties and desires. As such, the Cinderella masterplot has an enormous emotional capital that can be drawn on in constructing a narrative. But it is only one of many masterplots. We seem to connect our thinking about life, and particularly about our own lives, to a number of masterplots that we may or may not be fully aware of. To the extent that our values and identity are linked to a masterplot, that masterplot can have strong rhetorical impact. We tend to give credibility to narratives that are structured by it.

The term "masterplot"

There have been many terms used for what I am calling a masterplot. One currently in favor is "master narrative." But if you take seriously the important distinction between story and narrative, it should be obvious why "master narrative" would not work for this concept. A narrative is a particular rendering of a story. Works like *War and Peace* or *Harry Potter and the Goblet of Fire* are narratives. The masterplots that undergird these narratives are much more skeletal and adaptable, and they can recur in narrative after narrative. Roger Shank actually proposed the term "story skeleton" for something like masterplots (147–88). The term is a good one, but it does not convey the rhetorical power that accompanies a masterplot. Stephen Jay Gould's term "canonical story" catches something of that power by alluding to the concept of a "canon" with its connotation of official sanction (as in a culture's recognized canonical works).[7] But this suggests stories that are somehow certified, whereas masterplots often work in secret, influencing us without our wholly realizing it. Finally, the term "archetype," which used to enjoy more currency than it does now, comes quite close to the concept of a masterplot. The problem with "archetype" is its Jungian baggage, particularly the implication that these stories are warehoused in a collective memory that is part of our biological or spiritual inheritance. For all these reasons, I prefer "masterplot." It is not perfect. The term "plot," for example, is frequently used to mean "narrative discourse," especially among European narratologists. But "plot" very commonly means "story" in English, and I have drawn on that meaning, while "master" conveys something of the power of the particular stories that I am calling "masterplots."

There are some masterplots, very loosely conceived, that would appear to be universal: the quest, the story of revenge, seasonal myths of death and regeneration. But the more culturally specific the masterplot, the greater its practical force in everyday life. All national cultures have their masterplots, some of which are local variations on universal masterplots. The Horatio Alger story, for example, is a variation on the quest masterplot that speaks directly to cherished values in broad swathes of US culture. It takes its name from Horatio Alger, an enormously popular nineteenth-century novelist who published over 120 books. Most of these books narrativize the same masterplot featuring a youth (Ragged Dick, Tattered Tom), who, though born in poverty, rises by his own hard work and clean living to the highest level of social standing and often great wealth. The Horatio Alger story has been told and retold throughout American history. It is the story of such diverse figures as Andrew Carnegie and Abe Lincoln and it expresses in its shape convictions about life that are dear to many Americans. It is tempting to see these masterplots as a kind of cultural glue that holds societies together. They constitute, to quote Kermode again, "the mythological structure of a society from which we derive comfort, and which it may be uncomfortable to dispute" (113).

But no culture can be summed up in one masterplot. There are many other masterplots in American culture beside the Horatio Alger story. Some of them are not so dear to some Americans, but carry just as much affective power. When the black motorist Rodney King was caught and beaten by Los Angeles policemen in 1991, the incident activated a very different American masterplot from the Horatio Alger story. Yet this masterplot is equally American, and for many black citizens it expresses a feature of life in America that goes further and deeper than Horatio Alger. Looked at from the perspective of narrative, then, national culture is a complex weave of numerous, often conflicting, masterplots.

Skilled lawyers arguing before a jury, or politicians addressing their constituencies, or advertisers seeking to create a market can gain rhetorical leverage by handling the narratives they use in such a way as to activate cherished masterplots of their audience. The sharp differences in the reactions to the Simpson verdict and the intensity with which they were (and still are) held owe much to the fact that Simpson's "story" was bonded during the trial to several powerful, yet sharply divergent, masterplots in American culture. One that worked powerfully in Simpson's favor is the story of the black man who is unjustly punished for stepping "out of his place." In this masterplot, the blackness of the victim facilitates the punishment by allowing him easily to be tagged as a criminal. It is a story that has been told in many versions from the slave narratives of the nineteenth century to Ralph Ellison's *Invisible Man* (1952). Another powerful masterplot that came into play throughout the trial is the story of the battered wife. This masterplot was deployed frequently by the prosecution, with Nicole Simpson cast in the central role. A third is the story of unjust privilege accorded to celebrity and wealth, with Simpson back in the central role. This again is a frequent masterplot in American cultural life, though it is one that can be found in most cultures. In the Simpson trial, one of the more delicate challenges for the prosecution was figuring out how to cast as the central figure in this masterplot of unjust privilege a black man who grew up in a San Francisco ghetto.

Much of the power of these particular masterplots, as with so many, is their moral force. They create an image of the world in which good and evil are clearly identifiable, and in which blame can fall squarely on one party or another. During the trial, lawyers for the defense and for the prosecution variously invoked these (and other) masterplots as they shaped their narrative renderings of this story of murder. To the degree that one or another of these masterplots tends to shape our view of the world, we may find it difficult to weigh the evidence dispassionately. Some would argue that our identities are so invested in our personal masterplots, that when these masterplots are activated it is impossible to break out of the vision they create. But, then, others argue that there are too many cases of people changing their minds in the face of the evidence to believe that we are quite so imprisoned.

Types and genres

The concept of the masterplot is closely bound up with the concept of the **type**. A type is a recurring kind of character. Cinderella is both a type (embodied in the character of Cinderella) and a masterplot (her story). The battered wife is a type, and her story, with its repeated beatings, the alternating rages and repentances of her often alcoholic husband/lover (another type), is the masterplot. For a conclusion, this latter story has two current variants: her death at his hands and his death at hers. A masterplot comes equipped with types. When a type does not come to life in a narrative and we see the character only as a formula for a character, we call it a *stereotype*. The term is a good one. It comes from the history of newsprint and refers literally to a cast metal plate in which the print is fixed. When we see a stereotype in a narrative, we see something so fixed and predictable that it seems prefabricated. Masterplots can be rendered stereotypically as well. In such cases, all we see is the masterplot. The particular narrative in which it is conveyed brings little of interest to the story. But again we should note that we all differ in our responses to narrative. We all know intelligent people (including perhaps ourselves) who have been moved to tears by a narrative that for many other intelligent people is laughably stereotypical from beginning to end. This apparent failure of taste, or lack of sophistication, has a lot to do with masterplots and our personal vulnerability to some of them.

Another term closely related to masterplot is **genre**. A genre is a recurrent literary form. Epic and tragedy, for example, are narrative genres. There are many non-narrative genres as well (the sonnet, the expository essay). Genre, which comes from the French word for "kind," is a loose concept. It can apply to large categories like the novel (a very broad and inclusive narrative genre) and it can apply to subsets of these large categories, like the picaresque novel (the episodic adventures of a rascal, told in the first person) and the epistolary novel (narrated in letters). Moreover, a text can combine two or more genres.

> Thus a novel, for example, can be both picaresque and epistolary. Sometimes, but not always, genres are closely bound up with certain masterplots. Perhaps the oldest and commonest example of this is the quest. It is a literary genre, but it is also a particular kind of masterplot. The genre of the novel, in contrast, carries with it no assumption that it will conform to any particular masterplot whatsoever.

Narrative rhetoric at work

I described the O. J. Simpson trial as a contest of narratives in which the contestants draw on masterplots (among an arsenal of other rhetorical tools) to achieve the effect of normalization. This is invariably the case in legal trials, though courts of justice are not the only place that contests of narratives can be found. One finds them everywhere, from politics to family arguments. This is a subject I go into at length in Chapter Eleven. But sometimes one finds a contest of narratives carried on within a containing narrative. This can be a very effective tool in narrative's rhetorical repertoire, since in such cases the contest is often "no contest." After all, there is only one author running the show. This kind of managed contest is worth pausing to look at. Can you see the contest of narratives in the following news report? Who wins?

Khadafy Calls Confrontation wih U.S. a Libyan Triumph

New York Times News Service
TRIPOLI, Libya – Col. Moammar Khadafy claimed victory Friday night in his confrontation with the United States over the Gulf of Sidra.

In a rambling speech to a crowd of more than 1000 soldiers, sailors, Boy Scouts and party faithful bused in for the occasion, the Libyan leader repeatedly described the outcome of his showdown with the Sixth Fleet as "a triumph" . . . .

In his speech, Khadafy insisted that Libya had shot down three American fighter planes and that the Americans had sunk only a fishing boat. The United States has asserted that no planes were lost and

that two Libyan naval patrol boats were sunk.

"The Americans are lying," he said. "They can't believe a small country could shoot down three planes. We shot down three planes, and the six fliers are being eaten by the fish in the Gulf of Sidra.

"America has gone mad in the past few days. They shot a fishing boat and claimed it was a warship."

A few minutes later, Khadafy asserted that an American helicopter had been allowed to cross the "line of death" to pick up a wounded flier and a body.

The colonel said that two American rockets had been fired at the Libyan missile site at Sidra but that one had failed to explode. He said it was being given to the Russians, "so they can learn its secrets." . . .

The crowd Friday night, like others seen at rallies here in the last few days, was small and seemingly lacking in enthusiasm.

All those in the crowd appeared to be members of organized groups, like the soldiers and sailors, who could be rounded up and brought in.

Some people managed to slip away before the speech was finished, and on the edges of the crowd many smoked and chatted, paying little attention to the fiery oratory.[8]

Something happened in the Gulf of Sidra on 26 March 1986. There is a story here somewhere, though very few, if any, of us will ever have a narrative rendering of this story that can be fully confirmed. What we do have in this article is three narratives. There is the "official" US narrative account of the incident, which we glimpse only in one sentence of the third paragraph. There is Colonel Khadafy's narrative of the incident, rendered in "direct discourse" (in the words of the character Khadafy, who acts as a narrator within the piece). And there is the journalist's narrative, which both includes and exceeds the other two narratives. Let's look at the second and third of these.

Narrative Two. Before all else, we must acknowledge that this narrative is told not by the real, living Colonel Khadafy, but by a character, "Colonel Khadafy," within the article's larger narrative. Saying this is not to impugn the integrity of the *Times* reporter who filed the account but to acknowledge our first principle: that, insofar as it is narrated, any story is an act of mediation and construction, and this includes its characters. That said, we can see clearly here that the character/narrator "Khadafy" is working with the masterplot of David and Goliath: a small, struggling nation has taken on the most powerful nation on earth and with careful aim knocked three of its vaunted fighters out of the sky. Directly reinforcing the masterplot are two supplemental details: the Americans claimed to sink a warship but only sank a fishing boat, and the six fliers of the three downed planes are "being eaten by the fish in the Gulf of Sidra." Both incidents are unnecessary for the story (they are not *constituent events*), but "Khadafy" is moved to include them because they reinforce the David and Goliath reversal. Both attach an idea of smallness to the most powerful nation on earth, especially the image of mighty US pilots being eaten by little fish. Two other *supplementary events* provide indirect rhetorical support. Risking apparent contradiction, "Khadafy" states that an American helicopter had been allowed to "cross the 'line of death' to pick up a wounded flier and a body" and that an unexploded rocket had been forwarded to the Russians "so they can learn its secrets." However true or untrue these supplemental events may be, they do their rhetorical work. The first expresses the compassion (moral largeness) of a small nation, and the second indicates that the small nation has large friends.

Narrative Three. The journalist's narrative works to undermine the orator's masterplot and to replace it with the ranting of a type: the tin-pot dictator. As with "Khadafy's" narrative, here too the reigning motif is diminishment, though now working on "Khadafy" and effected largely through *setting*. In the last three paragraphs, the journalist sets in contrast to "Khadafy's" oratory the indifference of a small bused-in crowd, "lacking in enthusiasm." Notice how the setting is in part made up of tiny supplemental narrative events: "Some people managed to slip away before the speech was finished, and on the edges of the crowd many smoked and chatted, paying little attention to the fiery oratory." In this way, the journalist's narrative shrinks "the Colonel" even as "the Colonel" seeks in his own narrative to shrink his enemy.

Selection, too, is construction

To *New York Times* readers, the journalist's narrative probably has the greater texture of reality. And it may, in fact, be more accurate. But it is important to bear in mind that, as narrative, it is as constructed as the narrative "Khadafy" tells. The details we get, if not invented, are nonetheless chosen from a great number that were left out. They are privileged details that strongly color how we see the central figure in the journalist's story.

What this brief analysis shows is how multiple parts of a narrative contribute to its rhetorical effect. If you are not persuaded that in narrative every single thing signifies (as Barthes contends), you can still see from this analysis how minor details, parts that are quite unnecessary to the story – like *supplementary events* and the *setting* – can exert considerable rhetorical leverage on the way we read. It also shows how masterplots and types that an author shares with his or her audience are drawn on to establish the framework within which the narrative can be seen as credible. "Khadafy" selects a masterplot that plays to the powerful third-world desire that weakness on the global stage can prevail against the hegemonic strength of dominating nations. The journalist draws on a perhaps equally powerful desire among the *Times* readership to see the frightening figure of Khadafy as a clownish tyrant, ignored even in his own land.

Selected secondary sources

Wayne Booth's landmark 1961 study, *The Rhetoric of Fiction*, is almost equally a study of the rhetoric of narrative as it is found in novels. For an in-depth study of causality in narrative, see Brian Richardson's *Unlikely Stories: Causality and the Nature of Modern Narrative*. Jonathan Culler develops the concept of "naturalization" in *Structuralist Poetics: Structuralism, Linguistics and the Study of Literature*, Ithaca Cornell University Press, 1975, pp. 134-60. Hayden White's books are an extended study of the ways in which historians have drawn upon narrative coherence and other devices of narrativity to convey the sense of historical plausibility. A good sampler of his work on the importance of narrative form in the representation of history, and the one of his many books I would recommend reading first, is *The Content of the Form: Narrative Discourse and Historical Representation*. You might want to put beside White's work the psychologist Jerome Bruner's "The Narrative Construction of 'Reality'." A searching analysis of a masterplot (and implicit endorsement of my use of the term in this chapter) can be found in Peter Brooks's chapter, "Freud's masterplot: a model for narrative" in his *Reading for the Plot*. But masterplots frequently undergird literary, historical, and cultural studies. Variations on the Horatio Alger masterplot, for example, form the analytical spine of works like William A. Fahey's *F. Scott Fitzgerald and the American Dream* (New York: Crowell, 1973), Elizabeth Long's *The American Dream and the Popular Novel* (Boston: Routledge and Kegan Paul, 1985), Doris Kearns Goodwin's *Lyndon Johnson and the American Dream* (New York: Harper and Row, 1976), and Jane Flax's recent study of the Clarence Thomas hearings, *The American Dream in Black and White* (Ithaca: Cornell University Press, 1998).

Additional primary texts

Examples of narrative's power to account for things through its normalizing function are legion. It is, in fact, hard to think of narratives before this postmodern age that do *not* give a sense of causation. As I mentioned above, a common element in the narrativity of narrative is the sense of coherence, and particularly coherence that derives from a linear structure of cause and effect. One genre in which the normalizing function of narrative, including its structure of cause and effect, becomes especially intriguing is autobiography. Not infrequently an autobiography is a defense of an autobiographer who has made some controversial life choice. When John Henry Newman left the Church of England and converted to Catholicism, he was accused of bad faith and hypocrisy. His defense of his action was an autobiography titled *Apologia pro Vita sua* (1864), the title of which means roughly, "a defense of his life." Exactly one hundred years later, Malcolm X did much the same thing when he found himself in a similar situation after leaving the Nation of Islam. Defending himself meant laying out the stages of his life in *The Autobiography of Malcolm X* (1964) to show how they followed each other in an understandable causal sequence. A wonderfully comic fictional treatment of narrative's rhetoric of normalizing and explaining can be found in Eudora Welty's short story "Why I live at the P. O." (1939). Finally, much absurdist fiction draws on reader expectations of the normalizing function to do just the reverse. In its first sentence, Franz Kafka's famous tale "The Metamorphosis" (1915) hits the reader with a puzzle that is never explained: "As Gregor Samsa awoke one morning from uneasy dreams he found himself transformed in his bed into a gigantic insect."[9] Samuel Beckett's *Molloy* (1951) renders profoundly mysterious the whole question of cause – why we do what we do, including writing about why we do what we do – in back to back fictional autobiographies.

Just as most narratives of any length work with our expectations of causal order, so too do they work either with or against masterplots. Children's literature is crowded with variations on the story that success crowns hard work, beginning with "The Little Engine that Could" and "Mike Mulligan and his Steam Shovel." The more specific version of this, the Horatio Alger story, not only has its numerous variants in American popular literature, but also stinging critiques that take the story and drive it to a tragic or farcical end. F. Scott Fitzgerald's classic novel, *The Great Gatsby* (1925), is a devastating exposé of the masterplot's mythic status in American culture, as are two landmark novels by African-American authors: Richard Wright's *Native Son* (1940) and Ralph Ellison's *Invisible Man* (1952). As always, it is worth keeping in mind that any work that goes beyond stereotype is going to impress its individual differences on the masterplots it recreates in its narrative discourse.

Chapter 5

Closure

Conflict: the agon

If, with its immense rhetorical resources, narrative is an instrument of power, it is often about power as well. This is because, in almost every narrative of any interest, there is a conflict in which power is at stake. You might say that conflict structures narrative. The ancient Greek word for conflict (actually "contest" is closer) is *agon*, and how the agon played out formed the spine of any Greek tragedy. The presence on stage of a chorus reinforced awareness of the agon as the chorus debated with itself during the course of the play, one side of the chorus pitted against the other (Woody Allen richly satirized the role of the chorus in his *Mighty Aphrodite* [1995]). Characters in the narrative of Greek tragedy were assigned roles in the agon. Thus, there was a "prot*agon*ist" (hero) and an "ant*agon*ist" (the hero's chief opponent). Conflict in narrative, of course, does not necessarily take the form of a clear opposition of good guys and bad guys (though this is one defining feature of *melodrama*). And in many narratives, there is more than one conflict at play.

The agon, or conflict, has been so central a feature of narrative throughout its recorded history that it is reasonable to assume that it serves important cultural purposes. One very plausible possibility is that the representation of conflict in narrative provides a way for a culture to talk to itself about, and possibly resolve, conflicts that threaten to fracture it (or at least make living difficult). In this view of narrative, its conflicts are not solely about particular characters (or entities). Also in conflict, and riding on top of the conflict of narrative entities, are conflicts regarding values, ideas, feelings, and ways of seeing the world. There is, of course, no culture without many such conflicts. Narrative may, then, play an important social role as a vehicle for making the case for one side or another in a conflict, or for negotiating the claims of the opposing sides, or simply for providing a way for people to live with a conflict that is irreconcilable (as, for example, the conflict between the desire to live and the knowledge that we have to die). *Hamlet*, for example, features a set of conflicts between certain characters – Hamlet and his mother, Hamlet and his uncle, Hamlet and

Ophelia, Hamlet and Laertes — but it also deals with a complex set of cultural conflicts centered on the issue of revenge. In Chapter Twelve, I will take up this idea of a culture using narrative as an instrument to think about difficult issues. In this chapter, I want to focus more narrowly on the rhetorical impact of both the presence and the absence of closure in narrative.

Closure and endings

When a narrative resolves a conflict, it achieves closure, and this usually comes at the end of the narrative. We expect stories to end. We talk about good and bad, satisfying and unsatisfying endings. There are, for example, stories that snap shut at the end.

Taboo

His guardian Angel whispered to Fabian, behind his shoulder: "Careful, Fabian! It is decreed that you will die the minute you pronounce the word *doyen*."
"Doyen?" asks Fabian, intrigued.
And he dies.[1]

In this very short story, the conflict between an implacable decree and the unthinking wonderment of youth is resolved decisively when the fulfillment of the decree coincides with the last word of the narrative. Here's another:

Bedtime Story

"Careful, honey, it's loaded," he said, re-entering the bedroom.
Her back rested against the headboard. "This for your wife?"
"No. Too chancy. I'm hiring a professional."
"How about me?"
He smirked. "Cute. But who'd be dumb enough to hire a lady hit man?"
She wet her lips, sighting along the barrel. "Your wife."[2]

These are rather wonderful narratives, and certainly one of the things (if not *the thing*) that makes them work so well is how decisively they end. In each there is a clear (though not necessarily simple) conflict which is resolved emphatically with the final words of the narrative.

But closure does not have to come at the end of a narrative; in fact, it does not have to come at all. So it is important to keep the two concepts — the ending and closure — distinct.

Must narratives end?

Aristotle wrote that the well-made tragedy has a beginning, a middle, and an end. But this was an evaluation rather than a definition. Soap operas, by contrast, can go on forever. Some sagas, myth cycles, comic strips, TV series seem also to have no proper end. And the phenomenon of the "prequel" (the opposite of the sequel) suggests that even beginnings are not sacred, but can be pushed back endlessly into the past. Much as we, like Aristotle, want shape in our narratives we seem also frequently content with postponing the end – and therefore some final perception of narrative shape – indefinitely.

Closure, suspense, and surprise

The term "closure" can refer to more than the resolution of a story's central conflict. It has to do with a broad range of expectations and uncertainties that arise during the course of a narrative and that part of us, at least, hopes to resolve, or close. Closure is therefore best understood as something we look for in narrative, a desire that authors understand and often expend considerable art to satisfy or to frustrate. If the object is to satisfy this desire – which is often the case – it can't be satisfied too quickly, because we seem also to enjoy being in the state of imbalance or tension that precedes closure. In fact, narrative is marked almost everywhere by its *lack of closure*. Commonly called *suspense*, this lack is one of the two things that above everything else give narrative its life. The other thing is *surprise*. All successful narratives of any length are chains of suspense and surprise that keep us in a fluctuating state of impatience, wonderment, and partial gratification. We are held this way until the final moment of closure, though there are also instances, and not infrequently, when a narrative will fail to close altogether. And this, too, can have its satisfactions.

Decoding narrative. It will help at this point to refer to Roland Barthes's argument in his book *S/Z* that, just as we bring to a sentence a complex set of linguistic codes by which we understand it, so we bring to any readable narrative a set of narrative codes. These codes are necessary, not just to make sense of the narrative, but to extract meaning from it. He argues that there are five fundamental codes that author and reader share in order to make a narrative readable. Two of these codes that are especially applicable to us here are what Barthes called the "proairetic code" – having to do with expectations and actions – and what he called the "hermeneutic code" – having to do with questions and answers. In these two codes, Barthes referred to the ways in which narratives arouse both expectations and questions, and then either give us satisfaction or frustrate us. This is where the presence or absence of closure comes in. If expectations are fulfilled or questions answered, we say that closure occurs. Adapting Barthes, we can identify two important levels at which suspense and closure occur in narrative: the *level of expectations* and the *level of questions*.

Closure at the level of expectations

At the level of expectations we recognize, by numerous signals, the kind of action or sequence of events that we are reading (revenge, falling in love, escape, murder, a bad dream). Once actions start in a certain way, we expect what follows to be consistent with the overall code. When a beautiful young woman like Cinderella meets a handsome young prince, we expect falling in love to follow. Moreover, we see these two successive events as one part of an overall sequence of events, a *genre*, which in common language is called "romance" and which often but not always closes with marriage. It may seem coldly inappropriate to speak of such an event involving such lovely people as part of a code, but it is nonetheless true that we learn at a very early age to read and decode not just words but whole patterns like the genre of romance. This is another way to look at masterplots: as coded narrative formulas that end with closure. When the beautiful young woman is relocated from romance to the genre of tragedy, as Cordelia is in *King Lear*, we expect a very different kind of closure from romance. Depending on her role in the tragedy, we might well expect the worst. When at the end, Lear finds Cordelia dead in her cell and then dies himself, painful as this is, it fulfills expectations that have been built into the play. You could call it a painful satisfaction.

At least these expectations seem to be "built in" to the play, especially to modern viewers of *Lear* who come to the play for the first time, having heard what a bleak tragedy it is. But half of what gives life to expectations in narrative is their violation, for which the common word again is *surprise*. Conversely, directors, screen-adapters, audiences themselves, can force a story to conform to expectations. After all, the earliest version we have of Shakespeare's *Lear* does not refer to itself as a tragedy. And renaissance audiences, familiar with Geoffrey of Monmouth's *King Leir*, would have fully expected both Lear and Cordelia to live. So Shakespeare surprised his audience with his version of the story in a way that we can't be surprised since we are so familiar with the tragic version. Later, in 1681, Nahum Tate rewrote the conclusion of *King Lear*, not only saving Cordelia's life but also marrying her off to Edgar (who may not have been a prince but was certainly well born, unlike his wicked sibling). That version held the English stage for the next 160 years. Purists may object that this ruined the tragedy, but then Shakespeare could be said to have "ruined" Geoffrey of Monmouth's *King Leir* when he decided to kill both Lear and Cordelia.

With regard to expectations, then, there appear to be two imperfectly balanced needs: on the one hand to see them fulfilled, on the other to see them violated. When, at the end of Alfred Hitchcock's *Vertigo* (1958), Kim Novak falls for real from the mission tower, the audience's lingering expectations that it is watching one kind of romantic thriller – the kind with a happy ending – are rudely violated with a closure that retroactively instates a much darker genre. For some, this makes the film a hard one to see twice; for others, it is a stroke of genius. The extraordinary Dutch film, *The Vanishing* (1988), cast as a romantic quest to rescue a kidnapped lover, sickeningly violates expectations when the hero is buried alive at the end. Difficult as the film is to watch, however, the conclusion can be seen to be in accord with the dark moral obsession of the hero's deeply disturbed killer. In both of these films (at least for those for whom they work), the surprise of the conclusion casts a light backward over the whole film, giving it a new shape and tone as the sense of surprise wears away and the ending is seen to fit.

Certainly the key to suspense is the possibility, at least, that things could turn out differently. And surprise, which is such a common feature of successful narrative, is what happens when, to a degree, things do turn out differently. But for any audience there is a range of what they will tolerate in the way of surprise. When the same director (George Sluizer) remade *The Vanishing* for Hollywood in 1993, the producers gambled that a large American audience would not tolerate the original ending. Such at least was Hollywood's assessment when they gave it a happy ending, but the remake was not a box-office hit either. Meanwhile, *Vertigo*, which also did poorly when it was released, has aged into a classic and for some is Hitchcock's masterpiece.

So it is important to note that words like "code" and "formula" may work in describing how expectations are aroused, but they fail when applied to narrative itself. Codes and formulas thrive on their inflexibility. Because the Morse Code is always dependably unchanging, it could be relied on in the days of telegraphy. Likewise, the formula for methyl alcohol can be depended on so long as it stays the same. Change it ever so slightly and you've got a formula for something else. Were narrative to operate in the same way, we would have nothing but stereotypes and wooden clichés for our literature. Indeed, one could argue that, for there to be any kind of success in narrative, the codes and formulas that go into it have to be sufficiently flexible to permit all kinds of variation in the details. This would include not just variation in the things inessential to the *story* (*setting, supplementary events*) but variations in treating the story's *constituent events* as well. So Barthes was describing not how a narrative necessarily should turn out but what we expect as we read or watch. And, of course, without expectations in the first place we could not appreciate the variations. Yet this brings up a further difficulty with the word "code," since one of our expectations in almost all narratives of any complexity, is that our expectations will turn out to have been anywhere from inadequate to completely wrong. We expect, in short, to be surprised. This is still a dark area in the study of cognition, so in this book, I have avoided the connotations of "code" by using the word "level," as in the phrase "level of expectations."

Chekhov's famous advice

Chekhov told an aspiring writer: "If in the first chapter you say that a gun hung on the wall, in the second, or third chapter it must without fail be discharged."[3] This is a famous piece of advice and it has been repeated in many different versions ever since. But it is worth distinguishing between two ideas that are packed into this statement: first, that the mere presence of a gun arouses expectations that it will be used and, second, that an author must fulfill those expectations. The first is probably quite right, but the second seems to be a pretty mechanical rule. In fairness to Chekhov, he may have been overstating to make the point that authors must include only those elements in their stories that contribute to the overall affect ("Everything that has no direct relation to the story must be ruthlessly thrown away"). But certainly one can think of all kinds of ways that a gun introduced in Chapter One might *never* go off, and with great success. There could be, for example, a prolonged struggle at the end of which we discover that the gun isn't loaded, or, after many threats to shoot, a desperate would-be assassin throws the gun out of the window, or the gun produces a little flag with the word "Bang!" written on it, or it turns out to be a chocolate gun and is eaten after the quarreling lovers kiss and make up. So, yes, "discharging" is certainly something that a gun stands for in our minds, since we know that discharging is what guns are made to do. But narrative can succeed in many ways, not just by delaying the discharge (suspense) but by happily frustrating it altogether (surprise).

Closure at the level of questions

If at the level of expectations we anticipate what will happen, at the level of questions we anticipate enlightenment. These two may look alike and they may work very closely together. But they are also opposite. At the level of expectations, we lay down tracks in our mind for the ways in which the action will develop. These can be short little tracks for small pieces of action (now she is going shopping, now they are going to fall in love) or long tracks of *genres* and *masterplots* (this is a tragic story and it will close with the death of the protagonist). We can be surprised when our expectations are not fulfilled, but then usually, if the narrative isn't over yet, new expectations rush in on new tracks. Finally, as we saw with regard to *Vertigo* and the original *Vanishing*, a surprise at the conclusion can, if it works, reveal retrospectively tracks running through the narrative that we had not fully picked up on.

At the level of questions, we seek enlightenment. Who did it? Who killed Councilman Stubbs? At the level of expectations, we recognize that we are heading into the investigation of a crime and we expect that it will end with a revelation of the murderer. But at the level of questions, we want to know who did it. This is another kind of suspense in narrative. The level of questions is also a level of answers. Just as there can be a steady stream of questions, so too there can be a steady stream of answers. These answers may not be the right answers. They could be red herrings – a likely murderer but not the real one – as is frequently the case over the course of a mystery. Or they may be partial answers. But this thread of information (and disinformation) keeps us going until the narrative (in most cases) provides the answer and closure comes. A mystery story is only the most obvious genre in which the level of questions is activated. In reality, that level is activated in all narratives, and right from page one, or scene one, or shot one. Where are we? What's going on? Who are these people? What is their relationship? What do they want? But there are also larger questions that frequently come into play. In Dostoevsky's *The Brothers Karamazov*, large questions are pursued throughout the novel's 900 pages in a running debate that weaves in and out of the story's events. The most pressing of these questions is whether or not, in the cosmic scheme, anything and everything is permitted (even murder).

The absence of closure

Critics disagree about whether this question is answered by the time you have come to the end of *The Brothers Karamazov*. But the fact that closure does not have to happen in narrative makes it especially important to keep closure separate from the formal concept of an ending. Here, for example, is a short, fascinating narrative by Franz Kafka that ends quite emphatically but does not close the questions that it raises.

A Common Confusion

A common experience, resulting in a common confusion. A has to transact important business with B in H. He goes to H for a preliminary interview, accomplishes the journey there in ten minutes, and the journey back in the same time, and on returning boasts to his family of his expedition. Next day he goes again to H, this time to settle his business finally. As that by all appearances will require several hours, A leaves very early in the morning. But although all the surrounding circumstances, at least in A's estimation, are exactly the same as the day before, this time it takes him ten hours to reach H. When he arrives there quite exhausted in the evening he is informed that B, annoyed at his absence, had left half an hour before to go to A's village, and that they must have passed each other on the road. A is advised to wait. But in his anxiety about his business he sets off at once and hurries home.

This time he covers the distance, without paying any particular attention to the fact, practically in an instant. At home he learns that B had arrived quite early, immediately after A's departure, indeed that he had met A on the threshold and reminded him of his business; but A had replied that he had no time to spare, he must go at once.

In spite of this incomprehensible behavior of A, however, B had stayed on to wait for A's return. It is true, he had asked several times whether A was not back yet, but he was still sitting up in A's room. Overjoyed at the opportunity of seeing B at once and explaining everything to him, A rushes upstairs. He is almost at the top, when he stumbles, twists a sinew, and almost fainting with the pain, incapable even of uttering a cry, only able to moan faintly in the darkness, he hears B – impossible to tell whether at a great distance or quite near him – stamping down the stairs in a violent rage and vanishing for good.[4]

What closes here is the sequence of action. By mid-narrative, we have enough cues to recognize that this is a world of nightmare and to anticipate that, accordingly, things are not going to turn out well for A. Readers familiar with Kafka might guess this from the author's name alone. Sure enough, the chain of frustration and failure achieves closure with the angry departure of B and the despair of A. But along the way, all kinds of questions (with competing possible answers) have been raised in the reader's mind. Who are these people? What business do they have with each other? Is there more to this relationship? Why is the trip sometimes hard and sometimes easy? Why did A not recognize that B had arrived at his own house? Why can't A cry out? And how on earth, to go back to the title, is this a "common confusion"? The ending not only fails to close these questions, but opens them up even wider.

Kafka is an extreme example. In his world, little is ever known for sure, though some would argue that, at least on the level of metaphysical wonderment ("What are we here on earth for?", "Who is in charge?", "Why is there needless suffering?", "Why do we often feel guilty for no reason?"), the lack of closure in a Kafka narrative is an accurate representation of our general condition on this planet. But there are also those who argue that *any* truly valuable narrative is "open" to some degree. *King Lear* may close with tragic finality at the level of expectations, but some of the issues raised during the course of the play are left open at the end. For example, at one point, Gloucester in despair says,

> As flies to wanton boys are we to the gods,
> They kill us for their sport.   (IV, I, 38–39)

And though there is much in the narrative to support this view, the issue of whether or not any being or beings control our fates and, if so, whether they "sport" with us in this cruel way seems to remain permanently open by the end of the play. And this openness is not necessarily a bad thing. By not closing, the plays of Shakespeare, like so many other powerful narratives, don't tell us what to think but cause us to think. Narrative as such, to borrow a line from I. A. Richards, is a "machine to think with."[5] Conversely, we tend to think of narratives that close the issues they raise, or at least close them too easily, like satire or children's fables, as lesser works, with modes like advertising and propaganda, which seek to close unequivocally, somewhere near the bottom. But this raises in turn yet another vexed issue. Is there something necessarily wrong or inferior about a narrative that closes with moral clarity? Conversely, isn't it an easy thing to build confusion into one's narrative? In short, the presence or absence of closure by itself can not be taken as a standard of narrative failure or success.

The peril of buying a story

Stockbrokers sometimes talk about clients who make the mistake of buying a story rather than a stock. These are people who hold on to dead or moribund stocks because they have become caught up in the story of the stock. What such people want is for this story to close in the right way, with a recovery and eventual ascent to the point where the buyer makes a profit. So strong is this investment in the story of the stock that the investor forgets where her or his best interest lies (e.g., abandoning the story of the stock and investing the money in securities that show promise).

What we can say is that closure is something we tend to look for in narratives. We look for it in the same way that we look for answers to questions or fulfillment to expectations. This would appear to be a natural human inclination. For this reason, the promise of closure has great rhetorical power in narrative. Closure brings satisfaction to desire, relief to suspense, and clarity to confusion. It normalizes. It confirms the masterplot. At the same time, we don't want closure too quickly. We seem to like the experience of remaining in doubt while moving toward closure. But even as I write this, I have to stop and remind myself that "we" refers to an immense number of very different people. Some of us demand closure and have little tolerance for narratives that don't provide it. Others prefer Kafka. Most of us have a broad range of narrative tastes, depending on our moods. If I pick up a mystery to read on the plane, chances are I am going to be disappointed if I don't eventually learn who killed Councilman Stubbs. But then, to complicate matters even further, some of us can find closure where others cannot. In other words, we read in different ways. So far we have been discussing the rhetorical power of narrative, but power also resides in the reader. We will take up this subject in Chapter Seven when we directly address the issue of **interpretation**. But before we get there, we need to look at yet another set of considerations that seem to be part of the text (what some call "formal" considerations) having to do with **narration**, that is, "the *telling* of a story."

Recommended secondary reading

There are a number of good works devoted to the subject of closure in narrative. Among these are Mariana Torgovnick's *Closure in the Novel* (Princeton University Press, 1981), David H. Richter's *Fable's End: Completeness and Closure in Rhetorical Fiction* (University of Chicago Press, 1974), and Russell J. Reising's, *Loose Ends: Closure and Crisis in the American Social Text* (Duke University Press, 1996). A major work on the general human tendency to project a cosmic masterplot with satisfying closure at its end is Frank Kermode's *The Sense of an Ending*. My distinction between closure (or the lack of it) at the level of expectations and closure at the level of questions is indebted to Roland Barthes's brilliant anatomy of how we read narrative, *S/Z*. A good book on suspense in narrative is Eric Rabkin's *Narrative Suspense*.

Additional primary texts

There is hardly a narrative that is not powered by a story of conflict, and there are numerous longer works – notably among nineteenth-century French and English novels – that feature several conflicts, often in progress over the same story time. The first two-thirds of the English nineteenth century also saw the production of many novels – by Austen, Dickens, Wilkie Collins, Trollope and others – in which it appears by the end of the novel that the *implied author* is seeking closure not only on the level of expectations but on the level of questions as well. In the latter part of the twentieth century, however, these same novels – among them *Emma* (Austen, 1816), *David Copperfield* (Dickens, 1849/50), *The Moonstone* (Collins, 1868), *The Eustace Diamonds* (Trollope, 1873) – were opened up in readings by a whole range of critics who, despite their differences, were intent on refuting easy assumptions about the kind of wisdom that such novels communicate. This latter day attention to complexity and ambiguity seems to have flowed in the wake of the energetic experimentalism of twentieth-century writers, many of whom were determined to frustrate the quest for closure. Among these are André Gide's *The Counterfeiters* (1925), Samuel Beckett's *Molloy* (1952), Alain Robbe-Grillet's *In the Labyrinth* (1959), Vladimir Nabokov's *Pale Fire* (1962), Thomas Pynchon's *Gravity's Rainbow* (1973), and Michael Joyce's hypertext novel *Afternoon: a Story* (1987/93). Among the narratives that I personally have found most challenging with regard to the question of closure, because they seem capable of yielding strongly built, yet conflicting, interpretations, are Emily Brontë's *Wuthering Heights* (1849), Dostoevsky's *Notes from Underground* (1863), Henry James's *Turn of the Screw* (1898), Joseph Conrad's *Heart of Darkness* (1899), and John Guare's play and film, *Six Degrees of Separation* (1990/93). There are many more.

In this chapter, I have tended to stress problems at the level of questions, but there are certainly examples of authorial challenge at the level of expectations. The best, I think, is *Great Expectations* (1860/61), for which Dickens wrote two quite different conclusions. The first satisfied Dickens's own sense of what the novel has led us to expect; in it, Pip and Estella part without marrying. The other is the one that Bulwer-Lytton persuaded Dickens was the only one his readership would accept; in it, Pip sees "no shadow of another parting" from Estella.

Chapter 6

Narration

A few words on interpretation

We have all had the experience of arguing about the *meaning* or *meanings* of a narrative. In other words, we have argued about how to *interpret* the narrative. "Meaning" is yet another debatable term in this field, but in general we think of meaning as having to do with ideas and judgments. Do narratives have meaning in this sense? Do they communicate ideas and produce judgments? There are some who would say: No, a story is just a story and a narrative is just a narrative, just as a picture is just a picture and a song just a song. But this is a pretty hard position to maintain. To begin with, it is very hard *not* to take notice of the ideas that come up everywhere during the course of a narrative. As one reads, say, *The Brothers Karamazov*, it is very hard *not* to become engaged in the debate on the ethics of killing. As to the question of whether or not narratives actually arrive at judgments – that is, arrive at *closure* on the level of intellectual and moral questions – the answer is: some seem to and some don't. Certainly, narratives that are satire or propaganda or advertising make judgments, some of them with hammer blows. But we have also just been acknowledging that many narratives refrain from closing at the level of questions. So there is a whole class of narratives, some of them very powerful, that don't appear to arrive at judgments.

Nonetheless, a refusal to judge is quite different from having nothing to do with judgment. To go back again to *The Brothers Karamazov*, though we may feel that an issue is still open by the end of the novel, we are at the same time hard put to disengage ourselves from the effort to resolve the issue. In other words, it is hard to treat the novel's debate on the ethics of killing as pure entertainment. It is hard to look at the novel as if it were a kind of music, orchestrated simply for our enjoyment. It is in fact arguable that no narrative can achieve such a "purely aesthetic" status – that all narratives, however playful, carry ideas and judgments with them. Be that as it may, certainly part of the value of Dostoevsky's novel lies in the fact that, like so many narratives, it deals openly with issues that most of us do take very seriously. That the narrative may not close with a judgment is not the same thing, then, as saying that judgment is irrelevant to it. Indeed, its openness is itself a kind of judgment. It is a judgment that the issue is too complex to warrant final judgment at this stage of our understanding.

The two chapters that follow this one are focussed squarely on the interpretation of narrative. But the subject of narration, and particularly of the narrator, is so central to problems in the interpretation of narrative that I have begun this chapter with these few words on the subject of interpretation.

The narrator

In this book we are considering all forms of narrative, including those that do not have narrators. Still, the number of the world's narratives that employ narrators is vast. And in interpretive disagreements, if there is a narrator, almost invariably the **reliability** of the narrator becomes a focus of dispute. This is because the first point almost anyone in the field of narrative will agree on nowadays with regard to narrators is that they should not be confused with authors. The narrator is variously described as an instrument, a construction, or a device wielded by the author. Some theorists (like Barthes) put this emphatically: "The (material) author of a narrative is in no way to be confused with the narrator of that narrative" ("Structural Analysis," 282).

But wait a minute . . .

I wonder about Barthes's "in no way." If I start to tell you the story of my life, should I "in no way" be confused with myself? If I should write my story instead of telling it, does my written voice now become utterly separate from who I am? Some might argue that in fact there is "no way" I can entirely hide myself, even if I wanted to – that whatever narrative voice I choose to narrate my story, there would be discernable traces of the real me lurking in it. Mark Twain caught this paradox neatly in a letter to William Dean Howells: "An autobiography is the truest of all books; for though it inevitably consists mainly of extinctions of the truth, shirkings of the truth, partial revealments of the truth, with hardly an instance of plain straight truth, the remorseless truth *is* there, between the lines, where the author-cat is raking dust upon it, which hides from the disinterested spectator neither it nor its smell . . . the result being that the reader knows the author in spite of his wily diligences."[1] Twain's remarks provide a good caution and advise us to go carefully when we generalize on this subject.

Whether or not you want to go as far as Barthes when he says the author "is in no way to be confused with the narrator," there is still no doubt about it: when you narrate you construct. This is true whether you are making up a story about creatures from another planet or telling the intimate secrets of your life. And though you can certainly lie when you narrate, and liars always construct, constructing is not the same thing as lying. Just as language comes to us with words and grammar ready made, out of which we construct our sentences, so narrative is always a matter of selecting from a great arsenal of pre-existing devices and using them to synthesize our effects. One of these devices is the narrator.

The device of the narrator, like the subject of point of view, with which it overlaps in a number of ways, has been intensely studied in the last fifty years. Out of the many discriminations that have been made with regard to the narrator, the three most useful are those of *voice*, *focalization*, and *distance*.

Voice

Voice in narration is a question of who it is we "hear" doing the narrating. This is yet another subject that begins with a simple distinction, and then gets richer and more interesting the further you look into it. The simple distinction is grammatical, that of "person," of which there are two principal kinds in narration: *first-person* ("I woke up that morning with a violent hangover") and *third-person* ("She woke up that morning with a violent hangover"). There have been a few experiments with narration in the second person ("You woke up that morning with a violent hangover"). Some of the latter, like Michel Butor's *La modification* (1957) and Italo Calvino's *If on a Winter's Night a Traveler* (1979) are notable achievements, but for whatever reasons there hasn't been much enthusiasm for second-person narration. Perhaps as readers we do not take well to being addressed in this way, with someone else telling us what we are thinking and doing ("You were tired of being pushed around by bullies, always fearful, never showing any courage. Well you'd show them. You'd commit a really serious crime. That would set the record straight").

Regarding first-person narration, it is important to stress that it almost invariably includes third-person narration.

> I woke up that morning with a terrible hangover. The phone rang. It was George. He said he was sorry. He promised never to harass me again. He had turned over a new leaf, he was going regularly to AA, he had opened a bank account and already, just that morning, had made a deposit that he intended to keep there until he had been sober for three consecutive months.

Most of this is told in the third person ("He said he was sorry. He pro-mised ..."). But technically we would call it first-person narrative because the narrator has used "I" and "me" to refer to herself, and she has a par-ticipating role (however brief it may turn out to be) in the story. As you can infer from this example, the degree to which the narrator refers to herself can vary greatly in narratives. This passage could, for example, be the beginning of a story about George with no more references at all by the narrator to herself. In other words, it might approach the status of a third-person narrative. But what we call narrative in the third person is most often told by a narrator situated outside of the world of the story. Such an *external* narrator generally does not include an "I" or "me" ref-erence and, therefore, does not invite us to look at him or her (or it) as a character.

> She woke up that morning with a terrible hangover. The phone rang. It was George. He said he was sorry. He promised Sally he would never harass her again . . . .

But here again, classifying in this area can never be neat. Third-person nar-rators have been known to refer to themselves. Henry Fielding referred to himself and his views frequently as he narrated *Tom Jones*.

> It is now time to look after Sophia, whom the reader, if he loves her half so well as I do, will rejoice to find escaped from the clutches of her passionate father, and from those of her dispassionate lover.[1]

And even if third-person narrators strictly avoid using "I" or "me" in ref-erence to themselves, they can still, by the quality of their language, convey the kind of personality we could well find in a character:

> Poor girl, she woke up that morning with a terrible hangover. Would that the phone would never ring. But it did. It was George. He said he was sorry, and like the confused, naïve, trusting soul that she was, she believed him.

Though there are no first-person references to the narrator in this version, there is most definitely the sense of a personality doing the narrating, some-one who cares enough to be a little frustrated by the behavior of this trusting soul. This third-person narrator in turn processes the scene for us as it passes through the screen of her (or his) personality.

So, to summarize, grammatical person is an important feature of voice in narration, but more important still is our sense of the kind of charac-ter (or non-character) it is whose voice colors the story it narrates. In this sense, narrative voice is a major element in the construction of a story. It is therefore crucial to determine the kind of person we have for a narrator because this lets us know just how she injects into the narration her own needs and desires and limitations, and whether we should fully trust the information we are getting. In some cases, when the voice is strong or interesting enough, it may be that the narrator herself, rather than the story, is the center of interest.

"Omniscient narration" and the authorial persona

Third-person narration and *omniscient narration* are often used interchangeably, but there is a risk in this. There are many instances of third-person narration that are anything but omniscient (literally "all-knowing"). Some critics reserve the term "omniscience" and "omniscient narration" for eighteenth and nineteenth-century novelists, like Fielding, who seem to preside over their fictional universes like all-knowing gods. But even in the texts of these authors, much is kept from view. In other words, even if the narrator seems omniscient, the *narration* is far from it.

In fact, you'll note that the quotation above from Fielding's *Tom Jones* expresses a distinctly human and this-worldly personality. Is this Fielding's personality? Yes and no. It certainly came from Fielding. He devised the words. And yet it is also a construction that serves the purposes of narration. The real, historical Fielding was a complex individual with many voices. For the narration of his novel, he created a kind of mask or authorial *persona* (which means "mask" in ancient Greek).

Focalization

Focalization is an awkward coinage, but it serves a useful purpose that the vaguer and more disputed term *point of view* cannot. It refers specifically to the lens through which we see characters and events in the narrative. Frequently, the narrator is our *focalizer*. Just as we hear her voice, we often see the action through her eyes. But this is not by any means always the case. Notice how, in the following scene from *Madame Bovary*, Flaubert's narrator maintains a strict, external third–person narrative voice but lets us look through the eyes of someone else:

> She nudged him with her elbow.
> "What does that mean?" he wondered, glancing at her out of the corner of his eye as they moved on.
> Her face, seen in profile, was so calm that it gave him no hint. It stood out against the light, framed in the oval of her bonnet, whose pale ribbons

were like streaming reeds. Her eyes with their long curving lashes looked straight ahead: they were fully open, but seemed a little narrowed because of the blood that was pulsing gently under the fine skin of her cheekbones. The rosy flesh between her nostrils was all but transparent in the light. She was inclining her head to one side, and the pearly tips of her white teeth showed between her lips.

"Is she laughing at me?" Rodolphe wondered.

But Emma's nudge had been no more than a warning, for Monsieur Lheureux was walking along beside them, now and then addressing them as though to begin conversation."[2]

Our focalizer in the long paragraph here is not Flaubert's unnamed narrator but Rodolphe, a character in the story who is at that moment walking beside Emma, planning his campaign of seduction. The intensity of his gaze, and by inference something of the character and intensity of his feeling, are indicated by the minute, highly focused anatomical details that we are allowed to absorb through his eyes. Flaubert's narrator keeps our gaze aligned with Rodolphe's for the full paragraph, then reverts to the neutral vantage of the narrator: "But Emma's nudge had been no more than a warning, . . ."

As you can see from the example, focalizing can contribute richly to how we think and feel as we read. Just as we pick up various intensities of thought and feeling from the voice that we hear, so also do we pick up thought and feeling from the eyes we see through. And just as the voice we hear can be either a character in the narrative or a narrator positioned outside of it, so also our focalizer can be a character within or a narrator without.

Distance

Usually, the extent to which the narrator plays a part in the story has an impact on our assessment of the information she gives us. Distance, as I am using the term here, refers to the narrator's degree of involvement in the story she tells. This is something that is almost infinitely variable. Pip, for example, tells the story of his own life in Dickens's *Great Expectations* (1860); the servant Nelly Dean tells the story of the lives of others in *Wuthering Heights* (1848). Yet Pip is a grown man when he tells the story of his growing up, a wiser man who, both in time and maturity, has attained a distance from the youth who made so many mistakes. Nelly Dean, in contrast, tells a story that is still in progress and in which she has strong sympathies and even plays a part. Because of her closeness to the characters and events, the question of narratorial distance has proved to be more of a problem in Nelly's case than in Pip's. Much of the interpretive debate over *Wuthering Heights* has centered on the degree to which we can trust her representation of the story.

At the other end of the spectrum from *Wuthering Heights*, there are texts in which the author has sought to create a narrative voice totally cut off from involvement in the tale. Hemingway could achieve this with considerable austerity:

> Dick Boulton came from the Indian camp to cut up logs for Nick's father. He brought his son Eddy and another Indian named Billy Tabeshaw with him. They came in through the back gate out of the woods, Eddy carrying the long cross-cut saw. It flopped over his shoulder and made a musical sound as he walked. Billy Tabeshaw carried two big cant-hooks. Dick had three axes under his arm.[3]

This is the entire first paragraph of the short story "The Doctor and the Doctor's Wife." It shows how closely related are considerations of distance and voice. In order to create narratorial *distance*, Hemingway devised a narratorial *voice* that gives the impression of complete emotional *non*involvement in what it narrates. Each sentence is focussed on dispensing information, one following the other like bare statements of fact, each built on the same simple syntactic noun–verb structure ("He brought," "They came"). There are no evaluative terms to indicate personal judgment. Adjectives, which often give the impression of a feeling response, are at a minimum. And with the possible exception of "musical," the adjectives that are included ("long," "big," "three") are emotionally neutral, as are the common verbs ("came," "to cut up," "brought") and nouns ("camp," "logs," "gate"). In this example, impersonality and distance are very closely aligned.

Three technical terms that may help

With increasing frequency, the term **diegesis** (which Plato originally used to refer to stories that were told, not acted) has been used to refer to the world of the story – that "reality" in which the events are presumed to take place. Thus, if a character narrates who also plays a role in the diegesis (like Pip or Nelly Dean), it is called **homodiegetic** narration. If a voice situated outside the action narrates, as in the example from Hemingway, it is called **heterodiegetic** narration. Gérard Genette argued with much justice that the distinction between homodiegetic and heterodiegetic narrators is more adequate than that between first- and third-person narrators for specifying whether a narrator is inside or outside of the world of the story.[4]

Reliability

Voice and distance, especially, but also focalization have much to do with what Wayne Booth referred to as the narrator's **reliability**. To what extent can we rely on the narrator to give us an accurate rendering of the facts? To what extent, once we have ascertained the facts, are we meant to respect the narrator's opinions when she offers an interpretation? Is Nelly Dean too harsh in her judgment of Catherine? Is she too soft in her judgment of Heathcliff? Booth, when he introduced the concept of *unreliable narrators*, was careful to point out that such narrators "differ markedly depending on how far and in what direction they depart from their author's norms" (159). And certainly, in order to interpret a narrative, we must have as fine a sense as we can of where a narrator fits on this broad spectrum of reliability.

But the difficulty this task can pose makes you wonder why authors would ever choose to entrust their narratives to an unreliable narrator in the first place. Yet they do, and the number is legion of narrators who are bumblers, madmen, jealous lovers, mean-spirited relatives, and even pathological liars. If this century has seen an increase in the number of unreliable narrators, they have nonetheless been around for a long time. Clearly there are advantages, besides willful obscurity, in handing narrative responsibility over to an untrustworthy narrator. One important advantage in such narratives is that narration itself – its difficulties, its liability to be subverted by one's own interests and prejudices and blindnesses – becomes part of the subject.

In some texts, the implied authorial vision emerges quite clearly, despite the narrator's unreliability. This is true in James Hogg's extraordinary novel *The Private Memoirs and Confessions of a Justified Sinner* (1824). Robert Wringham, the central figure and diarist-narrator of the second part of the novel, convinced of his own election (that is, that he is one of the rare "justified" sinners in the strict Calvinist scheme, pre-approved for salvation), writes with self-satisfaction of activities that appall the reader. These include Wringham's murder of his half-brother. Though we are picking up the narrative from his "unreliable" words, we nonetheless develop a clear judgment of his true character, as well as that of the mysterious friend (the Devil) who keeps encouraging him in his evil ways. In this narrative, then, there is not only great distance between the narrator's views and those of the *implied author*, but we have a clear understanding of the distance.

At the other end of this spectrum, and more unsettling because of its failure to arrive at some closure on the level of questions, is Akira Kurosawa's film classic *Rashomon* (1951). In this film, two travelers try to get to the truth of what appears to be a story of kidnapping, rape, and murder, involving a bandit (played by Toshiro Mifune) and two newlyweds. The story of the "crime" is told four times – once each by the three participants and a single witness. Each narrative tells the story in a way that is radically different from the others, yet still richly persuasive. By the end, we are left with the four narratives in suspension. Asked which was the true story, Kurosawa answered: "All of these, none of these."[5]

Between Hogg's novel, with its unreliable narrator but clear communication of what happened and how it should be judged, and Kurosawa's film, with its four competing narrators and its failure to render any judgment, there is a great range of unreliable narrators with a great range of impact. But the difference between Hogg and Kurosawa yields a helpful distinction among unreliable narrators: those whom we trust for the facts but not for their interpretation (Hogg's justified sinner), and those whom we cannot even trust for the facts (the narrators of *Rashomon*). Dorrit Cohn has referred to the former as *discordant* narrators.[6] They are narrators whom we feel we can rely on for the facts of the case, but whose interpretation of those facts is probably in discord with what we infer would be the author's interpretation. Getting to this *implied author* is one of the central challenges of interpretation. We will address it in the next chapter, but first we need to take up two more considerations with regard to narration that can play a significant role in interpretation.

Free indirect style

Just as the focalization can shift from one pair of eyes to another throughout a narrative, as it does in the example from *Madame Bovary* above, so too voice can shift as readily. Most frequently this shift is accomplished by moving from the narrator's voice to that of a character by means of *direct* citation, either of thoughts or openly expressed words. You can see such a shift happen above when we read the words that Rodolphe speaks to himself: "What does that mean?" In this instance, Flaubert changes the voice we hear by directly quoting his character's unvoiced thought. But this kind of shift can also be done *indirectly* by filtering a character's voice through the third-person narrator. It can also be done *freely*, that is, without any quotation marks or other indicators like the usual "she thought/she said." This fluid adaptation of the narrator's voice in a kind of ventriloquism of different voices, all done completely without the usual signposts of punctuation and attribution, is called *free indirect style* (or free indirect discourse). The author simply allows a character's voice momentarily to take over the narrative voice. Flaubert was a master of this. Here is Emma later in the novel, musing on the insufficiency of another lover. Notice how Flaubert starts with the *direct* mode of citation and then moves into the *indirect* mode:

> "I do love him though!" she told herself.
>
> No matter: she wasn't happy, and never had been. Why was life so unsatisfactory? Why did everything she leaned on crumble instantly to dust? But why, if somewhere there existed a strong and handsome being – a man of valor, sublime in passion and refinement, with a poet's heart and an angel's shape, a man like a lyre with strings of bronze, intoning elegiac epithalamiums to the heavens – why mightn't she have the luck to meet him? Ah, fine chance!... [7]

Though this is written in the third person ("she wasn't happy"), the voice is unmistakably Emma's. You can hear her complaining ("Why was life so unsatisfactory?"), mildly despairing ("Ah, fine chance!"), and thinking throughout in the sentiments and overblown language of popular romance ("a man of valor, sublime in passion and refinement, with a poet's heart and an angel's shape"). Her thinking, feeling, and vocabulary momentarily seize control of what is still third-person narration.

When the narrative voice is so free and fluid, it makes you wonder about the status of the narrator and whether one can even speak of *a* narrator in the case of free indirect style. Also, because it is so fluid, free indirect style can at times present quite a challenge for interpreters who are trying hard to locate a unified sensibility on which to base their interpretation.

Stream of consciousness and interior monologue

Here are two terms that are often used interchangeably for a technique that is very close to **free indirect style**. It is most useful, though, to keep all three terms as distinct as possible. "Stream of consciousness" is a phrase first used by William James in 1892 to describe the way we experience consciousness (as a continual stream of associated thoughts, without rational ordering and permeated by changing feelings). "Interior monologue" was first used almost at the same time by the French novelist Édouard Dujardin in his novel *Les lauriers sont coupés* (1887) to describe a technique of *free direct* (not *indirect*) style in representing the stream of consciousness of his characters. Early in this century, Dorothy Richardson, Virginia Woolf, James Joyce, William Faulkner, and others began experimenting with **stream of consciousness novels** in which the flow of consciousness of one or more characters was the principal focus. They used *interior monologue* to represent that subject.

But aren't the passages above from *Madame Bovary* interior monologue? The answer is that they could be, but because they are brief departures contained within a third-person narrative, the overall technique is free indirect style. Interior monologue is more extended, more thoroughly given over to a character's stream of consciousness. It is therefore usually *direct* rather than *indirect*, and often characterized by a variety of innovative techniques. The final chapter of Joyce's *Ulysses* is forty pages of unpunctuated interior monologue devoted to the immediate evocation of Molly Bloom's consciousness: "... but I was sure he had something on with that one it takes me to find out a thing like that he said you have no proof it was her proof O yes her aunt was very fond of oysters but I told her what I thought of her...."[8] Such writing can be an even greater challenge to interpretation than free indirect style.

At what point does free indirect style become interior monologue? Here again, we have a gray area in defining our terms. In long stretches of some of Virginia Woolf's novels (for example, *Mrs. Dalloway* [1925] or *To the Lighthouse* [1927]) it is hard to decide which term is more appropriate.

Narration on stage and screen

Narration through a narrator, though not the rule in either film or theater, has been deployed often enough in these media. Plays like Thornton Wilder's *Our Town* (1938) and films like *Murder My Sweet* (1944) and Stanley Kubrick's *A Clockwork Orange* (1971) make highly effective use of a narrator. The major difference in effect between narration in these media and narration in print or through oral storytelling is the degree to which the presence of visual imagery absorbs attention. This is especially the case in film, where narration is most frequently *voice-over* narration in which a disembodied voice is heard in tandem with imagery which is often conveying in its own way incidents of the story. The term "voice-over" itself indicates that the sound of the voice must share the sensory arena with the visual. And in the great majority of cases, voice-over narration is only intermittent and serves usually as a framing device at the outset, giving way within minutes to a full reliance on the performance of actors to convey the story. The film theorist David Bordwell wrote that "in watching films, we are seldom aware of being told something by an entity resembling a human being."[9] And with good reason. Certainly films have often begun by drawing on the ancient appeal of being told a story, so that we start out hearing the voice ("I suppose nothing would have happened if I had never met her. I was down to my last buck, and then I saw her, seated at the counter ..."). But at the same time we are already seeing the characters, watching them move and hearing them speak, and quickly the old form gives way almost unnoticed. "Maybe if I told you this story . . ." says Nelly Dean to Mr. Lockwood in William Wyler's 1939 film adaptation of *Wuthering Heights*. Her voice carries on for awhile over a fade-out as the setting changes to a time long ago in the realm of story when the Earnshaws were a happy family. A variation on this device, using print rather than an oral storyteller, is the opening of the original (1977) *Star Wars*. Viewers begin by reading a text – "A long time ago in a galaxy far, far away . . ." – that lengthens out into the universe. At one and the same time, viewers are taken back to an age (for some, quite "long ago") when they first read adventures like this and drawn visually into a place far away (more recently, the device was used again at the beginning of the *Star Wars* prequel, *The Phantom Menace*).

Voice-over was common in Hollywood films of the 1940s and 1950s and is still common today in European films. But rare as it may be today in Hollywood or on the stage, it is important to keep in mind that, simply by representing human life, plays and films are also crowded with instances of narration. They include narration in the dialogue in direct proportion as we narrate in life, which is many times a day. The same holds true for written narrative. The difference, again, is that on stage and in film we see and hear the characters who are doing the narrating. Though we still have to fill in, imaginatively, the details of the stories they tell, we watch and hear them as they do their telling. We see the expressions on their faces and the gestures and meaningful pauses they make. In other words, the actors do work for us that, when we read, we have to do entirely by ourselves. To that degree, with plays and films it is generally easier to assess how we should feel about what is narrated, where the emphasis should fall, what is important and what is not, and how we should judge the characters involved. This is true at least insofar as we have a clear grasp of the character narrator we observe. There is little wonder, then, that a performance of a play, or an adaptation of a play or novel to film, is called an "interpretation" – a point that we will come back to later.

Selected secondary resources

Wayne Booth's *The Rhetoric of Fiction*, after almost forty years, still serves as a lucid introduction to the narrator and the problems connected with this topic. Booth's treatment of both distance and reliability make a good foundation. Another book from the 1960s, Scholes and Kellogg's *The Nature of Narrative*, provides a somewhat contrasting take to my own in their chapter on "point of view." For more recent work, the third, concluding section of Mieke Bal's *Narratology* provides a concise overview of the narrator and narration. Also look at the two chapters on narration in Rimmon-Kenan's *Narrative Fictions*. The classic study of free indirect style is Roy Pascal's *The Dual Voice*, but for a short, lucid exposition of the same phenomenon in everything but the name, see Hugh Kenner's chapter on "The Uncle Charles Principle" in his *Joyce's Voices* (Berkeley: University of California Press, 1978, pp. 15–38). Regarding narrative in film, David Bordwell in *Narration in the Fiction Film* uses the term "narration" differently from the way I do in this chapter, but his text is nonetheless one of the most accessible and useful texts on the subject. See also Edward Branigan's *Narrative Comprehension and Film*.

Additional primary texts

Here once again it is hard to single out texts for the demonstration of formal qualities that recur in almost all narratives. But narrators do get especially interesting when their reliability is open to challenge, and in widely discussed cases, the reliability of the narrator has been a crux issue in the interpretation of the narratives he or she tells. Among these are Werther in Goethe's *Sorrows of Young Werther* (1774), Ellen Dean in *Wuthering Heights* (1848), the Governess in James's *Turn of the Screw* (1898), Nick Carroway in F. Scott Fitzgerald's *The Great Gatsby* (1925), and Humbert Humbert in Vladimir Nabokov's *Lolita* (1955).

Self-conscious experimentation with the broad issue of art's reliability in representation has been increasingly intense in the twentieth century. Here are four remarkable novels that quite deliberately work against reader confidence in the narrator: Samuel Beckett's *Molloy* (1951), Alain Robbe-Grillet's *In the Labyrinth* (1957), J. G. Ballard's *The Atrocity Exhibition* (1972), and Italo Calvino's *If on a Winter's Night a Traveler* (1979). In a wonderfully comic novel, Flann O'Brien's *At Swim-Two-Birds* (1942), the characters actually manage to escape from their author's control while he sleeps and even plot his death. In Stephen Sondheim's musical *Into the Woods* (1986) the characters actually succeed in killing the narrator by feeding him to a giant. Finally, it is worth mentioning Luigi Pirandello's now classic trilogy, *Six Characters in Search of an Author* (1921), *Each in his Own Way* (1924), and *Tonight We Improvise* (1930), which was designed to set every feature of theatrical production in conflict: characters, actors, the author, the director, the critics, and the spectators.

The use of voice-over narration in films comes in considerable variety. Frequently the voice is that of a character, often the central character, in the *diegesis*. When Raymond Chandler's *Farewell, My Lovely* was adapted to film as *Murder, My Sweet* (1944), detective Philip Marlowe does the narrating. In Francois Truffaut's *Jules et Jim* (1962), the voice-over narration comes from a *heterodiegetic* entity, that is, someone outside of the action and whom we never see. A third mode can be seen in the classic French farce *La ronde* (1951) in which Max Ophüls borrowed a narrative device from the stage – what the French call a *meneur de jeu*. This is a figure whom we do see and who talks directly to us, but who is not a part of the story. He or she connects the threads of the story, provides bemused commentary, and sometimes engages in gentle moralizing. In my view, one of the most interesting and complex interweavings of narration and direct representation in film is *Six Degrees of Separation*, Fred Schepisi and John Guare's 1993 adaptation of Guare's 1990 play of the same name. It is, moreover, fascinating to compare the original play with the film, especially in the way the audience shifts from being the intimate recipients of narrative in the staged version to onlookers observing the response of filmed intimates. But both the play and the film are powerful renderings of the struggle to contain through multiple retellings an increasingly complex story as it evolves. It is a fascinating case study of the need to control the inexplicable through narration.

Chapter 7

Interpreting narrative

In defining interpretative meaning as a compound of ideas and judgment, we need to be careful – especially with the word "judgment," since for some this word can conjure up the image of a judge making blistering judgments. But judgment, in the broad sense that we are using it, is an attunement of feeling to its object. These feelings come in all shades and strengths. If narrative is no stranger to the ferocity of Old Testament judgments, its judgments can also be extraordinarily subtle:

> THIS IS JUST TO SAY
>
> I have eaten
> the plums
> that were in
> the icebox
>
> and which
> you were probably
> saving
> for breakfast
>
> Forgive me
> they were delicious
> so sweet
> and so cold

William Carlos Williams's short narrative poem about a theft of fruit says something far from earth-shaking about simple pleasures. It tells us of their importance, how hard it is to resist them sometimes, and (more deeply layered in the poem) the value of a relationship that has found ways to honor such understandable weakness. It renders a judgment, but one that is delicately nuanced. Perhaps "evaluation" is a better word.

For longer works, most of the terms we have been discussing so far in this book describe elements that greatly help when it comes to bringing out ideas and judgments in narrative. In this chapter, we will take up a few more concepts that are central to a general understanding of what is involved in the interpretation of narrative. Again, I will restrict attention to the most useful of these. But where the terms discussed in the last chapter are largely *formal* terms in the sense that they describe elements like "the narrator" and "focalization" that are part of the form of narrative discourse, in this chapter I will shift the balance to focus more on what we, as readers and audiences, actually do when we interpret a narrative.

The implied author

In the last chapter, we referred to the challenge readers and audiences often face in trying to locate a sensibility behind the narrative that accounts for how it is constructed – a sensibility on which to base their interpretations. A good term for the sensibility that we seek is the *implied author*. Obviously, given what we have covered in the foregoing chapter, we cannot necessarily rely on the narrator to act as a direct, or even an indirect, representative of the implied author. Even the most sober, seemingly reliable narrators can turn out to be profoundly *unreliable* (or at least *discordant*, to use Dorrit Cohn's term). The master butler who cautiously and precisely narrates Kazuo Ishiguro's *The Remains of the Day* (1989) loses credibility as a direct result of his seeming objectivity. His capacity to suppress emotion in the service of duty makes him incapable either of responding to love when it comes his way or of recognizing and responding appropriately to evil, which also comes his way. Ishiguro's is one of many narratives (Hogg's *Confessions of a Justified Sinner* is another) in which we are required to go beyond the sensibility of the narrator for a just assessment of the novel's import. But if the narrator cannot be relied upon, the real author – the person who actually created the narrative – may be equally uncertain as a guide. After all, the real author is a complex, continually changing individual of whom we may never have any secure knowledge. So we posit an implied author. This is a key concept in interpretation, *insofar as we are concerned with "authorial intention"* – an important qualification, to which I will return in the next chapter.

An implied author is that sensibility (that combination of feeling, intelligence, knowledge, and opinion) that "accounts for" the narrative. It accounts for the narrative in the sense that the implied authorial views that we find emerging in the narrative *are consistent with all the elements of the narrative discourse that we are aware of*. Of course, when the real living and breathing author constructs the narrative, much of that real author goes into the implied author. But the implied author is also, like the narrative itself, a kind of construct that among other things serves to anchor the narrative. We, in our turn, as we read, develop our own idea of this implied sensibility behind the narrative. So the implied author (the term comes from Wayne Booth) could as easily be called "the inferred author" and perhaps with more justice, since we often differ from each other (and no doubt the author as well) in the views and feelings we attribute to the implied author. But the key point is that, insofar as we debate the intended meaning of a narrative, we root our positions in a version of the implied author that we infer from the text.

Department of Amplification

But seriously, why do we need to say "implied author"? Why not just say "the author"? The best answer is that, if by "author" we mean the person who wrote the narrative (which we usually do), then we are referring to somebody with a rich and complex life, whose personality is no doubt as multi-faceted as our own, and who like us is constantly changing. The real author may be open to many views that are actually condemned in the narrative. The real author may even, within a space of time, find her own work repugnant and repudiate it. In the case of a Hollywood film, the real author may not be a person at all, but a committee. So we may never have a good understanding of the real author, but we do have a chance of understanding the author implied by the narrative, or at least of constructing a plausible author by inference. In film theory, Albert Laffay used the term "grand imagier," or "grand designer" to refer to an intelligence that is at once present and invisible behind what we see in a film.[1] In his book on *Ulysses*, David Hayman uses the term "the arranger" to "designate a figure or a presence that can be identified neither with the author nor his narrators, but that exercises an increasing degree of overt control over increasingly challenging materials."[2] If you are looking for yet another way around this problem of attribution, you may find Umberto Eco's concept of the "intention of the text" attractive.[3] But I find it awkward to attribute intention to a non-sentient entity like a text. For me, "implied author" comes closest to describing what an author projects as she writes and what a reader infers as he reads.

In the years since Booth introduced the concept of the Implied Author, there have been many determined attacks on the concept, especially in the 1980s and 1990s when the implied author was seen as no less a reductive, exclusionary concept than that of the author: one moreover that perpetuates the same illusion of human beings as whole entities with clear boundaries. David Bordwell's articulate critique of the concept in *Narration in the Fiction Film* sees the implied author as part of the mistaken imposition of the "classic communication diagram: a message is passed from sender to receiver." He calls instead for attending primarily to the narrative text itself, "understood as the organization of a set of cues for the construction of a story" (62). But my remarks in this chapter, including my treatment of the implied author, apply to a specific kind of reading, which I am calling "intentional." There are other kinds (I will take up two others in the next chapter), but reading intentionally is a very widespread activity, whether it calls itself intentional or not. We tend not to see a film as put together accidentally, or by chance, but by intention. And we do this even when chance may have played a key role in the film's construction. Our "habit" of referring to Truffaut or Ophüls in the same way as we refer to Joyce or Dickens as we try to put together a reading is a clear symptom of this trait. Whether it is culturally determined or in some way genetic, I cannot say. But the job of work in this chapter, and part of the next, is not to judge but to bring into view what is involved in this common approach.

Underreading

When we try hard to develop an adequate sense of an implied author behind a text, one thing that becomes very clear is how vulnerable texts are to their audiences. For much of the earlier part of this book I made the opposite case: that we are vulnerable to narrative texts, that is, that given their rhetorical resources they seem to manipulate us and in general to exercise a good deal of power over our lives. Narrative texts hold us through suspense, they make us sympathize with this character and hope to see revenge against that one, they withhold the closure we seek and then (sometimes) they grant it. Not only do the narrative texts we come across have this power, but some would argue further that throughout our lives we are prisoners of these cultural texts – that they even do a lot of our thinking for us. But the final twist to all this is that we do manipulating of our own. As readers, we exercise a power over narrative texts that is arguably as great as their power over us. After all, without our willing collaboration, the narrative does not come to life. And the price we exact for this collaboration is that we do not simply absorb the information in the narrative discourse but, almost invariably, we overlook things that are there and put in things that are not there. We *underread* and we *overread*.

It is easy to see why we should underread. It is simply very difficult to achieve and then to maintain an awareness of all the details of a narrative. In the words of Frank Kermode, who coined the term:

> It is not uncommon for large parts of a novel to go virtually unread; the less manifest portions of its text (its secrets) tend to remain secret, tend to resist all but abnormally attentive scrutiny, reading so minute, intense, and slow that it seems to run counter to one's "natural" sense of what a novel is. (*Art of Telling*, 138)

Looking again at the second quotation from *Madame Bovary* quoted in the last chapter, how many of us reading this four hundred-page novel would pick up on the strange phrase "elegiac epithalamiums" in Emma's wish list for the man of her dreams ("a man like a lyre with strings of bronze, intoning elegiac epithalamiums to the heavens")? More than a few readers, of course, might not even know these words. But my guess is that even if they do, most would underread at this point, letting the curious phrase slip by. But the reader intent on not underreading would have to ask: How did this odd phrase come into Emma's stream of consciousness and what is its effect? "Elegiac" is the adjective for "elegy," and an elegy is a lament, usually for someone who has died. But an "epithalamium" is a poem celebrating a wedding. What on earth would an "elegiac epithalamium" be? It seems to be a flat contradiction. Are these, then, just fancy words thrown together in the confusion of Emma's mind, conveying by their sound alone something of the grandeur of this ideal lover she imagines? Are they limited to expressing her pretentious shallowness? Or might they also express something that is on her mind – the deadliness of her own marriage to Charles Bovary? Or, finally, is this funny phrase a sly comment, sent to us from the implied author, who uses the confusion of Emma's mind to make a statement about the institution of marriage in provincial towns?

If we do pass over "elegiac epithalamiums," we do something that happens all the time in our reading and viewing of narrative. But Kermode was also thinking of major underreadings that have had the power to shape cultures and even to shape the course of history.

> The history of interpretation may be thought of as the history of exclusions, which enable us to seize upon this issue rather than on some other as central, and choose from the remaining mass only what seems most compliant. (*Genesis of Secrecy*, 20)

In these instances, we seek by exclusion to close the narrative at the level of questions, and in doing so we achieve an interpretation. Of course, even at a high degree of richness or sophistication, interpretation is a form of *closure* in that it is an assertion of meaning within which the text can be accommodated. Even if the interpretation is an assertion of the text's multiple ambiguities, that itself is an embracing formulation.

When interpretation requires the rough and ready exclusions that Kermode refers to, it is easy to see how vested cultural or personal interests might be consciously or unconsciously at work in them. Much of the motive in this, of course, is the desire to restore normality, to settle a text's disturbing quality and bring it into line. Gabriel García Márquez catches the need to interpret by exclusion in his story "A Very Old Man with Enormous Wings." Finding an ancient man with huge wings floundering in their back yard, Pelayo and Elisenda key their reading of the creature to his "incomprehensible dialect" and "strong sailor's voice": "That was how they skipped over the inconvenience of the wings and quite intelligently concluded that he was a lonely castaway from some foreign ship wrecked by the storm."[4] This is absurd, of course, but the demand for interpretive closure exhibited by Pelayo and Elisenda, with its attendant underreading, probably to some degree reflects a necessity of ordinary life.

Robert Musil, in *The Man Without Qualities*, went so far as to argue that narrative itself can be a kind of underreading insofar as it is rooted in the desire (and necessity) to underread the complexity of life.

> [W]hen one is overburdened and dreams of simplifying one's life, the basic law of this life, the law one yearns for, is nothing other than that of narrative order, the simple order that allows one to say: "First this happened and then that happened...." It is the simple sequence of events in which the overwhelmingly manifold nature of things is represented, in a unidimensional order, as a mathematician would say, stringing all that has occurred in space and time on a single thread, which calms us; that celebrated "thread of the story," which is, it seems, the thread of life itself. Lucky the man who can say "when," "before," and "after"! Terrible things may have happened to him, he may have writhed in pain, but as soon as he can tell what happened in chronological order, he feels as contented as if the sun were warming his belly. This is the trick the novel artificially turns to account: Whether the wanderer is riding on the highway in the pouring rain or crunching through snow and ice at ten below zero, the reader feels a cozy glow, and this would be hard to understand if this eternally dependable narrative device, which even nursemaids can rely on to keep their little charges quiet, this tried-and-true "foreshortening of the mind's perspective," were not already part and parcel of life itself.[5]

Put more sympathetically, underreading, like the desire to find (and if necessary create) interpretive closure in the narratives we encounter daily, is probably rooted in the fact that in life we have to act. In order to act, we need to know (or at least think we know) what the story is. Our survival as a species has probably depended on our doing this with sufficient speed and efficiency to get done what we need to get done in order simply to stay alive.

The primacy effect

One interesting form of underreading is what Emma Kafalenos and others call "the primacy effect," which is our tendency to privilege, in our memory of a narrative, the first impression we developed early in the reading or witnessing of it. In our memory, the primacy effect can override the much fuller, and sometimes quite opposed, understanding of the narrative we may have had when we originally read or viewed it. Thus, for many, the tragedy of Catherine and Heathcliff almost exclusively dominates their impression of *Wuthering Heights*, even though the novel is only half way through when Catherine dies, and the budding romance of Hereton Earnshaw and Catherine's daughter plays a major role in the novel's conclusion.[6]

Overreading

At the same time, we overread. That is, we find in narratives qualities, motives, moods, ideas, judgments, even events for which there is no direct evidence in the discourse. This, again, should not come as a surprise. We are different people with different backgrounds, different sets of associations, different fears and desires. If I grew up as an ungainly girl with few friends and I had a beautiful little sister, who always complained of her lot and who was always petted and who wound up marrying a handsome, wealthy prince, I might see Cinderella in a different light than others. I might even see her as a scheming hypocrite (though it would take a lot of underreading along with overreading to do so). I might and I might not. But you can certainly recognize in this example something that is very common. Overreading is a phenomenon that is frequently cued by the masterplots in which our fears and desires are most engaged. It is what allows some people to flesh out an incident involving inexplicable lights in the night sky with a chain of events involving extraterrestrial beings. It is what allows others to load up a stranger with an unflattering moral character, cued only by the color of his skin. Our minds seem to abhor narrative vacuums. We try to fill them in.

So, if the concepts of underreading and overreading seem obvious, we nonetheless tend to forget our own susceptibility to them in almost every argument we have about the meaning of a particular narrative. This brings us back to the issue of *closure*. Probably the most difficult thing about reading narratives is to remain in a state of uncertainty. If a narrative won't close by itself, one often tries to close it, even if it means shutting one's eyes to some of the details and imagining others that aren't there, underreading and overreading. This goes for novels, films, plays, narrative poems, histories, newspaper reports, legal cases, and even the plumber's account of how your drains got clogged. It is true, in fact, of our response to all but the shortest and simplest narrative texts. And maybe not even these. Looking back at those two short texts we cited in Chapter Five, can you safely say that you haven't missed anything significant in either of them, or foisted something upon them that isn't there?

Powerful as the tendencies to underread and overread are, it is well worth keeping in mind that we also have the capacity to revise our readings. In this light, one way to define *intentional* interpretation (which is the kind we have been discussing) is the effort to reduce both underreading and overreading to a minimum. It is a process perhaps best achieved by minds coming together in a mutual lending of perceptions. One person, a woman perhaps, reading the passage quoted in the last chapter in which Rodolphe gazes at Emma Bovary, might respond to it quite differently from someone else, a man perhaps, reading the same passage. Our hypothetical woman might feel the gaze as prying and oppressive, an act of visual appropriation, a reduction of Emma to her material being. Our hypothetical man, in contrast, might see the power and inscrutability of her image; he might feel something of Rodolphe's mixture of bafflement and desire. Similarly, some of us, reading the second passage quoted from the same novel, might look with repugnance on an ignorant and shallow mind, corrupted by cheap romance, refusing to grow up. Others of us might be moved by the plight of this vigorous woman, trapped in a stale marriage and the narrow hypocrisy of French provincial towns.

It is hard to say where overreading ends and underreading begins in these conflicting interpretations of the two passages. But we might finally conclude that each of them underreads more than it overreads. In other words, the implied author that we finally construct for this novel would be a complex figure who combines in his mind all these readings in a mixture that is at once provocative and disquieting. F. Scott Fitzgerald once wrote: "the test of a first-rate intelligence is the ability to hold two opposed ideas in the mind at the same time."[7] Whether this is true or not, it is the case that in works at this level judgment is rarely black and white.

Gaps

There is another reason why overreading is inevitable: narratives by their nature are riddled with gaps. Even if we come as close as we humanly can to avoid underreading and overreading, we still have to fill things in if we are to make sense of the narratives we read or see.

> That night we lay on the floor in the room and I listened to the silk-worms eating. The silk-worms fed in racks of mulberry leaves and all night you could hear them eating and a dropping sound in the leaves.[8]

In these first two sentences of Hemingway's short story "Now I Lay Me," a number of gaps open up. Where are we? Why are we lying on the floor? What do silk-worms sound like when they eat? What is a "dropping sound"?

Is it like the sound of rain? Why can't or won't the narrator shut out the sound of the silk-worms? If he (is it a he?) listens "all night," why is he staying awake?

As we read, the narrative discourse gives us some guidance for filling in these gaps. We learn that the narrator is recalling a time when he was convalescing "seven miles behind the lines." From a few historical markers and the fact that his orderly is an Italian who was conscripted when he returned home, we infer that these "lines" are the Italian front during World War I. We infer from the fact that they "were lying on blankets spread over straw," that the narrator and his orderly are in a makeshift ward in a structure (a house? a barn?) appropriated for the purpose. But much of these inferences, insofar as we build them in our minds, are constructed from what we know or imagine of houses or barns in Italy in the second decade of the twentieth century. We never receive any more information on the sound of silk-worms eating (except that it is different from that of guns in the distance), so if this gap is going to be filled in, we must use what we know, or imagine, about the sounds of things dropping on leaves.

And why can't he sleep? We learn a reason for this in the next two sentences:

> I myself did not want to sleep because I had been living for a long time with the knowledge that if I ever shut my eyes in the dark and let myself go, my soul would go out of my body. I had been that way for a long time, ever since I had been blown up at night and felt it go out of me and go off and then come back.

This explains why he knows that the silk-worms feed all night. But it also helps us, by inference, to account for why he may listen to them obsessively – because they help block out the more distant sound of the guns. As for the specific nature of his wounds when he was "blown up," this gap remains wide open. We do learn, with regard to the immediate impact of that event, that his soul went out of his body and then came back again, but for most of us we are again forced to do some filling in since few of us have had this experience.

The reading of narrative is a fine tissue of insertions like this that we make as we move from point to point. And though this can often lead to overreading, it also gives the experience of narrative much of its power. In other words, the energy narrative draws on is our own. Wolfgang Iser, who wrote at length about the gaps in narrative, put it this way: "it is only through inevitable omissions that a story gains its dynamism."[9] But it is also worth underscoring at this point that we have little clear understanding of what exactly the mind does when it reads. And if filling in gaps is one of the ways the mind makes narrative "dynamic," another way is to limit this filling in – not to go too far. When Satan is described in *Paradise Lost*, rising from the burning lake in hell, Milton gives an indication of his immensity by strategically limiting the information he gives us:

> Then with expanded wings he stears his flight
> Aloft, incumbent on the dusky Air
> That felt unusual weight   (I, 225–7)

Had he told us that Satan was 100 feet in length, had a wingspan of 85 feet, and weighed roughly 8 tons, Milton would not have communicated the same sense of immensity that he does in these three lines. He gains by leaving out, by suggesting and not specifying. Satan does not fly, but "stears his flight" like a ship; he is weighted with low "u" sounds, "incumbent on the dusky air"; and even the air, normally so unfazed by everything and anything, "felt unusual weight." As in a bad dream, we don't see but rather feel the satanic hugeness of this creature. Satan arouses awe to the degree that the reader does not fill in the descriptive details about him. So here is another interesting complication in the field of narrative. If narrative comes alive as we fill in its gaps, it also gains life by leaving some of them unfilled. In the art of narrative, less can be more.

Gaps and multiple interpretations

"[O]ne text is potentially capable of several different realizations, and no reading can ever exhaust the full potential, for each individual reader will fill in the gaps in his own way, thereby excluding the various other possibilities; as he reads, he will make his own decision as to how the gap is to be filled. In this very act, the dynamics of reading are revealed. By making his decision, he implicitly acknowledges the inexhaustibility of the text; at the same time it is this very inexhaustibility that forces him to make his decisions."

Wolfgang Iser (280)

Cruxes

We have been discussing the running texture of gaps that characterizes all narratives, but in the field of interpretation some gaps have proven to be more central than others. One such gap is the mystery surrounding the origins of Heathcliff in *Wuthering Heights*. All the information we have on this subject is that he was found by Mr Earnshaw, a "dark" lad, speaking "gibberish," "starving, and houseless, . . . in the streets of Liverpool."[10] Is

Brontë drawing largely on nineteenth-century English stereotypes of racial others here? Is Heathcliff a moor, a "lascar," a gypsy, an Irish castaway? Or is he royalty, as Nelly encourages him to think: "Who knows but your father was Emperor of China, and your mother an Indian queen" (98)? Or is he supernatural: "a man's shape animated by demon life – a Ghoul – an Afreet," as the author's sister Charlotte Brontë insisted in her preface to the 1850 edition (40)? Or, finally, is he simply English? The issue is important when we try to fashion some interpretive evaluation of Heathcliff's strange combination of brutality, love, and implacable narrowness of purpose. Is our nineteenth-century implied author trying to suggest that Heathcliff is not quite human? more than human? just as human as the rest of us? Or is she asking us to keep our minds open on this subject?

Gaps of this sort are *cruxes*. In criticism, a crux is an oft-debated element in a work that, depending on how we interpret it, can significantly effect how we interpret the work as a whole. There is a crux, for example, in "Now I Lay Me," the deceptively simple short story by Hemingway I discussed above. It consists of a gap between the significance of the narrator's war wound and the significance of a memory that dominates the latter part of the narrative. And the question posed by the gap is: How do these two rather different events belong together in the same story? The memory arises this way: to occupy himself while he is awake the narrator usually spends his time recalling in minute detail trout streams with which he is familiar by fishing them again in his mind. When this fails, he tries to pray for all the people he has ever known, and to do this he tries to remember everything that has happened to him and everybody that he has known. But in the narrator's rendering of this effort to remember, only one memory is narrated in detail, taking up three paragraphs. This is it: Once when his father was out hunting, his mother took all of his father's cherished collection of Indian artifacts and burned them.

> When my father came home and got down from his buggy and hitched the horse, the fire was still burning in the road beside the house. I went out to meet him. He handed me his shotgun and looked at the fire. "What's this?" he asked.
>
> "I've been cleaning out the basement, dear," my mother said from the porch. She was standing there smiling, to meet him. My father looked at the fire and kicked at something. Then he leaned over and picked something out of the ashes. "Get a rake, Nick," he said to me. I went to the basement and brought a rake and my father raked very carefully in the ashes. He raked out stone axes and stone skinning knives and tools for making arrow-heads and pieces of pottery and many arrow-heads.   (366)

Here, as so often in Hemingway, the narration is extremely restrained, even though it is narrated in the first-person. The narrator's *voice* is almost neutral, with scarcely any explicitly evaluative language. Consequently, we are called on to fill in gaps of feeling, that of the son watching his father, and that of the father as understood by the son. Filling in, we infer that this had to be a calamitous event for his father, now carefully laying out the burnt artifacts, noting that "The best arrow-heads went all to pieces." There must have been great fury, too, yet not one word of anger or even protest is lodged against the smiling woman who has destroyed years of caring and patient collection. And here is another gap: Is she crazy? Is she just insensitive? Or is she quite aware of what she is doing: a calculated and cruel exercise of authority, made even worse by her smile? Regarding this last gap, we get no assistance from the rest of the narrative (though we may well still fill this gap from our experiences). But I think we can with justice infer not only heartbreak and anger in the narrator's father, but also a paralyzing incapacity (fear? the sense of futility?) to stand up for himself in this situation, to express his anger and lodge a protest.

Filling gaps versus overreading

There is nothing that I can see in Hemingway's story to indicate that any of the three readings of the narrator's mother (crazy, insensitive, cruel) could be charged with *overreading*. Each works with the other elements in the story. But if I were to propose that she is a demon or, conversely, a noble figure, heroic in her housecleaning chores, I would have my work cut out for me. I would have to reconcile the former with the realistic texture of the narrative discourse, and the latter with its predominating focus on the men.

Here, once again, I have been working with what we are given in the discourse to fill in the kinds of gaps that Iser describes as the dynamic life of narrative. And, as Iser also points out, how I fill these gaps can alter the narrative itself. But the crux I referred to above lies not in these but in this: In the story as a whole, how does the wounding of the son that we learn about early in the narrative relate to the wounding of the father that we learn about later? These two incidents of wounding, the one physical and the other psychological, separated widely in "real" time, are the two major events we learn of in this very short story. Why has our implied author brought them together? Why has he chosen to dwell on this single unhappy memory, called up by a wounded soldier fearing that he will die if he closes his eyes? Are we meant to see these events as two *constituent events* in the narrator's life story? And if so, is Hemingway's story merely setting them down as two separate bad things that happened to our narrator? Or is the story aligning them in some other way? Are they two kinds of death? Are they two sides of the same deadly thing in the mind of this narrator? Has the trauma of being "blown up" under fire in the course of the "manly" pursuit of war re-ignited or in some way coalesced with the memory of his father, shotgun in hand and home from the hunt, being "unmanned" by the destruction of his hunting artifacts by fire? Is this story a variant on the *masterplot* of Samson, who was robbed of his strength by Delilah, or of Circe, who turned men to swine? If I am on the right track in my questioning, then for the particular male sensibility represented by the narrator, women and warfare are inter-identified as threats to life – the two kinds of fear, being at bottom the same fear. I am inclined to see the story this way. But where would I look to find additional evidence for this interpretation? To put this another way, how would I defend myself against the charge of overreading?

Repetition: themes and motifs

When you are having trouble interpreting, one thing that can often help is to look for what repeats itself. *Themes* and *motifs* are the two terms most frequently used for the repetitions in narrative. As technical terms, they are often used interchangeably, though "motif" is especially varied in its meanings. But as a general working rule for the discussion of narrative, a theme is abstract and a motif is concrete. Beauty, nature, violence, and love can be themes; roses, gardens, fists, and the phrase "Barkis is willin" can be motifs. Themes are implicit in motifs, but not the other way around. Motifs are, in Gerald Prince's words, the "minimal thematic unit" (55). Windows, for example, are a motif in *Wuthering Heights* and, given the way Brontë deploys them, they support a highly complex interplay of three themes: escape, exclusion, and imprisonment. When, for another example, the character Barkis in *David Copperfield* continues to repeat his cryptic phrase, "Barkis is willin'," it becomes a motif, a signature phrase for the theme of shy, honest-hearted devotion in love that Barkis exhibits in his pursuit of Peggotty. Identifying themes and motifs cannot in itself produce an interpretation, since the same themes and motifs can lend themselves to any number of different interpretations. But identifying themes and motifs can help enormously in establishing what a work is about and where its focus lies, and that in turn can be used to eliminate some interpretations and to lend support to others. In *David Copperfield*, Barkis makes one kind of statement about love, but in the context of the novel, we see a very different treatment of the theme of love in the seduction of Emily by the smoothly treacherous Steerforth. Together with other treatments of the theme, a complex picture of love begins to develop.

To go back to my reading of Hemingway's "Now I Lay Me," the question I left off with was: Am I making too great a jump in the way I try to fill in the gap between the narrator's war trauma and his memory of his parents? These are, after all, two separate points of focus in the development of the narrative. Can I find repetitions that lend support? Do other elements — *supplementary events* or descriptive detail — serve to bring these two major events together or to leave them islanded? To begin to answer this, if I move back just a short way in the narrative from the account of the narrator's father and mother, I will find that this memory is introduced by "the earliest thing" that the narrator can remember: "the attic of the house where I was born and my mother and father's wedding-cake in a tin box hanging from one of the rafters, and, in the attic, jars of snakes and other specimens that my father had collected as a boy" (365). By means of these objects two themes are juxtaposed — marriage and the passionate interests that a boy pursues by himself. And these are precisely the themes that will collide in the memory that follows.

After his account of the memory of his parents, the narrator recalls a conversation he had with his Italian orderly, John, also wounded and awake in the room. In this brief exchange, John not only talks about his own marriage but urges his "Tenente" (Lieutenant) to marry as well. "A man ought to be married. You'll never regret it. Every man ought to be married" (370). Marriage again. We now have three points where this theme surfaces. And then it pops up again. Following his conversation with John, the narrator writes that now "I had a new thing to think about and I lay in the dark with my eyes open and thought of all the girls I had ever known and what kind of wives they would make." But he soon goes back to trout fishing, because the streams were all distinct, "while the girls, after I had thought about them a few times, blurred and all became rather the same and I gave up thinking about them altogether" (371).

Why are all women the same woman for this man, while all streams are individually distinct? If to some degree we have to rely on our imagination to fill this gap, we also have to work with what the narrative provides, and the one woman we see in the story is the narrator's mother. If we have read that critical scene correctly, she is a frightening individual who not only destroys without warning what a man values, but also appears to have the power to rob a man of his strength. Is this, then, why all women blend into one for the narrator? Is this why he goes back in his imagination to the world of trout streams where nothing threatens, and he can rely on his physical strength and his wits to achieve his ends? In my reading, the answer to both questions is yes, but the important point is that I have developed a *thematic* analysis to support my original contention. I have looked at the rest of the story and asked: what repeats itself? This is also a way of asking: where is the implied author trying to take us, as we interpret?

In my reading, by making marriage so insistent a theme, the implied author underscores the importance of the one marriage the narrator seems to know best: that of his parents. Given the way that relationship is represented, I am in turn encouraged to close the gap between the threat of war and the threat of marriage: to see them, in other words, as similarly destructive from the point of view of the narrator. This reading would appear to be clinched by one additional step the author took when he capitalized on the special weight that endings have, by returning to the marriage theme one more time at the conclusion of the narrative. These are his final words and, in this interpretation of the story, they create a sad but powerful sense of closure.

> [John] came to the hospital in Milan to see me several months after and was very disappointed that I had not yet married, and I know he would feel very badly if he knew that, so far, I have never married. He was going back to America and he was very certain about marriage and knew it would fix up everything. (371)

Interpretation is a fine art involving many considerations. In this chapter I have concentrated on four of the most useful things to be aware of in interpreting narrative, but I have also drawn on concepts we have discussed earlier (the *narrator*, *distance*, the distinction between *constituent and supplementary events*, *masterplot*, *closure*). However, these can only provide material to work with. As you can see from my reading of "Now I Lay Me," much of interpretation is a process of subjecting the information one gathers to chains of inductive and deductive thinking. In this regard, narrative interpretation is no different from analysis in most other fields in which meaning must be culled from data.

Recommended secondary reading

With regard to the concept of the implied author, once again Wayne Booth's *Rhetoric of Fiction* is the germinal study, and in fact the work in which the term was first introduced. Booth took much heat for certain aspects of his treatment of the concept. A response can be found in his later book *The Company We Keep: an Ethics of Fiction* (Berkeley: University of California Press, 1988, see especially the chapter "Implied Authors as Friends and Pretenders," pp. 169–98). In contrast, David Bordwell's *Narration in the Fiction Film* can be read throughout as an effort to replace the centrality of the implied author and to correct the mistake of automatically applying a "communication model" to the experience of film. The terms "underreading" and "overreading" come from Frank Kermode's brilliant study, *The Genesis of Secrecy*. A major treatment of the role that gaps play in a reader's construction of narrative is found throughout Wolfgang Iser's *The Implied Reader*. For a superbly readable inquiry into famous nineteenth-century cruxes, many of which involve significant gaps, I recommend the series of books by John Sutherland – *Is Heathcliff a Murderer?*, *Can Jane Eyre Be Happy?*, and *Who Betrays Elizabeth Bennet?* (all published by Oxford University Press, 1996, 1997, and 1999, respectively). A classic treatment of repetition in the novel can be found in the last chapter of E. M. Forster's *Aspects of the Novel* (1927): "Pattern and Rhythm." More recently, two contrasting treatments of the subject of repetition that have now become common reference points are Bruce F. Kawin's *Telling it Again and Again: Repetition in Literature and Film* (Ithaca, NY: Cornell University Press, 1972) and J. Hillis Miller's *Fiction and Repetition: Seven English Novels* (Cambridge, MA: Harvard University Press, 1982).

Additional primary texts

All narratives that have problematic narrators – that is, narrators whose reliability is an interpretive crux – are narratives that present a challenge in the construction of the implied author. Many of the texts, then, featured in the last chapter are excellent case studies for the problem of constructing an implied author. And as we all underread, it is also the case that almost any narrative serves to demonstrate this fact insofar as it will contain potentially significant elements that can escape notice. The longer or more complex the narrative – as, for example, Homer's *Odyssey* (c. 8th to early 7th century BC), Murasaki's *Tale of Genji* (10th century AD), Stendhal's *The Red and The Black* (1830), Emily Brontë's *Wuthering Heights* (1848), Dostoevsky's *Brothers Karamazov* (1880), Thomas Mann's *The Magic Mountain* (1924), André Gide's *The Counterfeiters* (1926), Vladimir Nabokov's *Ada or Ardor* (1969), or Don DeLillo's *Underworld* (1997) – the more nearly impossible it is not to let important elements slip in interpretation. And as overreading is also inevitable, again almost any text will serve as an invitation to put in significance or even narrative material that is not demonstrable from the text. There are notable interpretive cruxes that are gaps. In *Wuthering Heights* (1847), does Heathcliff kill Hindley Earnshaw? In *The Turn of the Screw* (1898) did the Governess see a picture or hear a description of Peter Quint sufficient to allow her to construct a fantasy resembling him? There is no credible information in the text that would support such a reading, but this has not prevented interpreters from inserting such material to support the contention that there are no ghosts in James's novella, only projections of the Governess's perfervid imagination. Very wide gaps are often a distinguishing feature of modernist and post-modernist texts. A salient example of a narrative in which the gaps are too wide to fill with any degree of confidence is Samuel Beckett's *Molloy* (1951). What makes this narrative so intriguing is the way it invites constructions that bridge its many gaps, but never provides sufficient information to confirm any of these constructions. Michael Joyce's hypertext novel, *Afternoon, a Story* (1987/93), is another example, Julio Cortázar's *Hopscotch* (1963) is a third, and for a fourth, perhaps the most self-conscious of all novels on the subject of its own gaps: Italo Calvino's *If on a Winter's Night a Traveler* (1979).

Much of modernist fiction, in its movement away from the traditional linearity of eighteenth and nineteenth-century novels, also relies on the structural support of motifs. Joyce's *Ulysses* (1922) is perhaps the most famous example of a modernist text erected on a predetermined scaffolding of repetitions. But before it, *A Portrait of the Artist as a Young Man* (1916), Joyce's first published novel, is a richly poetic set of narratives in which colors, birds, water, other images, together with an array of phrases, gather a complex set of associations as they recur in different contexts. Other modernist texts that rely heavily on repetitions are Virginia Woolf's *To the Lighthouse* (1927), E. M. Forster's *A Passage to India* (1924), and Marcel Proust's immense serial novel, *In Search of Lost Time* (1913–27). But if modernists made repetition one of their trademarks, the device goes as far back as narrative itself. Works, especially, that come out of a tradition of oral story-telling, like Homer's epics and the Anglo-Saxon *Beowulf*, depend heavily on "oral formulaic" repetitions, which functioned primarily as devices to aid the memory and fill out the metrical line.

Chapter 8

Three ways to interpret narrative

There are many ways to interpret narrative, but almost all of them belong to one of three fundamentally distinct approaches: the intentional, the symptomatic, and the adaptive. Before I set these out, however, I need to focus on an assumption that has been lurking behind most of what I wrote in the last chapter. This is the assumption that narratives are "whole" in the sense that everything in a narrative somehow *belongs* and contributes to its meaning. Frank Kermode put this in the form of a question: "Why... does it require a more strenuous effort to believe that a narrative lacks coherence than to believe that somehow, if we could only find out, it doesn't?" (*Genesis of Secrecy*, 53).

The question of wholeness in narrative

This assumption of some kind of deep coherence or wholeness lies behind an old rule in the history of interpretation. Over 1600 years ago, Saint Augustine wrote with regard to scripture that meanings found in one part must "be seen to be congruous with" meanings found in other parts.[1] In other words, interpretations have to work for the whole text. In my reading of "Now I Lay Me," I applied this rule, trying hard to find an interpretation that was "congruous with" all the parts of the narrative. But suppose I wanted to make a more sweeping interpretation of "Now I Lay Me." Suppose I wanted to argue that the implied author in this story is not merely showing how a certain person, growing up in a certain way, can come to see marriage as a threat to his life but rather arguing through this narrative that any marriage is deadly for men because all wives are out to destroy their husbands.

If I followed Augustine's rule, I would have an immediate problem with this position because of the presence in the narrative of the narrator's orderly. John is, by his own account, very happily married. He could well be mistaken about this, but I can see nothing *in the narrative discourse* to indicate that his marriage is anything other than he says it is. To see the narrative as a vehicle for the larger, more sweeping thesis that women destroy men through marriage, John would have to be neutralized in some way. I would

93

need to find some indication that he is deceived, or lying, or crazy, or in some other way not to be trusted in the account he gives of his own happiness in marriage. I might be able to do this and then again I might not, but you can see how Augustine's rule provides a control over the multiplicity of interpretation that Iser says all narratives are subject to because of the existence of gaps. The rule does not eliminate the multiplicity (Augustine himself acknowledged this), but it does limit it. It is a significant check on *overreading*.

But is it necessarily true that narratives are whole? On what grounds can we assume they are? Some would argue that, far from being whole, all narratives are necessarily incomplete, fractured, and even self-contradictory. This multiplicity of meaning reflects not only our own human multiplicity (i.e., we are as self-contradictory as stories are) but also the fluidity of language itself. For these scholars, the inevitable gaps in narrative that I discussed in the last chapter are far more extensive than anything that can, or for that matter should, be controlled through ideas of wholeness. As for Augustine, the text he was trying to interpret was Holy Scripture, for which the Author is presumed to be divine, not mortal – a specialist in creating unity. For the rest of us, fallen and hopelessly fragmented as we are, wholeness is something that we impose on narratives, rather than something we find in them.

Whatever your own views are on the question of wholeness, I bring it up here at the beginning of this chapter because one's assumption of wholeness, or its lack, is closely tied to how one interprets narrative.

Intertextuality, imitation, and allusion

Attacks on the idea of textual wholeness were reinforced when Julia Kristeva first introduced the concept of *intertextuality* in 1967. What intertextuality refers to is the fact that all texts (films, plays, novels, anecdotes, or whatever) are made out of other texts. Just as a language pre-exists any narrative written in that language, so too do all of a narrative's other features precede it, from its overarching genres to its minute turns of phrase. They come out of a pre-existing cultural web of expressive forms. Seen in this way, narratives have no borders but are part of an immense, unfolding (and hence ever-changing) tapestry. Conversely, this larger cultural weave is an inextricable part of the (ever-changing) meanings of the narrative. To interpret intertextually is to bring out this complex embeddedness of a narrative's meanings in the culture from which it comes.

Of course, we have always recognized that narratives, like all works of art, draw on pre-existing genres and that they *imitate* or *allude* to

> pre-existing narratives. But the terms *imitation* and *allusion* shift the emphasis from an inescapable intertextual web that generates the narrative and produces its effects to an individually distinct narrative, shaped by an author through a process of skillful selection. Where intertextuality tends to minimize the author's role and the distinctive wholeness of the work, allusion and imitation tend to the reverse: featuring the author's control and the singular wholeness of the work.

Intentional readings

To key one's reading to an implied author, as I did in the last chapter, is to assume wholeness in the sense that one assumes that a single creative sensibility lies behind the narrative. That sensibility has selected and shaped its events, the order in which they are narrated, the entities involved, the language, the sequence of shots. When we read this way, we are reading *intentionally*. In other words, the ideas and judgments that we infer from the narrative are understood to be in keeping with a sensibility that intended these effects. Some would say that this is the only valid way to read a narrative. One argument is that this accords with the way we usually behave when we interpret: that is, we usually assume that a narrative, like a sentence, comes from someone bent on communicating. The novelist Paul Auster put it simply: "In a work of fiction, one assumes there is a conscious mind behind the words on the page."[2] Intentional reading accords respect to this author behind the implied author in the same way that most of us hope to be respected in the narratives that we ourselves tell.

As for situations where there are two or more authors, or even teams of writers and directors involved in making a film, the argument is that such collaborations implicitly construct a single sensibility as they proceed with their work. In other words, an implied author is one of the things that, consciously or unconsciously, these collaborators share, and they have it in mind when they edit things out of the narrative or bring things in. It is a device that allows the work to hang together. And if someone objected that life doesn't hang together, or that people (even authors) are anything but unified, a common answer is: Yes, but narratives can be. One might go on to argue that this, in fact, is one of the pleasures of narrative, as it is of art in general. Narrative is one way of creating order out of chaos, or as Robert Frost said regarding poetry: making "a temporary stay against confusion." The implied author, however complex or sophisticated the sensibility we attribute to her, is part of that order.

Reinventing the implied author

Every once in a while, a novel will be written by a series of authors, each producing a chapter one after the other, without prior consultation. Author A writes the first chapter, then mails it to author B, who reads it, writes the second chapter, then mails it to author C, and so on until it is done. Some of these efforts, like the mystery *The Floating Admiral* (1931) and the steamy American best seller *Naked Came the Stranger* (1969),[3] actually give strong support to the idea of the implied author as a functioning construct. Even without planning together, in other words, each successive writer tries to make his or her chapter consistent with the implied authorial sensibility that seems to be emerging.

In others, like *London Consequences* (1972), a good deal of the fun is tracking the ways in which successive authors undermine the implied sensibility and intentions of preceding chapters. One finds very much the same effect in "theater improv" (and, gamers tell me, in many role-playing games as well). In improv, entertainments in which a narrative is improvised by a small team of actors working with suggestions from the audience, the actors are required to obey an injunction against "blocking." That is, they must accept as part of the narrative the entities and events that have been made a part of the evolving narrative. But given these "facts," the challenge is to see how wildly one can wrench the story out of its course. The audience gives the players Aunt Matilda and her three beautiful nieces. Player A then tells the audience that Aunt Matilda is the brains behind an international band of smugglers and that her "nieces" carry bags of a controlled substance concealed in their dresses. Player B tells the audience that the controlled substance is Viagra. And so on. But in its perverse way, improv is an exception that proves the rule – the rule being not that we *should* look for the implied author but that we *seem predisposed* to do so anyway. From the first information we get, even in improv, we seem automatically to begin constructing an implied sensibility that accounts for the way the entities behave and the events unfold. Without this predictable inclination on the part of audiences, improv would not be half as funny as it is.

An additional appeal of intentional interpretation is that it provides one of the few widely accepted standards by which interpretations can be evaluated. By looking at a narrative as a whole and trying to grasp an intention behind it, we have a way of grounding a reading and making the case for its validity. If this kind of validity is of value, then Augustine's rule and the *implied author* provide their service. If, for example, the real author has credit with readers as someone whose writing is worth attending to, then it makes sense in such cases to seek to triangulate from the varied elements of the narrative, the sensibility that organizes them.

Validity and invalidity in interpretation

Establishing validity in interpretation can be a daunting task. And there are some who argue that finding valid interpretations is finally impossible. Others argue that pinning validity to an implied author is a way of controlling the text rather than discovering its meanings. However these arguments may be settled, there does seem to be a broad common-sense recognition among all parties to the debate that numerous instances of *invalidity* in interpretation can be recognized. Most of us would probably agree that the number of immediately recognizable *in*valid interpretations of, say, *Madame Bovary* is beyond counting. The novel is not, for example, about planetary exploration; it does not develop ideas in this sphere or render judgments. Nor is it about sea slugs. Nor is it about the wheat harvest in Russia. Silly as these possibilities sound, they tell us that there are definite limits to what we can propose as an interpretation of a text and expect people to listen.

Symptomatic readings

But say you acknowledge that intentional reading is a perfectly valid way to proceed and that, in the case of *Madame Bovary*, the fine balance of complex emotional response that we arrived at in Chapter Six accords with the implied author that Flaubert constructed in the course of writing his novel. Yet, at the same time, you want to argue that what is truly significant about the book is the anger and hatred it reveals toward women. You may point out that the suffering Emma is put through is far in excess of her "crime" and that her death and the black vomit that comes from her in the terrible last scene is a case of authorial overkill. This must, you argue, arise from a combination of fear and contempt for women that Flaubert shared with many men of his time and place. You may be right or you may be wrong, but the important point is that you are working here on an interpretation that is *not* grounded in the implied author. You are explicitly arguing that yours is an interpretation that the implied author would *not* agree with, but you are also maintaining that this is what is psychologically and culturally significant about the novel. The fact that the author may not agree with your reading, that he may in fact be shocked by it, could itself be taken as support for your position.

The world of interpretation has probably seen as many readings of this sort as it has of the intentional kind. Looking back at the short Kafka story "A Common Confusion," we may agree that our best intentional reading finds in it a universal statement about the mystery of our conscious presence in the world. This reading might run something like this: that an honest vision of the world and our place in it is one of absurdity, that we are born feeling guilty without cause and sentenced to suffering and death for no reason. Again, you may agree that this is an accurate intentional reading, yet want to argue that the implied author is misguided and that the whole tale is a symptom of neurotic acquiescence in an unjust and rigidly hierarchical society. You might then go on to argue that to give a place of privilege to the intentional reading of a universal condition of metaphysical absurdity is a cop-out. It is a way of blaming the universe for an evil that arises from social and economic conditions, conditions that the author might have tried to change had he not let himself off the hook by saying that they were an inevitable part of life in this universe. As above, you may be right or you may be wrong. But the point is that here again, as in your alternative reading of *Madame Bovary*, you have placed the text within a frame that allows for an interpretation at variance with an intentional reading. It is this frame – be it psychological, feminist, cultural materialist, conservatively moralistic, or whatever – that provides a different grounding from that of the implied author. We can refer to this kind of reading as *symptomatic*, in that the narrative is seen to express symptomatically the conditions out of which it comes.

Deconstruction

Much symptomatic reading is an example of what is loosely referred to as "deconstructive reading" in that it deconstructs the intentional reading to find in back of it a reading that the author had no conscious intention of constructing. The critical term "deconstruction" comes from Jacques Derrida, who saw it as an inevitability of all careful reading in a process that has no real conclusion. Derrida grounded this idea in a view of meaning as infinitely deferred and therefore infinitely unreliable as a foundation for any clear certainty of reference to the world that lies beyond it. But the term "deconstruction" has been widely appropriated by scholars and critics who, at least implicitly, retain varying degrees of confidence in the referential capacity of language.

Since symptomatic readings are not grounded in an implied author who accounts for all the elements in a narrative, the question of the work's wholeness becomes moot. Moreover, authors who are read symptomatically are frequently conceived of as fractured – split between what they intend (through the implied author) and what they reveal. The narrative at one and the same time shows and masks its symptomatic meanings. For example, on the intentional level it could be argued that Henry James's *The Turn of the Screw* portrays a heroic governess involved in a tragic effort to save her charges from demonic possession. But it could be argued at the same time (and it has been) that symptomatically this narrative reveals repressed sexuality, a lurid imagination, and a mania for power and control. Like intentional readings, such symptomatic readings thrive on *repetitions* in the narrative. But these repetitions are not parts of a whole, integrated work, but traces of the unacknowledged author (the real one) intruding on his work. Traces, for example, of Henry James's own combination of erotic fascination and erotic horror have been alleged to turn up in the governess's intense and intensely repressed sexual passion for her employer. She is after all obsessed with the sexual "crimes" of her predecessors (now presumed to be ghosts attempting to corrupt the children for whom she is responsible), and equally obsessed with the sexual "innocence" of these children and the necessity of preserving that innocence. These and many other repetitions of the theme of sexual obsession have led interpreters to find an anatomy of repressive Victorian taboos in a novella that the actual author himself called "a fairy tale pure and simple."[4]

Though they seem to be opposite ways of interpreting narrative, both intentional and symptomatic approaches are oriented toward a meaning that is presumed to lie *behind* the narrative. It lies either in the implied author or in the real author (or, channeled through the real author, in the culture out of which she or he came). In this sense, both are grounded. But symptomatic readings tend to place a greater weight on *paratextual* material for the reason that they are bypassing the internal organizing principle of the implied author. To go back to "Now I Lay Me," for example, if I wanted to make a convincing argument that the fear of the power of women we see in Nick is really Hemingway's fear of women, I would need to amass evidence from beyond the narrative. I might start with biographical information about Hemingway's own parentage, his vexed relations with his domineering mother, his apparently weak father (whose suicide might also work as evidence). I might look through his letters. I might go on to find repetitions in his work revealing a dichotomy between women to be feared because of their power over men (Lady Brett Ashley in *The Sun also Rises*, Mrs. Macomber in "The Short Happy Life of Francis Macomber") and conversely women who are arguably "made safe" by their devotion to a central male figure (Catherine Barkley in *A Farewell to Arms*, Maria in *For Whom the Bell Tolls*). Intentional readings can also find key support from paratexts, but symptomatic readings are hard to make persuasively without them.

Adaptive readings

But suppose you acknowledge that there is common sense in what I have been saying so far about these two modes, yet you are still quite taken by the idea that the narrator's mother is some kind of demon who presides over the entire narrative universe of "Now I Lay Me." She's a witch; she may even have a broom ("I've been cleaning out the basement, dear"). Her smile is satanic and her fire infernal. In an earlier house-cleaning mentioned in the paragraph preceding her appearance, his father's collection of "snakes and other specimens" is burned in a similar fire: "they popped in the heat and the fire flamed up from the alcohol. I remember the snakes burning in the fire . . . " (365). Is there not an *intertextual* fit here with *Macbeth*'s witches? "Fire burn and caldron bubble":

> Fillet of fenny snake,
> In the caldron boil and bake.
> Eye of newt and toe of frog,
> Wool of bat and tongue of dog,
> Adder's fork and blindworm's sting,
> Lizard's leg and howlet's wing . . . [(IV, I, 12–16)]

The narrator "could not remember who burned the things," but surely it was his demon mother. Moreover, she has sent the seemingly innocent orderly as an agent to guide the narrator to a doomed marriage with one of her weird sisters. The blast (under *fire*) at the front lines that sent his soul flying out of him was also her doing. Little wonder that he says his prayers "over and over," sending up his own incantatory counter-spell. These prayers are addressed to the only person who can help: his *Father* in heaven. This is the Father with the power, not the weak father who married his mother, but the one implied in the title of the story:

> Now I lay me down to sleep,
> Pray the Lord my soul to keep.
> If I die before I wake,
> Pray the Lord my soul to take.

As an intentional reading there are numerous problems with this interpretation. I fill gaps with overreadings (the broom, her agency behind the bomb that wounds the narrator), I rewrite the character of the orderly, I ignore contradictions (the narrator prays for *both* of his parents, after all).

As a symptomatic reading, this might be a little more plausible, since this fantasy of a witch chimes with the notion of an author obsessed with an irrational conviction of demonic female power. This after all is the same male nightmare that Shakespeare himself drew on when he fashioned his three witches out of the European intertext. Nonetheless, even from the symptomatic point of view, I have taken great liberties with the text and would have to struggle to find sufficient paratextual material to make the case for my reading. The important point in all this is that there is a line one can cross in doing interpretation, on the other side of which one is no longer supporting a reading from an analysis of the evidence but creating a reading by *adaptation*. But since some degree of creation is a part of all interpretation, finding this line puts us in yet another gray area.

As I enrich and embellish my reading of "Now I Lay Me," I am doing something which, in its poor way, is like what Shakespeare did when he adapted the history of Macbeth from the narrative history of Macbeth in Holinshed's *Chronicles*. When Shakespeare "interpreted" the story of Macbeth that he found in Holinshed, he was not interested in providing a reading that gave us insight into Holinshed's intentions. Nor was he trying to throw light on the way Holinshed's version of the narrative was symptomatically revealing. He was making his own version of the story by adapting it. This is what I was trying to do in my demon-woman reading of "Now I Lay Me." Had I tried to argue that this reading is endorsed by Hemingway's implied author or that it reveals the actual unacknowledged state of the author's mind, you might have had an uneasy feeling that I was trying to smuggle in my own creative work as Hemingway's. From time to time, we have all had this uneasy feeling in reading criticism. We feel that an interpretation purporting to be either intentional or symptomatic has crossed the line and become an adaptation of the tale itself with its own life. Some of these can be maddening, but some of them, despite the uneasiness they arouse, can be rather wonderful.

In weighing whether or not an interpretation has become its own free adaptation, it is important to stress that we are dealing with a question of degree. To return to a theme I have been foregrounding in this chapter and the last, all interpretation involves some level of creativity in the sense that we are all active collaborators in making meaning out of narrative. In reading or viewing or listening to any narrative, we are at once taking in and adding, tracing and shaping. There is a continuum here, and at a certain point we find that what we call interpretation is looking more and more like what we call creation. And yet interpretation is still present, even if it is flagrant misinterpretation. The critic Harold Bloom has argued that all great works of art are necessarily powerful misreadings of great works of art that precede them.[5] It was a remarkable way to describe the adaptive process in creation but it clearly traded on the close relations of creativity and interpretation. For at bottom all writers, not just great ones, who take a story and write their own version, are engaged in adaptive interpretation. This holds equally true for all those narrative artists who write non–fiction narrative. Historians, biographers, and journalists, digging up raw material in their research, find the skeleton of a story and then grasp it by rendering it as narrative. To tell a story is to try to understand it.

When does a play become another play?

Where the relations between interpretation and adaptation can be most vexed is in the theater. Staged narrative, in order to be realized, not only requires an audience, it requires a whole team intervening between the author's words and the audience. The team involves a range of sensibilities other than the playwright's to create the lighting, the sound, the sets; it includes actors for the parts and a director to orchestrate it all. If fidelity to authorial intention is at a premium, a dramaturge may be employed to assist in interpreting the text. But frequently the production of a play is an occasion for enormous creative investment. When does the balance tip from interpretation to new creation? Here is another line in another gray area. In 1988, Samuel Beckett tried to halt a Dutch company from staging an all-woman version of *Waiting for Godot*. His argument was that, with women playing the parts of an all-male play, it would not be the same work. "Women don't have prostates," Beckett remarked. And though the comment sounds sexist, one of the characters does in fact suffer from an enlarged prostate, and his suffering is so great that laughter is painful and urination an agony. At many other points, too, the references within the play are male. Since the play goes out under his name, one can understand Beckett's anxiety. Yet should Beckett have won his case (which he didn't) would this have meant that audiences would have been prevented from ever seeing this potentially interesting adaptation?

What I have tried to do in this chapter, as in all my chapters, is to focus on basic distinctions that apply regardless of one's intellectual approach to the study of narrative. A great deal (but not all) of Marxist, feminist, new historicist, and psychoanalytic criticism are varying forms of symptomatic interpretation. Their particular slants and inflections, what they choose to feature and how they go on from there are all constructed on top of a form of reading that is symptomatic. In general, it reads through or past the intending author, as well as the implied author that she constructs. But this is not always the case, and there are numerous examples of, for example, feminist readings of Virginia Woolf and Audre Lorde that propose impassioned arguments for intentional readings of their work. But an awareness of the differences between the fundamental kinds of approach that I have outlined in this chapter is critical because the reader/audience's relationship to the text, and consequently the kind of meaning involved, differ according to which approach one takes.

Secondary reading

My assessment of the field of interpretation in terms of three fundamentally different ways of reading is not explicitly developed in other surveys of interpretation. As noted above, what I am calling here symptomatic reading can be found widely across a range of approaches. Both Marxist and psychoanalytic approaches deploy symptomatic readings widely, if not by any means exclusively. More recently, feminist, new historicist, deconstructive, and queer theorist approaches deploy the same mix. Recent years have also produced a few resurgent defenses of intentionalist reading. What I have tried to find for this set of recommendations are books that endeavor to take the long view of the field. These necessarily do not limit themselves to narrative texts. One such book, a brief one, is Umberto Eco's *Interpretation and Overinterpretation* (Cambridge University Press, 1992). What makes this an especially lively text is its inclusion of responses to Eco from three distinguished, yet quite different, interpretive theorists: Richard Rorty, Jonathan Culler, and Christine Brooke-Rose. Another good survey is Wolfgang Iser's *The Range of Interpretation* (New York: Columbia University Press, 2000). And for a third, I would recommend Paul Armstrong's *Conflicting Readings: Variety and Validity in Interpretation* (Chapel Hill: University of North Carolina Press, 1990). Two more that are a little narrower but still distanced enough (in my opinion) are Paul Ricoeur's *Interpretation Theory: Discourse and the Surplus of Meaning* (Fort Worth: Texas Christian University Press, 1976) and Patrick Hogan's *On Interpretation: Meaning and Inference in Law, Psychoanalysis, and Literature* (Athens: University of Georgia Press, 1996). For deconstruction, a still serviceable introduction by example is *Deconstruction and Criticism* (New York: Seabury Press, 1979) that features five readings by five venerable critics: Harold Bloom, Paul de Man, Jacques Derrida, Geoffrey Hartman, and J. Hillis Miller. For a patient exposition in clear language, I would recommend G. Douglas Atkins's *Reading Deconstruction, Deconstructive Reading* (Lexington: The University Press of Kentucky, 1983).

Additional primary texts

Naturally, the whole world of narrative is grist for interpretive acts in all three of the modes I have described in this chapter. But there are some authors who, because of salient paratextual information about their lives, often invite readers to move from an intentionalist to a symptomatic approach. Awareness of Hemingway's masculine obsessions has often opened up his work in ways its implied author would probably find disquieting. The warfare between symptomatic and intentionalist readings of John Milton's *Paradise Lost* (1667) began in the eighteenth century with Blake's statement that Milton was of the Devil's party but didn't know it and has continued to the present time. An interesting case that parallels the controversy over Milton's epic is the work of Flannery O'Connor. O'Connor very emphatically stated that her work reflects her Christian orthodoxy, but many readers have had a hard time bringing such stories as "A Good Man is Hard to Find," "The Lame shall Enter First," or "A View of the Woods" (1955) into conformity with this position. Samuel Richardson's *Pamela* (1740), one of the foundational works of the novel, was seen by its author as a guide for young women to avoid the snares of libertines who may be their employers and social superiors. But many have seen in it the author's prurient fascination with sexual predation. Rousseau's intention in his *Confessions* (1781, 1788) to portray an honest man of spontaneous feeling has time and again run up on the reef of symptomatic readings that find him anything but. These examples of narratives that elicit a conflict of intentionalist and symptomatic readings can go on and on. I'll stop here. As for adaptive readings, the next chapter expands on this subject.

Chapter 9

Adaptation across media

Adaptation as creative destruction

If the creative leeway between script and performance is wide in the production of plays, it is enormous when adaptation crosses media boundaries.
This is necessarily the case. Reviewers who complain that a film or play
is a poor "translation" of the original, may miss the fact that adaptation
across media is not translation in anything but the loosest sense. In fact, it
can sometimes be the attempt to make a strict translation that winds up in
failure. George Bluestone formulated the strong "destructivist" position on
this issue over forty years ago:

> What happens . . . when the filmist undertakes the adaptation of a
> novel . . . is that he does not convert the novel at all. What he adapts is a
> kind of paraphrase of the novel — the novel viewed as raw material. . . . It
> has always been easy to recognize how a poor film "destroys" a superior
> novel. What has not been sufficiently recognized is that such destruction
> is inevitable. In the fullest sense of the word, the filmist becomes not a
> translator for an established author, but a new author in his own right.[1]

This holds for plays as well as movies. In the words of a still earlier critic
and director, Béla Balázs, "Shakespeare, reading a story by Bandello, saw
in it not the artistic form of a masterpiece of story-telling but merely the
naked event narrated in it" (Bluestone, 63). Adapters, in other words, if they
are at all good, are raiders; they don't copy, they steal what they want and
leave the rest. It is rather like what I did (or at least tried to do) in the last
chapter when I freely interpreted (that is, adapted) Hemingway's "Now I
Lay Me."

Directors and theorists go hot and cold on this issue. Among the directors of "New Wave" cinema (c. 1948–62), there was strong agreement with
the line of Bluestone and Balázs. The Swedish director Ingmar Bergman
went so far as to declare that "Film has nothing to do with literature; the
character and substance of the two arts are usually in conflict."[2] More recently, Anthony Minghella put the relationship of literature to film a little
more cautiously, but not much. Commenting on his experience in adapting
Patricia Highsmith's *The Talented Mr. Ripley*, he said: "You've drunk the

drink, and the taste that's left in your mouth is what you go with."[3] But still other directors and theorists, like André Bazin and Dudley Andrew, have argued that instead of positing an unbridgeable gulf between the media we should look at the possibilities of connection between them and even creative symbiosis. In such a spirit Sergei Eisenstein published a landmark essay in 1944 that demonstrated how the early film giant D. W. Griffith learned his film technique from a novelist – one, moreover, who was dead long before film was invented: Charles Dickens.[4] And in the same spirit, Dudley Andrew has called for an end to "battles over the essence of the media or the inviolability of individual art works" in favor of a focus on what adaptations tell us about the media and about how we see and communicate.

Borrowing, intersecting, transforming

Dudley Andrew has distinguished three different kinds of film adaptation, which may help you think about the subject: 1) *Borrowing* is close to the *intertextuality* of all art, the kind of casual appropriation of stories, ideas, situations that would appear to be inevitable in any creative act. 2) *Intersecting* is what filmmakers do when they try to come as close as they can to the original, using the different medium of cinema to bring out as faithfully as possible the world and texture of the original. Andrew's demonstration text is Bresson's film version of Bernanos's *Diary of a Country Priest*: "an experience of the original modulated by the peculiar beam of the cinema. Naturally a great deal of Bernanos fails to be lit up, but what is lit up is only Bernanos, Bernanos however as seen by the cinema." 3) *Transformation* is adaptation that seeks to deploy the full power of cinematic techniques and material both to remain faithful to the original and at the same time to make a full transformation of it in the new medium.[5]

For a critic, then, to judge a work on the basis of its faithfulness to the original, it is important to determine whether faithfulness was in fact the goal. Otherwise, one should judge on other grounds. These can still involve a comparison with the original. An adaptation can be less or more profound, less or more sentimental, less or more fun, and so on. *Romeo and Juliet*, *Much Ado about Nothing*, and *Twelfth Night*, are on many grounds superior to the novellas of Matteo Bandello that Shakespeare raided for his story material. Shakespeare's *Troilus and Cressida*, however, is not clearly superior to Chaucer's *Troilus and Criseyde*. But from what we can determine of Shakespeare's intentions, to say that he did not translate, or capture, or do justice to the works he stole from, including Chaucer's, is not to render a valid criticism.

It is nevertheless understandable why this criticism is so common. A major reason is the problem of titling. When Beckett complained that the all-woman *Godot* produced in Holland was not his play, he was making a valid point about a play titled *Waiting for Godot*. Even introducing one woman into the cast creates fundamental harmonic changes in the play. And though the court went against Beckett, one wonders if there is not a way of indicating the Dutch difference in the *paratexts* of performance. In the title, for example, and the attribution of authorship (e.g., "*after* a play by Samuel Beckett"), one could let audiences know that there are two separate plays in this instance and two separate sets of creative agency. This problem is greatly compounded when narratives are adapted across media lines. From the start, the film industry has omnivorously consumed novels to produce movies. And for obvious reasons of marketing, it has often used the titles of successful novels as titles of the films adapted from them − *Wuthering Heights, Of Mice and Men, For Whom the Bell Tolls, Gone with the Wind, Great Expectations, Tom Jones, A Clockwork Orange* − the list goes on and on. Yet the differences between these films and the novels of the same name are far greater than those between the Dutch *Godot* and Beckett's original.

In this chapter I discuss a few of the reasons why there should be such great differences when you adapt across media.

Duration and pace

A work of prose fiction, like a novel, can take any amount of time to read. It is portable. You can put it down and pick it up again, read slowly or quickly, go back and reread, even skip ahead to the end. In the theater, plays and movies are neither portable nor interruptible. Given the expense and logistics of production, plus the limits of audience endurance, the outside limit for narrative length in these media is usually two hours. There have been exceptions, like the Royal Shakespeare Company's eight and a half hour version of Dickens's *Nicholas Nickleby* or Eric von Stroheim's *Greed* (1924), which in its first ten and a half hour version surpassed the reading time of the novel it adapted, Frank Norris's *McTeague* (1899). *Greed*, however, was the kind of exception that proves the rule, since the studio quickly cut it down to two and a half hours. Early in the development of cinema, the length of feature films became standard across the industry and today, despite the portability and viewing flexibility of VCRs and DVDs, it holds steady. In addition, the primary venue for the cinematic narrative event is still the theater, and the continuous, unbreakable experience that theater demands exerts control not only over the length of the narrative but its pacing. This also holds for films made for TV, which, despite the private intimacy of the performance venue, are not (yet) designed to be taped and played under the control of the viewer.

The difference in duration alone has major implications for adaptation. Longer prose narratives, like novels, can be "loose, baggy monsters," as Henry James mockingly described the works of his competition. They create a world that you can freely enter and leave, and that can include a multitude of characters involved in a number of concurrent threads of action. In the nineteenth century, American, European, and Russian novels quite commonly weighed in at more than eight hundred pages. Many were first published serially over a period of twenty months. The great classic Chinese novels often included hundreds of characters. Adaptation to the shorter, continuous forms of stage and screen is, then, a surgical art. Even to adapt narratives of considerably less length and complexity, authors of scripts must ruthlessly cut the originals. *Wuthering Heights* at four hundred pages is a short nineteenth-century novel, yet William Wyler's award-winning 1939 film version amputated the original halfway through the narrative at the point where Catherine dies. Except for the death of Heathcliff, the whole second half of the novel with its diversity of character and incident is missing. This necessary economy alone would have made Wyler's film a fundamentally different narrative from the book. The same is true for nineteenth-century stage adaptations of *Wuthering Heights*, which stopped at the same point.

But Wyler had to reduce even further, not only to squeeze four hundred pages into 104 minutes, but also to insure that the audience would not get lost. Ironically, it is theater's absolute control over the pacing of the narrative experience, keeping the audience prisoners in their seats, that gives audiences enormous power of their own over the content of that experience. The result is a kind of tyranny of the story line, which must be kept clear enough to be grasped in one continuous experience. Conversely, novel readers tolerate a great deal of material unrelated or only peripherally related to the story line. Anecdotes, meditations, conversations, descriptions can all be piled on to the narrative platform of a novel without necessarily cutting into its appeal (and market value). There have been in fact highly successful novels with wide audiences, like *The Life and Opinions of Tristram Shandy* (1759–67), in which the central story is so encumbered by extraneous material that it barely comes alive. This rarely works in plays or films, at least commercially, and the exceptions tend to appeal to restricted audiences. So, even with their shortened story line, Ben Hecht and Charles MacArthur, the screenwriters for the 1939 *Wuthering Heights*, found that they had to cut still further, throwing out much material that comes before Catherine's death. This included the birth of Hareton Earnshaw, Heathcliff's accidental rescue of him when he falls from the landing, Nelly's vision of Hindley at the crossroads, Heathcliff's hanging of Isabella's dog, his confrontation with

Edgar Linton at the Grange, and much else. However, what the film in its finished form does bring out clearly is what readers of the novel often find themselves struggling to understand: the story's *constituent events*. We see much more clearly than in the novel how one event leads to the next, and this is a direct result of the time constraint that filmmakers have to deal with.

The relations between novelists and the film industry have had their low moments. There are a number of reasons why they should, but a critical one has been this need to make the story line move with greater clarity and simplicity in a film. One way to explain the difference is the quality and degree of *retardation*, or the slowing down of the narrative discourse, that the media can tolerate. Retardation is one of the great pleasures of narrative. It allows us to settle in and think about what we are taking in; it also can play a key role in the development of *suspense*. But the limits beyond which retardation becomes a liability vary from medium to medium. Like most narrative, film tolerates (indeed thrives on) retardation, but its tolerance is much more restricted than that of novels. Adjusting to the very different quality of retardation in film is something with which few novelists, regardless of their brilliance, have been fully comfortable.

Character

What do you see when you see a character in a novel or a short story? Given our current knowledge of the way we imagine things, there is much about this question that is impossible to answer. But it is clear that in some way we draw upon pre-existing *types* that we have absorbed from our culture and out of which, guided by the narrative, we mentally synthesize, if not the character, something that stands for the character. What we synthesize is to a greater or lesser extent unique, yet as a rule sufficiently flexible to accommodate new information.

> Mr Heathcliff forms a singular contrast to his abode and style of living. He is a dark skinned gypsy in aspect, in dress and manners a gentleman; that is, as much a gentleman as many a country squire: rather slovenly, perhaps, yet not looking amiss with his negligence, because he has an erect and handsome figure, and rather morose.[6]

This is one of the earliest descriptions we have of Heathcliff in *Wuthering Heights*. What do we see and understand from this passage? It provides what seem to be contradictions of nineteenth-century type: a "dark skinned gypsy," yet a gentleman; slovenly in dress, yet "erect and handsome." If we are not seriously underreading, we must deploy some kind of mental flexibility that allows us to hold these traits loosely together in our minds. Moreover, this description is transmitted through Mr Lockwood, who proves himself elsewhere to be an *unreliable narrator*. A silly and shallow man,

Lockwood goes on astonishingly to see his own traits of modesty and reserve in Heathcliff. Realizing this, we must be additionally wary, keeping our sense of Heathcliff open, rejecting selectively some of what Lockwood says (for example: "his reserve springs from an aversion to showy displays of feeling"). As the story progresses, we cobble together from these and other descriptions, combined with Heathcliff's words and actions, a fascinatingly complex entity – highly intelligent, passionate, articulate, avaricious, haunted, murderous and cruel – who somehow seems to hold together as a character. But when we see the character on stage, or see Olivier play him on the screen, much of this flexible indeterminacy is foreclosed. The character is to a considerable degree fixed for us, both visually and aurally. This kind of fixing of a character through image, of course, happens when written narratives are illustrated, either in hard copy or hypertext.

Lawrence Olivier, *Wuthering Heights* (United Artists, 1939) courtesy of the Academy of Motion Picture Arts and Sciences.

It is also much harder to get inside a character on stage or on screen. Actors' soliloquies can approximate the associative flow of private thoughts, and dream sequences can represent an internal struggle, but they rarely match the kind of extensive explorations in depth that can unfold over many pages of confessional fiction, letter-fiction, diary fiction, or stream of consciousness fiction. Tied to the dominance of visual and aural sensation, audiences of stage and film must apprehend human interiors by inference, much as we do in the course of our lives. For the dramatist and filmmaker, this constraint, like all constraints in art, can be the source of discipline and inspiration. Francois Truffaut's decision to end *The Four Hundred Blows* with the face of the child was a brilliant stroke in this regard. The view is external, but the face becomes a screen in which the audience reads the child's abandonment and what must be, at some level, his despair.

Must film actors have stronger personalities than stage actors?

Is there a difference between character as we see it acted on stage and character as we see it acted on screen? Leo Braudy makes the interesting argument that, if film actors don't necessarily have stronger personalities than stage actors, they must at least draw more on their personalities. This is because of a fundamental difference in production: "The stage actor memorizes an entire role in proper order, putting it on like a costume, while the film actor learns his part in pieces, often out of chronological order, using his personality as a kind of armature, or as painters will let canvas show through to become a part of the total effect."[7] If Braudy is right about this, then the need for a kind of armature of personality would be even greater for actors in film series, like the James Bond films, and perhaps even greater still for actors in TV series.

Figurative language

Quite similar to this difference between media in the representation of characters is the difference that verbal narration has when it draws on figurative language, particularly on metaphors. Often on the page what is internal to a character comes out in metaphorical language. In *The Turn of the Screw*, for example, the governess-narrator describes in the following passage both her charges as she first found them and then how the situation changed:

> They had the bloom of health and happiness; and yet, as if I had been in charge of a pair of little grandees, of princes of the blood, for whom everything, to be right, would have to be enclosed and protected, the only form that, in my fancy, the afteryears could take for them was that of a romantic, a really royal extension of the garden and the park. It may be, of course, above all, that what suddenly broke into this gives the previous time a charm of stillness – that hush in which something gathers or crouches. The change was actually like the spring of a beast.[8]

The challenges of "translating" this passage in dramatic or filmic terms, without using dialogue, soliloquy or voice-over, are immense. How do you show the mind fantasizing the future as "a romantic, a really royal extension of the garden and the park"? How do you translate for the stage or screen the sense of an indeterminate (and therefore much more frightening) beast, crouching amid that peaceful beauty and then springing? And how do you do all this while maintaining the strict economy that plays and films require? In this regard, what prose narrative loses in the immediate physical vitality of sight and sound it gains in figurative flexibility.

It is a mistake, however, to think that stage and screen are entirely without this resource. As long as there are characters in a narrative, they can in their turn become describers and even narrators who use words. They have in fact given us some of the most powerful figurative language ever employed in narrative. In Shakespeare's *Antony and Cleopatra*, here is how Enobarbus begins to describe Antony's first view of Cleopatra:

> The barge she sat in, like a burnished throne,
> Burned on the water. The poop was beaten gold,
> Purple the sails, and so perfumèd that
> The winds were lovesick with them. The oars were silver,
> Which to the tune of flutes kept stroke and made
> The water which they beat to follow faster,
> As amorous of their strokes.[9]

This is not what anyone would call detached, objective reporting. Enobarbus draws on a diverse arsenal of figurative tropes – personification, hyperbole, metaphor, catachresis – to saturate the wind and water with the feelings of the "amorous" and "lovesick" Antony. But to appreciate it in the theater, we must to some degree detach ourselves from what we see before us on stage (Enobarbus and Agrippa in a house in Rome) and engage in the same sort of mental theater that we do all the time with verbal narrative. And as with the case of characters like Heathcliff, brought to earth photographically in film, the filming of Cleopatra's "barge" cannot hope to compete with Enobarbus's words.

Cleopatra (Twentieth Century Fox, 1963) courtesy of the
Academy of Motion Picture Arts and Sciences.

Drama and screen can also deploy their visual resources in an effective counterpoint to language like this. In the scene above, a sturdy, domestic this-
worldly Roman set can put Enobarbus's language into sharp relief, making
the imagined African river scene it describes seem to belong to a different
world, exotic and mythological. Such contrasts can give wonderful energy
to a scene. When Romeo spies Juliet on the balcony, he cries,

> But, soft! What light through yonder window breaks?
> It is the east, and Juliet is the sun!
> Arise, fair sun, and kill the envious moon,
> Who is already sick and pale with grief
> That thou her maid are far more fair than she.[10]

Personification again, hyperbole, metaphor, but all of them deployed while
the object of description is right there before our eyes. It can even help if
Juliet is not exceptionally beautiful, since the difference between her quite
mortal beauty and the romantic excess of her lover's words can say a great
deal about the power of love.

Gaps

As noted in Chapter Six, gaps are everywhere in prose narrative. There is no way that a narrator can avoid calling on listeners or readers to help bridge one gap after another. But what if we had the *characters* in the story actually before us, alive, and the *action* unfolding with no difference between the time it takes and clock time? What happens is that many of these narrational gaps disappear. This is what happens on stage. The difference in effect is great, and it makes you see why some narratologists would rather not include staged action as a type of narrative, but instead fall back on categories like "mimesis" or "the presentation of events" to categorize what they are. It is important to bear in mind, though, that most prose narratives also include stretches of dialogue, some of them quite long. At these moments, prose narrative approaches the kind of gaplessness in staged narrative. There usually are, of course, a few major gaps in plays. Scene breaks and act breaks sometimes separate installments of the action by great swathes of time. There have also been quite fluid stagings of time shifts in any number of twentieth-century productions. With a modest set, John Guare's play *Six Degrees of Separation* can easily slide from one time and place to another with no breaks over 120 pages of script. But despite devices like this that have given some playwrights considerable flexibility, the unit of drama is still the scene. And scenes take place in real time. So, by and large, adaptation of a novel to the stage requires finding and shaping the scenes that carry action and intensity. Again, it is a highly selective process.

In this area of gaps, cinema revolutionized narrative in the theater, releasing mimesis (performed narrative) from clock time and reconnecting with the narrative fluidity of prose narrative. This came as a surprise. The earliest feature-length films were little more than filmed theater. But they quickly evolved. In the process, as Eisenstein pointed out, they drew inspiration from nineteenth-century fiction. This is because so much of the art of film is an art of gap management that Eisenstein called "*montage*." In French, montage literally means "assembly." In film, it is the art of assembling a multitude of different lengths of film to make the continuous narrative we see. Eisenstein argued that the effect of moving from one image to the next was not the sum of the two images but something quite new. In this way, an entire car chase through a city can be conveyed by a few selected moments. Conveying continuous events like a car chase, a climb upstairs, a fall from a window, a sudden embrace, or a conversation through the use of montage makes for great efficiency in the deployment of a film's 90 to 120 minutes. But suggesting the continuity of events is only one aspect of the art of montage. Putting disparate shots next to each other can also convey meaning, and often with considerable power. In *Apocalypse Now* (1979), the onrush of helicopter gunships flying to the strains of Wagner's *Die Walküre*, suddenly gives way to the sight and sound of Vietnamese schoolchildren in a village compound. The contrast not only conveys the continuous action of an assault on the village but also suggests a moral discrepancy between the invaders and the invaded. In sum, the ease of narrative movement that montage permits approximates the freedom of movement novelists enjoy as they jump ahead, fall back, speed up, slow down, or drift from character to character. And though the voice of the narrator can still take us many places the camera cannot go, it cannot match film's immediacy of sound and sight.

A narrative art form that draws, like hypertext fiction, on both film's visuals and prose's narrative flexibility is the comic strip. Long neglected as a "legitimate" art, comics are only now beginning to be theorized as they gain a certain level of respect through the innovative work of artists like Scott McCloud, Frank Miller, and Neil Gaimon. At the center of this theory is, once again, the principle of the gap. McCloud, in his *Understanding Comics*, vividly demonstrated this centrality of the gap in his explication of the "gutter" – the necessary gap that regularly falls between succeeding images.

Persistence of vision

Moving pictures don't really move. All the motion that we think we see on the screen is in fact a succession of still pictures. Its appearance as motion relies on the principle of "persistence of vision." Images persist on the retina for roughly one tenth of a second after their initial impact. This is enough to carry over from one frame of a film to the next, tricking us into seeing motion where, were it not for this persistence of vision, we would see only a jerky succession of still pictures. In other words, even here, at this molecular level of cinematic narrative, we are engaged in bridging gaps.

Focalization

In Chapter Five, I described focalization in verbal and written narrative as the point from which (or the eyes through which) you are given the illusion of seeing the action. It commonly, but not invariably, includes traces of the sensibility – the thought and emotion – of the chosen viewer. In drama,

From *Understanding Comics* by Scott McCloud.

there is of course no *illusion* of seeing since what you see is empirically real, a narrative embodied by actors who perform largely in real time. But also, in drama, focalization is largely constant. You see the entire narrative from the fixed perspective of your seat in the auditorium. There are ways that stage technology can be used to shift our focus from one point to another. Changes in lighting can draw your attention from one point on the stage to another, from one group of actors to another, and darkness can limit what you see. These devices can be very important, manipulating our attention, and to that degree, visually controlling our reception of the narrative. But by and large focalization in drama is centered, and fixed, in our own unmanipulated vision. As in all trade-offs between media, here too constraint creates discipline, and playwrights and directors sharpen the practice of their craft by having to work within a fixed visual space. But also a great deal of the thrill of drama comes from the fact that we are present at a spectacle involving real people in a three dimensional space, witnessing it unfold as if we were right there.

The situation is quite different in film. Montage, which liberated film time, liberated film space as well. In other words, just as it gave film its great freedom to construct narrative through an artistry of gaps, montage also gave film a freedom of focalization. Though we may sit in a theater, confined to one perspective from which to see the screen, the camera eye acts as our on-screen focalizer. Through the almost unlimited freedom of editing, our eyes can be shifted from one point of observation to another with a speed and fluidity that rivals that of prose fiction. And as in prose fiction, film focalization can take us anywhere (note, for example, the opening of *Contact* [1997], during which we rapidly move away from the earth out into the universe). The camera eye is often a cold eye, with no trace of a human sensibility, though some have argued that there is always something of the voyeur in this "external" focalizer. But film can readily adopt the point of view of any of its characters with shots aligned with his or her eyes. Camera eyes can get drunk, weave about, lose consciousness. Particularly vivid examples of what Mieke Bal calls "character-bound focalization" (105–14) in film can be found in *The Blair Witch Project* (1999). For great stretches of this film, the hand-held cameras of the young filmmakers, who are also characters in the film, give us both what they see and, through movement, something of the intensity of their panic. And in the night shots, including those in the house at the end, our vision is almost identical to theirs, confined as it is to the lights on their cameras. Death comes with the final out-of-focus shot of the fallen camera.

But *The Blair Witch Project* is what could be called a *tour de force*, stretching the limits of the medium to create remarkable effects. Though film shares much of the flexibility of prose and verbal narrative in moving easily from external to character-bound focalization, it is very difficult for film to achieve the depth of internal focus that can come so handily in a novel:

> [H]er communication had the oddest effect on him. Vaguely and confusedly he was troubled by it; feeling as if he had even himself been concerned in something deep and dim. He had allowed for depths; but these were greater; and it was as if, oppressively – indeed absurdly – he was responsible for what they had now thrown up on the surface. It was – through something ancient and cold in it – what he would have called the real thing.[11]

This passage from *The Ambassadors* (1903) is pretty typical Henry James. The way his language here tries to seek out and express the inexpressible underscores another trade-off between the media. The absence of vivid empirical immediacy of sight and sound in the novel is made up for by the flexibility it gains in relying on the fluid representational capacities of our imagination.

Constraints of the marketplace

Culture constrains all narrative. Audiences set limits on what is acceptable and what is unacceptable, and by their response they select which narratives get repeated and which fall away. Nevertheless, departures from cultural norms catch on and enter a culture's narrative pool. How this happens is as mysterious as it is exciting. But as culturally transgressive fads catch on they become in their turn cultural (or sub-cultural) norms, and as such serve to underscore the general rule – that audience expectations exert great control over the form and content of narratives as they are disseminated through a society. No doubt it has ever been thus, going back to the earliest oral transmissions.

The marketability of narrative, combined with new technologies of narrative delivery, put a complex spin on the whole issue of narrative's cultural constraints. In the European renaissance, two contrasting sets of marketable narrative technologies enjoyed extraordinary growth: the book and the staged play. Both had to meet bottom-line fiscal targets, for which a paying audience was indispensable. But these audiences, though they overlapped, were different, as were the costs of production for these two technologies. The private experience of written narrative (especially with silent reading – a comparatively recent development) allowed for a range of niche markets for books, small subcultures that often adhered to values quite divergent from the norms of the larger culture. Books also had a "shelf life." In a seventeenth-century bookseller's shop, they could wait patiently for readers to come and purchase them. But staged plays were big events that happened at set times. They required an immense investment of both funds and labor: a paid company of actors and a theater, which must be built, purchased, or rented. They also needed to bring in the broadest cross-section of society if they were going to meet expenses. This difference in the technology and marketing of these two narrative media has only grown with time. At present, printed narratives far exceed staged theatrical productions in both number and variety. A paperback book costs roughly $10 to $20; cheap seats in urban theaters run between $20 and $80.

But if the impact of this commodity difference is noticeable in top-end theatrical venues, one must still be very careful in generalizing from this commercial difference that books will always be more formally adventuresome than plays. Brilliantly innovative books have often had notoriously difficult times attracting a publisher. Conversely, small theaters have taken wonderful risks. A classic example of the latter opened at the Théâtre de Babylone in Paris on 5 January, 1953. Offered two plays by a little-known writer and unstaged playwright, actor-director Roger Blin chose the one with the least scenery (one scrawny tree) and cheapest costuming (old clothes for two pairs of tramps). A play in which nothing of any significance happens in two long acts, it opened to mixed reviews. But its reputation gradually caught fire and it has since become the signature play of the twentieth century, *Waiting for Godot* by Samuel Beckett (Beckett was awarded the Nobel Prize for Literature in 1969). Events like this are not uncommon in the theater. If the market exerts a powerful force that tends to soften the edges of produceable plays, it is not the only force operating in the circulation of narrative. Producers, especially in small, marginal theaters, regularly take risks with radically new material. There are limits, then, to the predictability of markets for the same reason that narrative seems inevitably to change. To borrow a phrase from Ezra Pound, we seem to want our artists to "make it new."

If the cost of producing plays is high, the cost of producing films can be astronomical. In fact, films represent such an enormous outlay in capital that the reliance on type characterization and only mildly adapted masterplots is commonplace in the industry. Written by teams and tested on audiences, films from the large companies fall into "high concept" molds, deploying characters, actors, and situations with proven market potential. Even with an exceptionally good adaptation, like Wyler's *Wuthering Heights*, the original narrative often has to be tamed and domesticated to make it commercially viable. Brontë's Heathcliff is a deeply disturbing mixture of attractive and horrifying traits. He delivers "a shower of terrific slaps on both sides" of a young girl's head. He probably kills Hindley Earnshaw. And about the youthful Cathy and Linton, he can say things like this: "It's odd what a savage feeling I have to anything that seems afraid of me! Had I been born where laws are less strict, and tastes less dainty, I should treat myself to a slow vivisection of those two, as an evening's entertainment."[12] In Olivier's film version of Heathcliff, none of this savagery survives. Almost exclusively the jealous lover, the Olivier Heathcliff arouses more pity than fear. The only violence we see him commit are two soft slaps of Catherine's face (unthinkable in Brontë's Heathcliff), which he then proceeds to atone for by deliberately scraping his wrists against broken window panes (again, unthinkable in the novel). Without the disturbing dimensions of Brontë's Heathcliff, Olivier's Heathcliff aroused feelings that were in much closer conformity with the 1930s Hollywood *masterplot* of thwarted love.

But here again we must beware of hasty generalizations. Despite the immense market pressures that amplify cultural constraints on film content, remarkable departures slip through. Numerous films from *The Cabinet of Dr. Caligari* (1919) to *Brazil* (1985) provide ample evidence that studios and producers don't always avoid risk. Adaptations like *Clueless* (1995; of Jane Austen's *Emma*) and *The Loved One* (1965; of Evelyn Waugh's novel of the same name) show that adaptation to film is not necessarily an art of contraction. If it is still the case that a far greater range of disturbing material is dealt with in the private forms of written narrative, it is far from true that the more expensive public forms of narrative invariably eliminate the subversive and counter-cultural.

Selected secondary resources

An excellent secondary source on film adaptation is the chapter on adaptation in Andrew Dudley's *Concepts in Film Theory*. A good compendium of articles on this and related subjects is Timothy Corrigan's *Film and Literature: An Introduction and Reader* (New Jersey: Prentice-Hall, 1999). George Bluestone's classic study, *Novels into Film*, is now over forty years old, yet still highly serviceable.

Additional primary texts

Over the history of the stage and of film it may be the case that adaptation is more the rule than the exception. In stage to screen adaptations, the examples are countless (Tennessee Williams's

A Streetcar Named Desire, Eugene O'Neill's *Long Day's Journey into Night*, David Mamet's *Glengarry Glen Ross*, the list is endless). Shakespeare's major plays alone have multiple screen versions. Of these, I would make three sets of selections: Laurence Olivier and Kenneth Branagh both directed and performed in their own adaptations of *Henry V* (1944 and 1989, respectively). Olivier's version is especially notable in the way it opens with a performance in the Globe Theatre that at a certain point gives way to filmic "reality." There are also interesting historical differences in the representation of war. The 1944 version was filmed during WWII and reflects Britain's embattlement as well as its nationalistic war spirit. The 1989 version, filmed in peacetime, implicitly plays off against Olivier's version with a much more sober awareness of the moral and emotional costs of war.

Akira Kurosawa's very free adaptations of *Macbeth* as *Throne of Blood* (1957) and of *King Lear* as *Ran* (1985) are bookends of his career. They make for a fascinating study of cross-cultural adaptation, complicated by Kurosawa's situating of both stories in medieval Japan. For comparison adaptations, I would recommend Orson Welles's 1948 low-budget version of *Macbeth* (starring himself) and Peter Brook's 1971 *King Lear*, a strong production with great depth of acting talent. Perhaps one of the strangest adaptations of any theatrical text is Jean-Luc Godard's 1987 *King Lear*, with a script by Norman Mailer and performances by Peter Sellers and Woody Allen.

There are even more novels and short stories converted to film than plays. One fascinating sequence of adaptation began in 1968 when Stanley Kubrick and Arthur C. Clarke adapted Clarke's story "The Sentinel" as *2001: a Space Odyssey*. Clarke then wrote a novel version of the film adaptation of his own story, *2001*, and followed it with a sequel, *2010: Odyssey Two*, which in turn was filmed in 1984 as *2010: The Year We Make Contact*, directed by Peter Hyams. Clarke continued the series with *2061: Odyssey Three*. An excellent example of a film adaptation that clarifies an extremely complex and to a degree mystified order of constituent events in the original novel is Anthony Minghella's version of Michael Ondaatje's *The English Patient* (novel, 1992; film, 1996; Minghella both wrote and directed the screenplay). There are a number of fine examples of adaptations of highly successful novels that succeed in their own right through the freedom of their adaptations. Among these are Tony Richardson's adaptation of Evelyn Waugh's *The Loved One* mentioned above (novel 1948, film 1965, screenplay by Terry Southern and Christopher Isherwood), Stanley Kubrick's adaptation of Anthony Burgess's *A Clockwork Orange* (novel 1962, film 1971), and, also mentioned above, Amy

Hackerling's transposition of Jane Austen's English novel of manners *Emma* (1816) to a Beverly Hills high school milieu in her 1995 film *Clueless*. For a contrasting effort to "translate" *Emma* faithfully to the screen see Diarmid Lawrence's 1997 TV adaptation. Finally, for a truly tormented effort to adapt Joseph Conrad's novel of turn-of-the-century colonial exploitation, *Heart of Darkness* (1899), to the American war in Vietnam, see Francis Ford Coppola's *Apocalypse Now* (1979).

Chapter 10

Character and self in narrative

One truism about narrative is that it is a way we have of knowing ourselves. What are we, after all, if not characters? That is, we seem to be characters, and characters are one of the two principal components in most stories, the other being the *action*. An extreme position is that we only know ourselves insofar as we are narrativized. But this cannot be entirely the case since scientists can dissect and anatomize humans in static non-narrative conditions and in this manner develop extensive understanding of the physical, chemical, and biological components of what we are. So, to put the generalization more accurately, *it is only through narrative that we know ourselves as active entities that operate through time.* In this regard, even scientists who study us need to see us in narrative. Psychologists conducting rigorously controlled experiments on human behavior situate their subjects as characters in stories. Sometimes these are very tiny stories indeed, but the skeletal structure of narrative governs even the most limited patterns of stimulus and response ("The infant's face showed signs of wonder when the ball appeared to pass through a solid object").

In this chapter we shall look at a few of the important issues and questions that arise in connection with the narrative representation of both character and that mysterious (some would say illusory) property of character usually referred to as "the self."

Character vs. action

Ever since the distinction between *character* and *action* in narrative was first introduced over two thousand years ago, theorists have tended to give priority of importance to one or the other. For Aristotle, it was quite clear that the action ("the incidents of the story") took precedence over character:

> Character gives us qualities, but it is in our actions – what we do – that we are happy or the reverse. In a play accordingly they do not act in order to portray the Characters; they include the Characters for the sake of the action. So that it is the action in it, i.e. its Fable or Plot, that is the end and purpose of the tragedy; and the end is everywhere the chief thing.[1]

For Leslie Stephen, writing in England at the end of the nineteenth century, the balance was just the reverse. The great object of narrative action was the revelation of character. Stephen was a man of his time and place, and became in 1881 the first editor of England's *Dictionary of National Biography*, whose founding was itself highly symptomatic of this shift in emphasis. The first of its kind, the DNB was the narrative equivalent of England's National Portrait Gallery, for in Stephen's words, a biography "should be a portrait as reveals the essence of character."[2]

A third position is that character and action are inseparable. Stephen's contemporary, Henry James, argued that no one could learn the art of novel writing by learning first to make characters and second to devise the action. Characters and action were, finally, indistinguishable, "melting into each other at every breath":

> What is character but the determination of incident? What is incident but the illustration of character? ... It is an incident for a woman to stand up with her hand resting on a table and look out at you in a certain way; or if it be not an incident I think it will be hard to say what it is. At the same time it is an expression of character.[3]

It is hard to deny the logic of this. Insofar as the incidents involve people, how those incidents play out is driven by the nature of the people involved. Characters, to put this in narratological terms, have *agency*; they cause things to happen. Conversely, as these people drive the action, they necessarily reveal who they are in terms of their motives, their strength, weakness, trustworthiness, capacity to love, hate, cherish, adore, deplore, and so on. By their actions do we know them.

But though he argued strongly for this "organic" view of the novel, James also, like Stephen, gave pride of place to character. Though action is inseparable from character, what gave action its importance for James is the revelation of character. In this regard, for James, too, a novel is like a portrait: "What is either a picture or a novel that is *not* of character? What else do we seek in it and find in it?" (16). In their stress on character, James and Stephen may be taken to represent our modern, western "age of individualism," but it is nonetheless the case that character thrives and has thrived in narratives across many cultures, not only making the action move, but absorbing attention as it does so. The title of Homer's epic *The Odyssey* did not mean to the ancient Greeks what it means today, "a long trip full of adventures," but rather, "an epic poem about Odysseus."

Eponymous heroes and heroines

One sign of the way in which character dominates attention in the novel is the frequency of *eponymous* heroes and heroines (central figures whose names are featured in titles). This trend goes back to the beginnings of the novel in the seventeenth century with works like Aphra Behn's *Oroonoko, or the Royal Slave* (1678), continues through the eighteenth century with novels like *Robinson Crusoe, Pamela, Tom Jones, Humphrey Clinker, Tristram Shandy, Rameau's Nephew, The Sorrows of Young Werther,* and on through the nineteenth century with *Emma, David Copperfield, Jane Eyre, Adam Bede, Daniel Deronda, Cousin Bette, Old Goriot, Madame Bovary, Tess of the D'Urbervilles, Thérèse Raquin, Anna Karenina.* This list goes on and on, and no doubt reflects a "modern" fascination with the individual. All the same, it is worth noting that featuring the protagonist in the title of a narrative has a long pedigree. It is not only largely the case among renaissance tragedies (*Macbeth, Doctor Faustus, The Duchess of Malfi*) but also among those Greek tragedies that Aristotle discussed when he asserted the priority of the action (*Oedipus the King, Agamemnon, Medea*). Eponymous heroes are less common in Asian narrative traditions, but the great Japanese classic of the twelfth century is *The Tale of Genji.* And in medieval China an oft-retold oral tale was the seventh-century *Story of Mulian.* The recurrence of these eponymous heroes is a small but telling symptom that the tendency to feature character in narrative goes far back in time and crosses cultures.

Whether it is true or not that character dominates narrative, it is true that character is generally harder to talk about than action. Action is the unfolding of an event or sequence of events. It is what happens in the story. Some narratives may postpone revealing the complete sequence until the very end, when we finally see who it was who killed Councilman Stubbs. And some narratives, frustratingly, don't reveal all the links in the action. But the presumption is that, once revealed, the action of the story of the murder of Councilman Stubbs can be described in terms of a linear chain: A → B → C → D (where D is the Death of Stubbs). This is a relatively simple description of causation, and there are narratives with multiple strands of action, which can be difficult to hold in the mind (how easily can you retell the plot of *King Lear* or certain episodes of *The X-Files*?). But, once we have sorted out all the strands and charted their courses, we still face the difficulty of describing the nature of the entities that motivate the events, that is, the characters. Characters are, usually, harder to understand than actions. They are themselves some of narrative's most challenging gaps.

> "Please," he implored, "give me one more chance!"
> Suddenly she felt a headache coming on.

The action here is: A (his pleading) → B (her headache). But when we ask why his pleading should lead to her headache, then we are asking what kind of characters we have here whose combined agency should make this cause and effect sequence possible. At this point, we have to move from a horizontal to a vertical analysis, descending down into the character to construct a plausible sense of her complexity. Does the headache arise out of guilt? Does she feel (irrationally perhaps) that she is a cold, unsympathetic woman who should care more for this poor guy? Or is she furious at what she sees as an attempt to manipulate her, and does the headache come about because she can't express her anger? Or does she love him passionately, and does the headache come from the effort not to collaborate with his weakness? Or is this a headache of despair (as in: "this is the story of my life")? Probably most of us reading through this passage do not probe this far at the time we read it but read on with the assumption that her character will gradually become clearer. Or perhaps her character is already clear enough for us to have a precise idea of what's going through her mind. But it may eventually turn out that an interpretation of the narrative stands or falls on how we fill this gap. In short, external causes are usually easy to spot; it is the causative chemistry *inside* that is hard to figure. We cannot see inside character. We must infer.

Flat and round characters

Character does not always present this kind of difficulty. E. M. Forster introduced the term *flat character* to refer to characters who have no hidden complexity. In this sense, they have no depth (hence the word "flat").[4] Frequently found in comedy, satire, and melodrama, flat characters are limited to a narrow range of predictable behaviors. Examples can be found throughout the novels of Dickens, flattened further by refrains (*motifs*) like "Barkis is willin'" that sum the character up. The philosopher Henri Bergson speculated that we laugh at such characters because they represent a reduction of the human to the mechanical. Whether he was right about this or not, such characters do seem to exist on the surface of the story, along with objects and machines. There are no mysterious gaps to fill since what you see is what you get. They declare themselves in their motifs, as if to say – to borrow a motif from Popeye the Sailorman (another flat character) – "I yam what I yam."

Forster's counter term to flat characters was *round characters*. Round characters have varying degrees of depth and complexity and therefore, in Forster's words, they "cannot be summed up in a single phrase" (69). In Ralph Ellison's novel *Invisible Man*, for example, the round central character takes apart Popeye's signature motif, "I yam what I yam," using it to evoke his own conflicted relationship with his African-American cultural heritage, of which yams are both a powerful symbol and an actual component.[5] The pun of "yam" and "I am" is in turn one small component in a complex web of conflicting ideas, feelings, and values out of which we, along with the Invisible Man, try to put together an understanding of his character. It is the interest of this sort of complexity that has led many critics to rank round characters above flat ones. And though flat characters can be awfully funny, and satire can provide focus and bite by reducing a target to a flat character, the complexity of round characters seems closer to the way people really are.

But then the subject of how people really are leads us to another complication and another question.

Can characters be real?

Another way to ask this question is: How and where do characters exist? Do they exist in the real empirical world where people walk about and do things or do they exist the way many conceive stories to exist, as constructions that reside only in a mental realm – in the minds of writers as they write, of readers as they read, of audience-members as they watch, of people as they look at other people? At the very least, this would seem to be the case for fictional narrative. The words on the page describing Madame Bovary or transcribing her words do not refer to a character in what we call the real world, either past or present. There neither is nor was a real Madame Bovary, only marks on a page. These marks do not so much *refer* to Madame Bovary as stimulate or catalyze a representation of Madame Bovary in the mind of the reader. She does not exist *before* the marks but *after* them, and repeatedly, with many variations big and small, in mind after mind. This is also the case on stage and on screen. Of course, in these media much of the work of imagining is performed for us, so that we are "filled in" regarding what the characters look like, at least with their clothes on (usually), and sound like. But in these media, too, we also perform the narrative operations of filling in other gaps, and of *overreading* and *underreading*, just as we do with the people we encounter in our lives. The model, then, for the construction of character in fictional narrative might look something like this:

reader/viewer + narrative → reader/viewer's construction of a character

---

But wait a minute

Can't the marks on the page and the representations on stage and screen be said to *refer* to the character *as the author imagines her*?

Surely there must have been a Madame Bovary that Flaubert referred to in his mind as he transcribed the marks that catalyze her for us. So vivid was she in his mind that he once wrote: "Madame Bovary, c'est moi" ("Madame Bovary, that's me"). But here again we are in a gray psychological area. It is true that authors have testified to the powerful life that characters seem to have in their minds, even before they write a word. And yet these characters also have the capacity to surprise their authors. "Guess what Flem Snopes did last night," William Faulkner once said to his friend Phil Stone, referring to a novel in progress. And as I mentioned in an earlier chapter, Tolstoy records that shortly after Vronsky made love to Anna Karenina, to the author's great surprise his character began preparing to kill himself. Tolstoy recalled writing on feverishly to find out how the scene would end. These may both be versions of Forster's famous comment – "How do I know what I think till I see what I write?" – but they indicate that the issue of "reference" with regard to character in fictional narrative is at the least a vexed issue. Here, as elsewhere in this book, I argue that the most adequate way to conceptualize an *intentional reading* is to see characters as constructions that we make, catalyzed by the text and in conformity with another construction that we also make, the *implied author.*

But now if we try to set down the model that governs characters in *non-fictional* narrative, reference to a realm outside our imagining would appear to be inevitable:

reader/viewer + narrative → reader/viewer's construction of a real person

However poorly they are composed or however poorly we may read or view them, histories, biographies, newspaper reports, legal briefs, documentaries, film biographies all purport to tell us about real people. But are real people characters? Or is character something that only exists in narrative? Do characters in non-fictional narratives inform us or do they create illusions? There have been many arguments that the latter is the case. Remember Sartre, whom I quoted as arguing that there are no "true stories." If there are no true stories, there are necessarily no true characters. In Sartre's landmark novel, *Nausea* (1938), a protagonist (Roquentin) is engaged in writing the biography of a late-eighteenth-century historical figure (Rollebon). As the novel progresses, Roquentin finds that he is incapable of integrating the contradictory aspects of Rollebon's reported behavior. In short, there is no character there, just a chaos of unreconcilable actions. Sartre argued that this is the condition that we all find ourselves in when we think honestly, or at least clearly, about ourselves and others. Character, for him, is an idea imposed on human beings; it has a clarity and crispness that does not comport with reality.

Types

If you follow this argument far enough – that no character can match the complexity and changeableness of people as they really are – then all characterization, however "round," involves some degree of flattening. It is here that the subject of *types* is especially relevant. All cultures and subcultures include numerous types that circulate through all the various narrative modes: the hypocrite, the flirt, the evil child, the Pollyanna, the strong mother, the stern father, the cheat, the shrew, the good Samaritan, the wimp, the nerd, the vixen, the stud, the schlemiel, the prostitute with a heart of gold, the guy with a chip on his shoulder, the orphan, the yuppie, the Uncle Tom, the rebel. These are just a tiny selection of a vast multitude of current types in western English-speaking culture that migrate freely back and forth across the line between fiction and non-fiction and between literary art and other narrative venues. Yet when applied to real people, types would appear inevitably to "flatten" them. At the least, one can argue that compressing people into types denies them their full humanity. We have certainly seen, over the millennia, the terrible consequences of branding (the word is apt) human beings as types – Gypsies, Jews, Kafirs, Gooks, Serbs. Whether the dictionary definition of the word is a neutral ethnic category (like Jew or Serb) or inherently a slur (like Gook), to limit someone to a character type is to deny her capacity to surprise us with behavior that exceeds the limits of the type.

This is a powerful argument. But then another question arises: are human beings capable of characterizing *without* the use of types? Do we know how to think about people in a type-free way? Trying to describe your friend to another friend, you say, "Oh, he's a big spender, but generous, too, and he wouldn't hurt a flea" and in the process you have deployed three types. Robert Musil spent much of his life writing a very long unfinished novel titled *The Man without Qualities*, which was to be about a man lacking in sufficient repeatable traits to allow us to see him as any type at all. Yet Ulrich (the presumptive Man without Qualities) is a scientist, a skeptic, a lover, a jealous man. Sartre's Roquentin, who comes like his author to disbelieve in character, looks in the mirror and sees an alien moonscape with nothing recognizably human. Yet we, reading the book, see a writer, an idealist, a foe of hypocrisy, a jazz lover, a deep thinker. It is very hard to exclude types in representing the human. Samuel Beckett appears to have sought something like this in a short, puzzling work titled "Ping":

> All known all white bare white body fixed one yard legs joined like sewn.
> Light heat white floor one square yard never seen. White walls one yard
> by two white ceiling one square yard never seen. Bare white body fixed
> only the eyes only just. Traces blurs light grey almost white on white.
> Hands hanging palms front white feet heels together right angle . . .[6]

Some have seen Christ as a type behind this prose poem, others have seen
a marionette in a box. But without some kind of action, it is hard to make
much of a case either way. This is an important point. To help him avoid
received narrative types (if this was in fact what he was trying to do) Beckett
had to eliminate narrative.

It may be that characterization and thinking in types is part of our mental
equipment, and it may also be that the rich complexity and constantly
changing nature of human beings can never be adequately captured by this
narrative equipment. But this is not the same thing as saying that character
is inevitably deceptive and that narrative can only deal in illusions because
of this. It is true that character in purportedly non-fiction narrative can be
false, misleading, unfair, and slanderous. But is it *invariably* false, misleading,
unfair, and slanderous? Are there not degrees of accuracy and inaccuracy
in characterization? A biographer, poring over the letters and diaries of
his subject, the letters of her correspondents, newspaper reports about her,
legal transactions involving her, and other documents and physical evidence,
begins to triangulate a series of events in which his subject acted and was
acted upon. He makes out some degree of *agency*, in her and other characters,
and finally begins to see how they connect as a *story* or collection of stories.
When he finally writes down the *narrative* of this story, he engages in the
third mode of *interpretation* I discussed in Chapter Seven: he interprets by
adaptation. This is what biographers and historians do. If they are sufficiently
scrupulous, they are constrained and guided by the facts as they know them.

This is not to say that there will not be — always and inevitably — a range
of interpretation regarding this woman's life that will allow for a number of
other plausible narratives. And it stands to reason that the less data we can
dig up, the greater will be the number of plausible narratives we can write,
since there are fewer facts to constrain us. But regardless of how great this
range of plausible narratives is, there will always be a far greater range of
implausible narratives that must be jettisoned — if, that is, we want to get
close to what actually happened in the real world. We know very little about
Shakespeare, but when we tell the story of his life we cannot plausibly say
that he came from Mars, or Venus, or Peru, or that he played basketball or
brushed his teeth with Pepsodent. Though it can be fun to think of him
coming from those places and doing those things.

One more word on types before we go on. As important as aspiring to a certain type can be for many of us (the fearless soldier, the crusading lawyer, the incorruptible politician, the supermom), there is also a natural and understandable resistance to being "typed." Who wants to be written off as a nerd or a yuppie or a ne'er-do-well or even an angel? It puts us in a box and denies our freedom. In satire, of course, putting someone in a box like this is one of the ways the author gains rhetorical force, but the force gets all its power precisely because people hate being packaged, especially when it is against their will. And types can be very flat characters. But they don't have to be – and that is the point of this paragraph. Characterization by type can accommodate a great deal of human complexity. If one looks at the narratives of Shakespeare, Tolstoy, Chaucer, George Eliot, one sees that the central figures can all be referred to by some dominating type – the machiavel (Richard the Third), the adulteress (Anna Karenina), the pious fraud (the Pardoner), the dusty scholar (Casaubon). Yet these characters are rarely simply types, but syntheses of types. Homer's Achilles in *The Iliad* may be the type of the military hero, but he is also a compound of the professional soldier, the stubborn man, the prima donna, the passionate man, and the devoted friend. The part played by Tom Hanks in *Saving Private Ryan* (1999) is also the type of the military hero, but compounded of the modest man, the school teacher, the reluctant soldier, and the dutiful man. We have here two characters in two stories of war who each conform to the type of the military hero. Yet we also have two very different individuals. This seems to accord with the way most of us think about our friends and the people we know well, however we may struggle to characterize them for others. "Oh, he's a big spender," we say of our friend, "but, you know, he doesn't just throw his money away. He spends it on things he really values. And he watches his pennies, too. So I guess he isn't *exactly* a big spender. . . ." As for the devils we hate or the angels we adore, the task of representation is usually easier.

Autobiography

If the problem of matching types to our perception of reality can be a burden for us in narrative accounts of those we know, it can be even more of a burden when we give narrative accounts of ourselves. It can be, that is, if we are not in fact exemplary types ourselves (which is unlikely), or at least willing to under- or overread our lives in order to appear as one (which is less unlikely). Certainly the history of autobiography, like that of biography, is full of accounts of lives that are a little too good to be true. Political autobiographies by still active politicians tend to fall into this category. Ghost-written, published on the eve of a campaign, such a narrative is probably not going to include those disturbing events in the candidate's life that might contradict the desired image. We learn that he was born in poverty, rose up through hard work, knows the value of a dollar, yet is compassionate, cares for his mother, etc. – just the *type* you want in government. As always, there is a selection of *masterplots* to go with such types.

But in general, if you want to write your autobiography without the sense that you are fictionalizing by displacing yourself with a type that is either more heroic, more honest, more pathetic (recall W. N. P. Barbellion), more whatever – if you want to do this, it can be hard work. When Mary McCarthy gathered together the autobiographical pieces she had been publishing in the 1940s and 1950s, she found that she had allowed types to fictionalize reality (her father as a dashing, romantic type; herself as an orphan). Her solution when she bound these pieces together in her *Memories of a Catholic Girlhood* (1957) was to correct the record in a series of addenda after each chapter. The result is a fascinating double perspective: on the life and on the difficulties she faced and actual falsehoods she committed in trying to render that life. Sartre solved the same problem in a different way when he set about writing his own autobiography. Written twenty-five years after his novel *Nausea* had demonstrated the impossibility of such an enterprise, the narrative account he gave of himself in *The Words* (1964) ended at age eleven. From this point up to the present, Sartre claimed, he had been imprisoned by the illusion that one could actually live one's life in conformity to some noble type playing the leading role in a masterplot.

The idea that there is an inherent conflict between type and reality, that the use of types in characterization can obscure the reality of one's self or others, is a comparatively recent and culturally localized dilemma. In 400 AD, when Saint Augustine invented the enduring form of the autobiography of a convert by writing his *Confessions*, his declared object was not to demonstrate his uniqueness but to show how his experience played out *according to type*. In his case the type was that of the Christian convert, and it belonged in turn to a masterplot that involved initial ignorance, news of the right path to salvation, repeated straying, repeated guidance from others, repeated renewal of effort, hard thinking, temptation, struggle, suffering, and a climactic moment of conversion, marked by divine intervention and followed by the firm decision to renounce the old ways and take up the new.

One of the advantages of writing according to type is its efficiency. Applying the model of the convert to his life meant for Augustine that he could throw out as irrelevant thousands, even millions, of events and micro-events that had happened to him. Autobiography was a matter of "collecting" or "re-collecting" from his memory those crucial events in the story of his life that conformed to the masterplot of conversion and that allowed him to ful-fill the requirements of the type at the center of that story. The *Confessions* of Saint Augustine is an enormously rich narrative, full of insightful brilliance, and valued greatly today for this richness. But this narrative and expository richness are not meant to obscure the conformity of its author to a story lived out by others. You do not find in Augustine's narrative any of Mary McCarthy's anxiety about obscuring the truth through the imposition of literary types. Rather the narrative is meant to confirm the authenticity of both type and masterplot, which it does by keeping its narrative eye focussed on them.

By contrast, the avoidance of self-typing in autobiography can result in an enormous increase in narrative detail. Sometimes this can get unwieldy. When Jean-Jacques Rousseau set out to write his own *Confessions* in 1766 he did so with the declaration that "I am not made like any one I have been acquainted with, perhaps like no one in existence; if not better, I at least claim originality, and whether nature did wisely in breaking the mould in which she formed me can only be determined after reading this work."[7] Of course, one type that he is still, of necessity, hanging on to here is that of the honest man. The result was more than a thousand pages of detail from his life, some of it extremely embarrassing. Moreover, before he was done, people were already reading what he had written (in circulating manuscript copies) and forming their own dreadful ideas about the *type* of man he was. So he now had to write even more pages just to correct these miss-impressions. It was a long losing battle, but it underscored another problem in writing one's autobiography – the problem of the reader. Readers will *underread* and *overread*, they will find types where none were intended, and there is no guarantee that adding to the narrative will remedy this.

Endless projects of the self

The idea of the interminable autobiography received its comic apotheosis several years before Rousseau began his *Confessions*. In Laurence Sterne's *Tristram Shandy* (1759–67), his fictional autobiographer found the going slow indeed, taking three and half volumes to get as far as one day old: "I am this month one whole year older than I was this time twelve-month; and having got, as you perceive, almost into the middle of my fourth volume – and no further than my first day's life – 'tis demonstrative that I have three hundred and sixty-four days more life to write just now, than when I first set out; so that instead of advancing, as a common writer, in my work with what I have been doing at it – on the contrary, I am just thrown so many volumes back – was every day of my life as busy a day as this – And why not? – and the transactions and opinions of it to take up as much description – And for what reason should they be cut short? as at this rate I should just live 364 times faster than I should write – It must follow, an' please your worships, that the more I write, the more I shall have to write – and consequently, the more your worships read, the more your worships will have to read."[8] Shandy's dilemma was as amusing as Rousseau's was tragic, but both authors raise key questions: What is important in life narrative? Are there *constituent events*? On what basis do you select some events and leave others out? This problem persists to the present day. By 1994, the Reverend Robert Shields of Tennessee had completed forty-two volumes of his personal diary and was still going strong, recording every hour of every day every single thing he did from the moment he got up in the morning to the moment he went to bed. More recently, people like Jennie of "Jennicam.org" have gone one better than the Reverend Shields by putting their lives on the Web, as it is lived. Jennicam records in a constant series of still shots what Jennie is doing twenty-four hours of every day and night. It is hard to call what she does narrative; it is rather a kind of cold focalization in real time. Yet, as in any narrative, much is still left out. This includes what happens off screen, what happens in the intervals between shots, not to mention what goes on inside in her organs, including the circulation of her blood and the love-life of her mitochondria. And of course we miss much of what goes through her mind.

Life writing as performative

Probably the best response to the question "When is enough enough in the narrative of oneself?" is another question: "What is being done with the narrative?" All writing in some way or another, and often in more ways than one, is a form of action taking place in the world. It is in this regard *performative*. It has functions and effects, and some of these are intended, some are not. Life writing is no exception to this rule. Saint Augustine had a very clear purpose in writing his *Confessions*, and for that purpose it was admirably designed. It performed well. But suppose you say: all I want to do is tell the truth about *myself*. The questions would still remain: what kind of truth and to what end? Saint Augustine had a powerful sense of the truth as divine, and insofar as the story of his conversion is a story of his journey toward this divine truth, it is telling the truth as he conceives it. But Rousseau was also struggling to tell the truth about himself, by his lights. His purpose and his sense of what constituted the truth were quite different from Augustine's. His purpose was to convince his readers of his uniqueness, and his honesty. His sense of the truth was fidelity to the facts, or at least the earnest attempt to be faithful to the facts, both big and small. Did his autobiography perform well? Yes and no. In the years since its publication, Rousseau's *Confessions* has persuaded a number, though by no means all, of its readers that it is the record of a courageously honest man. But in his lifetime it did not persuade the people that counted in his life, at least not sufficiently for Rousseau.

To sum up, if we can never tell the *whole* truth (for what is it, after all?), and if there are no universal standards of selection (that is, standards that can be applied to all of us regarding what is important in our personal histories), it is still the case that autobiographies are performative. They always are doing something (either well or ill) for the writer at the time of the writing. Therefore, it is always a good idea to keep a weather-eye out for the kind of act we are reading and the contexts it fits into. It may, for example, be dead wrong in an historical (autobiographical) sense that W. N. P. Barbellion died on 31 December, 1917. But, as an act, his premature announcement of his death is revealing. It is a falsehood that tells something of the truth. In the context of a life of thwarted ambition, it reveals the intensity with which this autobiographer hoped to achieve some kind of tragic distinction. Barbellion showed great promise as a zoologist, and when that career failed because of his disease, and when it became clear that he was not even going to have time to begin writing the English version of Balzac's *Human Comedy*, all he had left was his disease. Even before he knew how bad his disease was, he was half-seriously complaining that it wasn't bad enough:

> I have dabbled in a variety of diseases, but never got one downright – but only enough to make me feel horribly unfit and very miserable without the consolation of being able to regard myself as the heroic victim of some incurable disorder. Instead of being Stevenson with tuberculosis, I've only been Jones with dyspepsia. . . . Why can't I either have a first-rate disease or be a first-rate zoologist?[9]

Seeing *The Journal of a Disappointed Man* in this context, we can see how his concluding falsehood becomes the expression of a kind of truth. But note, too, how in making this move I have passed from an *intentional* to a *symptomatic* reading. Reading in this way – that is, with an eye out for a text's performative status – frequently involves passing back and forth between intentional and symptomatic modes of interpreting. And though historical or autobiographical truth is important in such an analysis, the analysis serves the recovery of "auto-graphical" truth, that is, the truth about the writer *as she or he writes*. As always, it must be emphasized, this truth is speculative. Regarding the ending of *The Journal of a Disappointed Man*, I cannot nail down my interpretation of what it tells us, but I think I could strengthen this reading, and I could certainly think of a multitude of less convincing interpretations.

Selected secondary resources

After Forster's *Aspects of the Novel*, the most commonly cited book on literary character was for years W. J. Harvey's *Character in the Novel* (Ithaca: Cornell University Press, 1965). Since then, much has been written, taking many different stances. Three books worth consulting are Thomas Doherty, *Reading (Absent) Character* (New York: Oxford University Press, 1983); Baruch Hochman, *Character in Literature* (Ithaca: Cornell University Press, 1985); and James Phelan, *Reading People, Reading Plots: Character, Progression, and the Interpretation of Narrative* (University of Chicago Press, 1989).

On autobiography, there are again numerous good books. A landmark collection of important essays is James Olney, ed., *Autobiography: Essays Theoretical and Critical* (Princeton University Press, 1980). Still earlier is Elizabeth Bruss, *Autobiographical Acts: The Changing Situation of a Literary Genre* (Baltimore: Johns Hopkins University Press, 1976). Bruss captures the great formal range of self-writing and its performative specificity to both historical context and authorial intention. John Paul Eakin wrote two companion books on autobiography – *Fictions in Autobiography: Studies in the Art of Self-Invention* (Princeton University Press, 1985) and *Touching the World: Reference in Autobiography* (Princeton University Press, 1992) – the first focussing on the ways in which this non-fictional form draws on fiction, and the second focussing on the ways in which this often fictional form actually relates to the "real world." Finally, among the many good and often provocative texts on women's autobiography, I'll recommend Shari Benstock, ed., *The Private Self: Theory and Practice of Women's Autobiographical Writings* (Chapel Hill: University of North Carolina Press, 1988).

Additional primary texts

A fascinating autobiographical effort to reconcile inherited types from one culture with one's sense of one's life in another is Maxine Hong Kingston's *The Woman Warrior* (1976). Audre Lorde's *The Cancer Journals* (1980) is a powerful act of resistance against all efforts to categorize the author in reference to her illness. The attempt to establish an identity free of socially imposed templates that Lorde's and Kingston's narratives represent so vividly can be found throughout the autobiographical literature of minority or marginalized figures. The nineteenth-century American genre of the slave narrative is almost invariably structured around the effort of writers to establish their identity in opposition to the narrow stereotype called up in many white minds by the color of their skin. One I would strongly recommend is *Narrative of the Life of Frederick Douglass*. Douglass published four versions of his personal narrative during his lifetime, and they are fascinating to compare. The 1845 *Narrative* can be found together with selections from three of the other versions in Michael Meyer, ed., *Frederick Douglass: The Narrative and Selected Writings* (New York: Random, 1984). An early, and powerful, record of self-invention that can be placed beside those of Augustine and Rousseau, is *The Life of Saint Teresa of Avila by Herself* (c. 1565). The field of autobiographical narrative is extraordinarily rich. If I had to select two more to recommend, one would be *Black Elk Speaks* (1932), a deeply moving "as-told-to" autobiography that records the personal reaction of a warrior and shaman to the final historical stages in which the United States secured its grip on the Oglala Sioux. The effect is that of a tragedy involving the apparent failure of the entire metaphysical system within which the narrator's identity has been constituted. The other text is Edmund Gosse's *Father and Son* (1907), which, like Kingston's *Woman Warrior*, is structured on the commonest of autobiographical masterplots: the effort to realize one's identity in spite of the often contrary expectations of one's parents.

Chapter 11

Narrative contestation

A contest of narratives

Here is a narrative. It is a hot day in the summer of 1892. Father and stepmother rise and have breakfast at 7:00. The elder daughter is away visiting; the younger arises just before 9:00 and has a light breakfast. Her father, an elderly man by now, almost seventy (the younger daughter is 31), goes off downtown on business. A banker, he is an important and wealthy man in this sleepy Massachusetts town. The younger daughter talks briefly with her stepmother, who tells her she has received a note asking her to go visit someone who is sick that morning. After telling the maid to wash the windows, the stepmother then goes upstairs. Later that morning, the father comes back. He is tired from his walking, and his daughter helps him to lie down on the couch in the parlor. She then sets up her ironing board to begin ironing a few handkerchiefs, but soon stops to go out to the barn in search of a piece of lead to fix a screen. Coming back twenty or thirty minutes later, she hears something – a scraping sound, or maybe a groan. She goes into the parlor and there she sees her father, lying half on and half off the couch, his head bloody and smashed almost beyond recognition. Numb with shock, she goes out into the hall, calls the maid, and has her go for the doctor. A neighbor, seeing her distress and seeing the maid rush off, comes over. When the maid returns, the daughter, vaguely remembering that her stepmother had returned, sends the maid and her neighbor upstairs to fetch her. There they find the body of the stepmother on the floor of the guestroom, her duster near her hand, her head also horribly smashed in. As it turns out, she has been dead for roughly an hour and a half, since shortly after she went upstairs that morning. Within fifteen minutes, the police arrive. There is considerable fear mixed with distress, since the assassin may still be hiding somewhere in the house, and it is only after a thorough search that fear begins to subside. At the same time, with no assassin apparent, no signs of forced entry, and no robbery, suspicion begins to fall on the younger daughter. This is a terrible mistake. She is a good woman, devoted to her father and on civilized terms with her stepmother.

Her free time has been devoted largely to church activities and good works. There isn't a blemish in her 31 years of life. Moreover, there is not a spot of blood on her, and her hair is perfectly in place. How could she kill these people with multiple blows of a hatchet or an axe and not have any blood on her or show any signs of exertion? And where is the weapon? Certainly it is not one of the old rusty, dusty hatchets in the basement that also show no signs of blood. Had they been used, when could she have cleaned and replaced them in the short space of time available to her? How could she have added the rust spots and the dust after cleaning them? No, this must have been the crime of an outsider, someone who had a personal antipathy to her father, and who, seizing the opportunity of an unlatched side door, had entered the house and hidden. Surprised by the stepmother, he killed her, then lay in wait till the father came home, killed him, and fled the way he came. Witnesses reported seeing at least two strange males near the house. Moreover, her father, if respected, was not a well-liked man. He was stingy, focussing most of his life's energy on making a lot of money. Only two weeks before, he had had a heated argument with someone to whom he had refused to give a loan, brusquely ordering him to leave the house. In short, this is a horrifying story made even more horrifying by the ordeal of innocence falsely accused.

Here is another narrative. It tells the story of a woman, outwardly unremarkable, but inwardly full of bitterness and hatred almost to the point of madness. This is a woman who never forgave her father for remarrying when her mother died. She is the same woman who, seven years before, when her father had given his half interest in a house to her stepmother, had stopped calling her "mother," addressing her from then on formally by her last name. The estrangement she feels is so strong that she rarely dines with her parents, as was the case on the fatal morning. Her stepmother, in her view, is "a mean good-for-nothing thing," as she told a friend five months earlier.[1] And so strong is her antipathy that on the same morning as her stepmother's murder she corrects an officer investigating the crime: "She is not my mother. She is my stepmother. My mother is dead" (106). This is a woman internally aflame, full of murderous intent. Only two days before the murder, she confided to a friend that she feared that there were enemies of her father about and that something terrible was about to happen in their home. Was she setting up expectations? The day before the crime, she tried to buy one of the most lethal poisons known, prussic acid, claiming that she wanted to use it to clean the edge of a sealskin cape. The pharmacist quite properly refused to sell it to her as it is never sold except by a doctor's prescription. Could this poison have been intended for anything else but murder? Lacking it, she was ready on the fatal morning of 4 August, 1892, to kill by other means. The note that was supposed to have summoned her stepmother to a "sick call" was a pure fabrication intended to throw the maid off the scent and to explain the absence of her stepmother during the interval between the two murders. No such note is ever found, nor does any party ever step forward to confirm that they had sent it. She kills her stepmother shortly after the latter goes upstairs to dust the guestroom at about 9:30. Then she hides the weapon. Her dress has been protected from blood by a wrapper or another dress that she also hides. When her father comes home an hour and fifteen minutes later, she sets up her ironing, waiting until he is nearly asleep on the couch. She does not go out to the barn, surely a hellish place to spend twenty or thirty minutes on one of the hottest days of the year. Instead, she fetches her hatchet from its hiding place and kills her father. The bloody protective wrapper or dress and the hatchet are now hidden in a place or places that only she knows of. Coolly, she summons the maid. There are no tears. Nor does she show any sign that she is afraid some assassin may be about. Later, knowing full well that her stepmother never went out, she says that she thought she heard her stepmother return earlier and asks the maid and her neighbor to please go upstairs and check on her. They find what she knew they would find, her stepmother's body, where she left it. The case is clear. She is the only one who had both the motive and the opportunity to commit this double homicide. The whole idea of a different assassin is preposterous. He would have had to come in unnoticed, kill the stepmother, then hide in the house for an hour and a half for the father to come home, kill him, still unnoticed, not taking anything of value, nor leaving the weapon, but fleeing in broad daylight, his clothes bloody, a bloody hatchet in his hand. It could only have been the daughter. A final incriminating circumstance comes three days later, after she is informed that she is a suspect. She burns a dress in the stove. Is it the bloodstained dress? She says it had paint on it. But this sounds like yet another lie.

This is the famous story of Lizzie Borden, who was tried in the summer of 1893 for the murder, a year earlier, of her father and her stepmother. As you can see, this story is not really one story but rather a contest of stories played out in a contest of narratives. In this, it is no different from any trial or legal dispute. They all start out like cousins of Kurosawa's film *Rashomon*, complex narratives in which *the agon is itself a conflict of narratives*. Prosecution and defense are the *antagonists* and *protagonists* (depending on your point of view) who, in their turn, operate like authors, challenged to narrate their stories so effectively that they win credence from their audience, which is either a judge or a jury.

Unlike *Rashomon*, however, where each narrative is told in turn, a trial is structurally more complex, since prosecution and defense overlap in the composition of their narratives. Not only are they permitted to tell versions of their stories in both their opening and closing statements, as well as in the direct examination of their own witnesses, but they are also permitted to cross-examine witnesses called by the opposition. In this way, the whole larger narrative rendered in the transcript of the trial is the record of a continual switching back and forth from one narrative version of events to the other as the opposing sides seek either to support their own narrative or to undermine their opponents' narrative. Thus, for example, the prosecution in the trial of Lizzie Borden calls Dr. Bowen, one of the first on the scene of the crime, as a witness to the color of dress Lizzie was wearing on the morning of the crime. This move is an effort to establish that the dress provided by the accused as the one she wore is of a different color from the one she was actually wearing that morning. In making this move, the prosecution works to support two segments of the action in its narrative: that the accused destroyed the dress she wore and that she later caused the wrong dress to be submitted in evidence. This would strengthen both their rendering of the events and their rendering of Lizzie's character as that of a cunning and deceitful person. But the defense now capitalizes on the presence of this witness in its cross-examination to gain a description of Lizzie's state shortly after the discovery of the bodies. Defense elicits the fact that Dr. Bowen, after observing the body of Mrs. Borden, came down to find Lizzie surrounded by four women:

> Q. What were they doing?
> A. They were working over her. I don't – fanning her and working over her. I don't know exactly what; rubbing her wrists and rubbing her head . . .(151)

Thus, only minutes away from the prosecution's work on its narrative and the diabolical character at its center, the defense introduces an important supplementary event into its own narrative. The effect of this is to say that we have here no cold-blooded murderer but a loving daughter, very naturally distressed by her discovery.

The transcript of any trial is full of micro-narratives of these sorts that sprout out everywhere you look, pulling credibility from one overarching narrative to the other in a rhythm that carries through the entire collective event. Here is an example of directly competing micro-narratives. In looking for the weapon, four hatchets were found in the basement along with a hatchet head with only the stub of a handle. As it turns out, the latter, though having no sign of blood on it, rusty and covered with ashes, is the only one that fits the cuts on the bodies. In their summation, the defense tells the tale of the handleless hatchet in this way:

> It was carried off to the police station and left there on the floor, called of no account, and they went through the preliminary examination on the four [hatchets] that I have laid aside, and found in them sufficient evidence to convict this defendant until Professor Wood appeared upon

> the scene, and when he told them there was nothing on them, then they
> had got to look for something else. Then they went and got this handleless
> hatchet... and as a last resort they come in here timidly and haltingly at
> the opening of this case, and say, "We bring you this handleless hatchet,
> but we do not tell you whether it is the hatchet or not." (315–16)

This is a story of pathetic folk, desperate to make their case. Now the
prosecution must fire back with its own narrative rendering of the same
sequence:

> They took that hatchet to the police station. It lay there unnoticed,
> because they supposed – they had a right to suppose – Professor Wood
> had told them, Dr Dolen had told them, their own eyes had told them
> that there was in the hands of the expert in Boston a hatchet covered with
> blood and hairs [not human, as it turned out]. And so this remained
> there. But the first hatchet came down from Boston, and we produced the
> evidence that one hatchet was out of the case. Then Hilliard said, of
> course, as it was the business of an honest and impartial detective, "See
> what about this hatchet; take it down." And Professor Wood took it down
> and examined it and has reported to you the results. (369)

This is the story of responsible folk, doing their work carefully and method-
ically.

These small segments are an example of how, throughout any trial, short
narratives vie with other short narratives. As such, a trial can be described
as a huge, unpolished narrative compendium featuring the contest of two
sets of authors, each trying to make their central narrative of events prevail
by spinning narrative segments for their rhetorical impact. They fight this
out in a tug of war in which the many discrete parts of their two narratives
are alternately constructed and deconstructed as they work toward their
final summations. As such, a trial is an immensely complicated narrative
structure.

But when you look at it closely enough, a trial has even more narrative
complication than this.

A narrative lattice-work

At one point in the trial of Lizzie Borden, the prosecution calls Hannah
Reagan as a witness. A matron at the Fall River police station, she re-
ports overhearing the following conversation between Lizzie and her sister,
Emma, while Lizzie was in the matron's charge:

> Lizzie: Emma, you have gave me away, haven't you?
> Emma: No, Lizzie, I have not.
> Lizzie: You have, and I will let you see I won't give an inch. (234)

After this, according to Reagan, Lizzie gestured with her finger that they should be quiet. She then turned her back on her sister and did not speak to her for the rest of the morning. Here, then, is a short separate narrative that is not a part of the events immediately connected with the narrative of the two murders. But the prosecution introduces it, clearly, to suggest that Lizzie has indirectly admitted her guilt.

The defense, in its turn, could have chosen to focus on the ambiguity of this exchange between Lizzie and her sister, but they make another, stronger move. During cross-examination, they elicit the information that Reagan immediately went to the press with this story, and that later she retracted it in a signed statement declaring that it was false. By shifting the focus to a *framing narrative* that contains Reagan's original narrative, a narrative in which Reagan is no longer narrator but active player, they seek to undercut her reliability. By converting her into an *unreliable narrator*, the defense hopes to bury her initial narrative under the immense problems of narrative credibility that we discussed in Chapter Six. In its turn, the prosecution, during "re-direct" (a return to "direct examination" of the witness), seeks to restore Reagan's reliability as a narrator by adding its own supplementary details to this framing narrative. Prosecution brings out the fact that the document signed by Reagan was prepared in advance by a friend of the defense, who pressed it on her saying, "If you will sign this paper it will make everything right between Miss Lizzie Borden and her sister" (236). Here, in other words, prosecution gives evidence to imply defense's *unreliability* in telling this framing narrative.

The narrative of Hannah Reagan is one of a great number of subsidiary, yet sometimes very important narratives, that were drawn on to supplement the central competing narratives in the trial of Lizzie Borden. In this way this trial, like any trial, necessarily generated a whole lattice-work of narrative extending outward from the core events. Some portions of this lattice-work are more important than others, and to the extent that their narrative reliability is either undermined or supported, the overall structure is rickety or sturdy. In the case of Hannah Reagan's narrative, the defense, by adding more narrative lattice-work to frame its own rendering of her tale, created sufficient doubt to damage the utility of Reagan's story for the prosecution, despite prosecution's repair work on its version of the framing narrative. Still more damaging is the competing testimony introduced later of Lizzie's sister, who claimed that no such incident took place.

Out beyond such narratives as Hannah Reagan's there are still more narratives that never make it into the sphere of judicially acceptable evidence. These are narrative satellites like that of the French Canadian farmer who claimed to have seen a man in the woods twelve days after the crime with a hatchet in his hand and blood on his clothes, repeating the words "poor Mrs Borden." Another is the story of Lizzie's attempt to buy prussic acid the day before the murders. By order of the judge, for one legal reason or another, such narratives are not allowed to be part of the long narrative the jury hears. Yet despite their unacceptable status as evidence, they remain *paratexts*, part of that immense constellation of narrative business connected with the trial that the public at large may eventually read and wonder about.

In addition to all these evidential narratives, the trial itself as it proceeds becomes *reflexively* narrativized. That is, one side or the other will look back from time to time to relate their own or their opposition's actions to gain a rhetorical advantage. "I heard what Miss Emma said Friday," says the prosecuting attorney in his summation,

> and I could but admire the loyalty and fidelity of that unfortunate girl [sic; she would have been 42] to her still more unfortunate sister. I could not find it in my heart to ask her many questions. She was in the most desperate strait that an innocent woman could be in, her next of kin, her only sister, stood in peril and she must come to the rescue. She faintly tells us the relations in the family were peaceful, but we sadly know they were not. (336)

Here one sister is dressed with the kind of generosity of spirit that damns the other sister. Emma's generosity in this reflexive narrative rendering of the trial is matched only by the generosity of the prosecutor, who "can not find it in [his] heart" to press the case (even, one must presume, at the risk of letting a murderer go unpunished). This generosity is in turn extended out to the jury who "sadly know" the truth. In this and numerous other ways, both sides exploit the trial itself as a narrative resource. In his very last words, the prosecuting attorney tells a prophetic story about the jurors themselves and in the process extends his narrativization of the trial out into the future:

> And, entering on your deliberations with no pride of opinion, with impartial and thoughtful minds, seeking only for the truth, you will lift the case above the range of passion and prejudice and excited feeling, into the clear atmosphere of reason and law. If you shall be able to do this, we can hope that, in some high sense, this trial may be adopted into the order of Providence, and may express in its results somewhat of that justice with which God governs the world. (392)

Shadow stories

In the trial of Lizzie Borden, as in most trials for murder in the first degree under US law, the heavier narrative task is placed on the prosecution, who must not simply tell a story, but tell one that is complete. It must have a central figure, fully equipped "beyond a reasonable doubt" with the motivation, opportunity, means and capability to commit the crime – that is, to engage in a complete action with a beginning, a middle, and an end. The defense is not under the same obligation. Their central figure is not necessarily required to do anything significant. She has breakfast, she sets out her ironing, she looks for a piece of lead. If the discovery of her father's body is significant, it is not a willed action on her part but rather an accident that happens to the unfortunate woman. She calls down the maid, she sends for the doctor, she waits. This is all narrative, of course, but it doesn't tell much of a *story*. It is all *supplemental events*. The real story, the one we are itching to know, is a murder mystery. Who killed the Bordens? But all that the defense has to show with regard to this question is that it would have been possible for some one else to have committed these crimes. They don't need to specify who it was or why they did it, only that some other party could have done it. From the defense point of view, then, the story of the murder is a shadow story. It is a story that is incomplete, missing key elements. "It is not your business to unravel the mystery," defense tells the jury at the beginning of his summation. "You are not here to find out who committed the murders. . . . You are simply and solely here to say, Is this woman defendant guilty?" (287–8). In this narrative, the story of the murder is hidden in the shadows.

Trials are full of shadow stories. At the request of the prosecution, the judge introduces a shadow story in his instructions to the jury when he tells them that a person "may be convicted upon evidence which satisfies a jury beyond a reasonable doubt that the act was done personally by another party, and that her relation to it was that of being present, aiding, abetting, sustaining, encouraging" (388). At a stroke, the shadowy outlines of another story begin to glimmer. This is a story in which Lizzie acted in collusion with someone else to commit the murders. But who it was she colluded with (her sister? someone else? more than one?), and who actually did the killing, and why they did it (sympathy? a separate grudge? money?) are terminally missing. Most of the disputed tales in the narrative lattice-work of the trial are to a certain degree shadowy. The story of Hannah Reagan is never resolved. In connection with Lizzie's account that she stayed up in the barn on one of the hottest days of the year, there is the ancillary story of the two boys, called by defense to testify that they went up into the barn on the day of the murder and found it cooler than it was outside. Were they lying? Were they consciously or unconsciously trying to help the defense? Or were they, well, boys – getting things wrong in the way boys do?

That a trial is full of shadow stories, narratives that are sometimes terribly incomplete as narratives, is not necessarily a detriment to either side. Shadow stories are used all the time, often subliminally and by indirection, as when the prosecution describes (narrativizing reflexively) the jury's visit to the barn in June:

> Some kind friend – and I make no misconstruction of it, I do not for a moment suggest it was done with intent to mislead you – some kind friend had opened the front door and windows so that you should not be suffocated by the heat when you were there on that comparatively cool day of June, compared, I mean, with August. (351)

Note how, by denying, he suggests. Protesting his own lack of suspicion, he indicates by negation the shadowy possibility of some "friend," more cunning than kind, who purposely adjusted the atmosphere in the barn to support the defense.

Motivation and personality

A shadow story, it can be argued, is only an extreme example of the inevitable condition of any narrative. As discussed in Chapter Six, reading narrative is a matter of filling in *gaps*. Here I am using "shadow story" (necessarily a vague concept) to mean a story in which the gaps in the narrative are so great as to prevent the story from achieving some general reader satisfaction that it is complete. Yet it must never be forgotten that it is we, the readers, who do the completing of any story by filling its many inevitable gaps. I bring this up at the start of this section because arguably the most important gap that we are called upon to fill in a narrative of criminal law is motive. As I argued in Chapter Ten, character and motivation are often more difficult to make out than actions and events. You can establish with a certainty that specific events happened – that two people were killed by violence. You can often establish to a certainty what they were killed with – in this case, a weighted sharp instrument, most likely a hatchet. These are gaps for which we get a lot of assistance from the evidence. But in the narrative of a trial, motive is necessarily out of sight. It is inferred from evidence, but can never be produced. It is something that you can neither hold nor see. Of course sometimes motives can be obvious, just as sometimes people can appear to be so simple that their motives are transparent. But it is also true that people can be highly complex. Moreover, there is always the possibility that someone who appears simple is in reality complex.

In addition to the problem of motive, the prosecution also faces the additional, and often more complex, challenge of narrativizing personality. Motive in itself is not sufficient. One may have the motive to commit

murder and yet lack the kind of personality that would enable one to carry
through with it. Indeed, one shadow story in the Lizzie Borden trial is that
of a woman who passionately hated her stepmother and bitterly resented
her father's remarriage and his partiality to this hated stepmother – in other
words, a woman who had a strong motive to see them dead – yet who did
not have the kind of personality that would permit her to murder them.
The prosecution, then, had to work hard to establish not only motive –
Lizzie's hatred for her stepmother and her resentment of her father – but
also the capability of carrying through such a crime. To this end, they
featured what seemed to be Lizzie's "lack of affect" – the fact that she did
not scream when she found her father's body, that she sat and waited in the
house after this discovery, that she could correct the investigating officer
when he called Mrs. Borden her "mother," in short, that "she was cool,"
to quote Officer Fleet (173). It is hard work, because this lack of affect is
a narrative gap that can be filled with other psychological accountings –
as, for example, shock. And, as the defense doesn't hesitate to point out,
prosecution's task is made all the more difficult by the fact that Lizzie's
record up until August 4, 1892, indicates a women who "led an honorable,
spotless life; she was a member of the church; she was interested in church
matters; she was connected with various organizations for charitable work;
she was ever ready to help in any good thing, in any good deed" (253).

Civil trials: stories without motivation

In US criminal law, as in the criminal law of many countries,
establishing criminal intent or motivation (what is referred to as *mens
rea*) is essential to the prosecution's case. But the same is not
necessarily true in US civil cases. Civil cases concern themselves with
events, actions, and conduct, and often do not need to go further. The
questions asked in tort cases are: Did injury occur through this action
and Is the defendant liable? If the event at the heart of the case is
brought about through negligence – my poorly parked car drifting into
my neighbor's – it makes no difference if my character is unblemished
and my intentions free of any malice toward my neighbor. I or my
insurance company will still have to pay for my neighbor's fender if
the case goes against me.

If, however, my car rolls over my neighbor and my negligence is
egregious, perhaps even part of a pattern of negligence, then we may
have a criminal case here, with the charge of criminal negligence.
Then my character, at least, will need looking into.

Masterplots and types

The problem in criminal law of establishing motivation and the requisite personality for the deed makes the deployment of masterplots especially important. As we noted in Chapter Three, *masterplots* come equipped with *types* – characters whose motivation and personality are an integral and often fixed element of the masterplot. As such, they can be powerful rhetorical tools when activated. They can absorb the complexity of a defendant's human nature into the simplicity of type. In the trial of Lizzie Borden, the prosecution pulls out all the stops in the deployment of masterplots and types. Even the handleless hatchet is made to fit into a masterplot – no less a one than the story of Christ. This happens during prosecution's attack on defense's scornful belittlement of the hatchet: "What is the sum of it all? A hatchet head is found in that cellar, despised and rejected of men at first, because a false king was set up for them to worship, and it was only when he was deposed that they thought of trying what was there in this one" (370). Here prosecution invokes the prophecy of Christ that is commonly purported to be in Isaiah – "He is despised and rejected of men; a man of sorrows and acquainted with grief" (Isaiah, 53:3) – which would have rung a responsive chord in the hearts of this nineteenth-century American jury. But as so often with this kind of rhetorical move, it depends for its effect on not thinking too closely about the implications (is the handleless hatchet an agent of redemption, sent by a merciful God? and are we to "worship" it?).

In constructing Lizzie from available masterplots, defense has an easier time of it, since so much of the visible record would indicate some conformity between Lizzie's life and the masterplot of the virtuous daughter. She pursued her household chores, attended church, did good works, cared for her father (who met his death wearing her ring on his finger, given to him when she was twelve). Defending counsel underscores this in his summation: "The heart waits to learn what theories they will get up about this woman without evidence. First, create your monster, and then put into him the devil's instincts and purposes, and you have created a character. But start with a woman, with woman's impulses and a daughter's love, and your imaginings are foreign and base" (313). Note how defense plays the gender card here, arguing that women by their nature are incapable of such base acts. Even in his grammar he makes evil incompatible with womanhood – "put into *him* the devil's instincts."

Counsel for the prosecution counters by taking up this gender assumption directly: "While we revere the sex," he tells the all-male jury, "while we show our courtesies to them, they are human like unto us. They are no better than we; they are no worse than we." So far so good, but by this state of equality in the scale of goodness, prosecution does not mean to imply that women's characters are the equivalent of men's. There is a whole range of less appealing female types and stereotypes ready to hand for him to draw on, and this he proceeds to do: "If they [women] lack in strength and coarseness and vigor, they make up for it in cunning, in dispatch, in celerity, in ferocity. If their loves are stronger and more enduring than those of men, am I saying too much that, on the other hand, their hates are more undying, more unyielding, more persistent?" (327). Establishing the type, he follows through by invoking a widely known narrative rendering of a chilling masterplot:

> I read in my library of history and fiction that many of the most famous criminals have been women. I am told by the great master of human nature, the poet who was almost superhumanly wise, that when the courage of a man failed, it was the determination, the vigor, the relentless fury of a woman, that struck the king down, that her husband might succeed to the throne.   (327)

Calling up the masterplot of Macbeth and the type of Lady Macbeth, prosecution not only invests his argument with the aura of Shakespeare's "superhuman" wisdom, but holds up to these men in the jury the model of a woman who can both kill men *and* dominate her husband. How effective it was, we can only guess. The prosecuting attorney draws on male masterplots and types as well in constructing Lizzie – Cain (340, 342), Judas (346) – but he throws most of his effort behind the elaboration of a specifically female type, stressing its otherness from types that the all-male jury might be capable of identifying with. In this way, he meets the challenge of the strangeness of the murders, their improbability. Projecting this type of woman permits the construction of an antagonist whose psychology is as mysterious as the crime. "You are neither murderers nor women," he says to the jury, "You have neither the craft of the assassin nor the cunning and deftness of the sex" (357). Here he not only links murderers and women, but also places both categories outside normal male experience. He thus renders invalid any effort by "normal" men to draw on their experience or empathetic understanding in dealing with these radical others. Women can do things far beyond the capabilities of ordinary men. How was it, for example, that Lizzie was not covered in blood? "I cannot answer it. Women's deftness, the assassin's cunning, is beyond us" (363). Where is the handle to the handleless hatchet? "There are plenty of ways in which a woman can conceal that sort of thing" (364).

In non-fiction narrative, as a trial purports to be, the ultimate form of inexplicable motivation is madness. It follows that mad people can bring about the weirdest "true" stories, stories that defy our common understanding of how people (even women) are motivated. Defense knows this, and in its opening comments tries to neutralize the power of this type by emphasizing its improbability:

> Fact and fiction have furnished many extraordinary examples of crime that have shocked the feelings and staggered the reason of men, but I think no one of them has ever surpassed in its mystery the case that you are now considering. The brutal character of the wounds is only equaled by the audacity, by the time and the place chosen, and, Mr Foreman and gentlemen, it needed but the accusation of the youngest daughter of one of the victims to make this the act, as it would seem to most men, of an insane person or a fiend.   (253)

Prosecution, undeterred, seizes on this possibility as well. Lizzie was not simply a woman, which was bad enough considering a woman's characteristic cunning and ferocity, she was also crazy: "We find her then set in her purpose, turned into a maniac, . . . and so the devil came into her, as God grant it may never come to you or me, gentlemen" (374). And this is how Lizzie Borden has gone down in history: the crazy lady who killed her parents for no reason at all. Before the trial, she was already immortalized in a rhyme that has survived to the present day:

> Lizzie Borden took an axe,
> And gave her mother forty whacks.
> When she saw what she had done,
> She gave her father forty-one.

This, too, is a narrative. It tells the story of someone so ferocious and so bizarre in her motivations that all it took to kill her father was her satisfaction with the job she had done on her mother. The jurors, however, thought differently. They acquitted Lizzie, and she went on to live comfortably in her father's house for another thirty-four years.

Revising cultural masterplots

Suppose that Lizzie Borden was truly (not just legally) innocent of the murder of her father and stepmother. And suppose further that she was nonetheless convicted of these crimes and eventually hung. And suppose still further that it subsequently became clear from interviews and other evidence that the jury had been in part swayed by prosecution's characterization of women as by their nature more ferocious than men, more cunning, and more inclined to nurse a grudge. Here would be a situation in which the power of the culture itself, residing in the deeply inculcated beliefs of a dominant element of that culture (from which were drawn the male members of the jury), would have prevailed *without at all violating the letter of the law*. We have made a number of suppositions in this instance, but there are many who would argue that fidelity to the law is no guarantee that those on the margins of cultural power – those marked by race, ethnicity, sex, sexual inclination, religion, or some other sign – will achieve justice in a way that comports not just with the letter of the law but also with democratic ideals of fairness.

How would you change such a state of affairs? One way, of course, would be to change the legal system so that women and others on the margins of power are included in juries. Change the audience for these narrative contests, in other words, by enlarging the pool from which it is drawn. And this has happened, though it is not so much a revolution as a greater fidelity to the original US constitutional right to be tried by a jury of one's peers. But another way to lessen the power of cultural assumptions in these legal contests would be to change the audience by changing the way it thinks. And since the prejudicial types that play a role in judicial unfairness are embedded in cultural masterplots, it has been argued that the way to make a deep cultural transformation is through the dissemination of counter-narratives, narratives that undermine or counterbalance the dominant masterplots of a culture and thus weaken the power of prejudicial types. Given how throughly narrative forms saturate our thinking about the world, it would seem logical that stories of the disempowered would be excellent instruments of cultural transformation. In the last couple of decades, two movements, Critical Legal Studies and Critical Race Theory, have both stressed the power of narrative to mitigate the kinds of injustice to which the legal system is, or has been, blind – kinds of injustice like that of my suppositional Lizzie Borden. Broadly, "the storytelling movement" in legal study is founded on the belief that

> [n]arrative has the unique ability to embody the concrete experience of individuals and communities, to make other voices heard, to contest the very assumptions of legal judgment. Narrative is thus a form of countermajoritarian argument, a genre for oppositionists intent on showing up the exclusions that occur in legal business-as-usual – a way of saying, you cannot understand until you have listened to our story.[2]

A trial, then, for all the narrative contestation that goes on within it, may still exclude important counter-narratives simply by cultural inertia. What is advocated by the storytelling movement is the dissemination of narratives that would enlarge the ways in which a culture thinks about the people within it, opening up possibilities of justice that a mere following of the rules would not allow.

The argument that has raged over the storytelling movement has focussed on several interrelated issues. One is the extent to which the legal system should broaden the range of stories allowed into legal decision-making. Should, for example, the lawyer defending my suppositional Lizzie Borden be allowed to call up witnesses to give first-person narrative accounts of how they have been victimized by gender stereotyping? If so how many? Are there any limits to what they may include and how they narrate? Must they typify? How is the typical determined? Another issue is whether or not stories should, or for that matter could, be used as a basis for law. As Martha Minow has argued, "commitments to narrative revel in particularity, difference, and resistance to generalization." As such, they are a risky foundation for law, which is a structure of propositions and therefore necessarily abstract: "Stories alone do not articulate principles likely to provide consistency in generalization to guide future action; stories do not generate guides for what to heed or what additional stories to elicit. Stories on their own offer little guidance for evaluating competing stories."[3] In reply, it is argued that precisely because of the hard abstractness of the law we need the human leavening that narrative allows. This is implicitly acknowledged already in the sentencing phase of capital cases. Because the life of the accused is at stake in such cases, there is considerable latitude in allowing the introduction of narrative material that might mitigate the argument for capital punishment. A third issue turns on just how completely we are the prisoners of the masterplots we grow up with. In the extreme position, our reason is helpless when it comes to changing the predispositions that have been loaded into our minds through stories. It is therefore only through stories that these predispositions can be changed. On the other side, it is argued that, powerful as stories can be, we are also amenable to reason. Indeed, because stories can be so powerful, working as they do directly on our emotions, it is essential that we give final authority to rational argument.

As of this writing, both sides in this argument are still quite far from agreement. And it may well be that there can be no final consensus about where lines can or should be drawn in these issues. This is yet another field with many gray areas. Of course, just because there are gray areas and there may be no hope in gaining some final exactitude is no argument against taking the issues seriously and trying to sort out answers.

Battling narratives are everywhere

The legal trial is by no means the only arena in which stories are made to do battle. One finds these contests almost everywhere. What distinguishes legal contests is the intensity of concentration both of and on narrative and the degree to which the contest is regulated. A trial has an umpire, the judge, who interprets an array of rules that governs the narrative contest over which he or she presides. The judge rules on what can or cannot be included, on who can speak, when they can speak, how they can speak, on how parts of the narrative may or may not be elicited from subsidiary narrators or the witnesses, and so on. But in less regulated forms, narratives are in combat in most compartments of life, public and private. Academic debate is frequently a narrative contest with, depending on the field, varying degrees of refereeing. Most obviously in the field of history, researchers spend their professional lives coming up with new narrative renderings of old stories, often with newly discovered *supplementary* or even *constituent events*. Less obviously, much of the theoretical work in fields ranging from physics to economics is a contest in the rendering of deep structural stories (as, for example, that every action has an equal and opposite reaction or that bad money drives out good). These are stories that undergird a multitude of the longer and more particularized narratives of everyday experience. Establishing these universal stories involves an extended *agon* of narratives (results of experiments, accounts of business failure) set against each other.

Political contests, though they ostensibly focus on issues, are often a chaos of narrative contestation. There is some regulation of these contests on the floor of congress or parliament, but on the campaign trail, the contest of narratives can be unreined. Much of the energy of a campaign is devoted to the manufacture of narrative discourse within which opponents situate the excellence of their own character and, more often than not, the sad insufficiencies of their rival's character. Commercial advertising is a constant warfare of micro-narratives showing sad tales of folks deceived into paying hidden charges to their long distance carriers or happy tales of folks empowered by their automobiles. Finally, what is writ large on grand legal, intellectual, political, or commercial stages, is also a common occurrence of everyday life. When neighbors quarrel, or friends fall out, or family members recall their grudges, or lovers recriminate, it is almost invariably a matter of people trying somehow to certify their narrative version of events against competing versions.

> "You said such cruel things to me. And then you flounced out of the room."
>
> "I was only trying to help you. And I didn't flounce. My hip is bad."
>
> "Bad hip, my eye. You flounced. And you were smirking."
>
> "I wasn't smirking, I was in pain. I bit my tongue at lunch. You saw how swollen it was."

Some of us get into these contests more than others. But one way or another, professionally or in our personal lives, we find ourselves in contests of narrative. Some of these make us wiser. Some don't.

Selected secondary reading

Major works in the field of "Law and Literature," which includes both proponents and critics of critical legal studies and critical race theory, are Ronald M. Dworkin, *Law's Empire* (Cambridge, MA: Harvard University Press, 1986); Sanford Levinson and Steven Mailloux, eds., *Interpreting Law and Literature: A Hermeneutic Reader* (Evanston, IL: Northwestern University Press, 1988); Stanley Fish, ed., *Doing What Comes Naturally: Change, Rhetoric, and the Practice of Theory in Literary and Legal Studies* (Durham, NC: Duke University Press, 1989); Peter Brooks and Paul Gewirtz, eds., *Law's Stories: Narrative and Rhetoric in the Law* (New Haven: Yale University Press, 1996); and Richard A. Posner, *Law and Literature*, revised edition (Cambridge, MA: Harvard University Press, 1998).

Additional primary texts

About Lizzie Borden, the text I drew on for examples in this chapter is *Trial of Lizzie Borden*, edited by Edmund Pearson. This book has long been out of print and contains an introduction that is quite partial to the prosecution. But it has an ample selection from the trial, including stretches of direct and cross examination, opening and closing remarks by both the prosecution and defense, the judge's instructions to the jury, and Lizzie's testimony at the inquest. There have been many theories about these murders. One not entirely implausible argument contends that neither Lizzie nor her sister, Emma (another perennial candidate), nor Dr Bowen, nor Bridget, nor a stranger killed the Bordens, but rather Andrew Borden's illegitimate son. This is Arnold R. Brown's *Lizzie Borden: The Legend, the Truth, the Final Chapter* (Nashville: Rutledge Hill Press, 1991).

One good text on another famous trial that is currently on the market and that includes both trial transcript excerpts and related material is *Commonwealth vs. Sacco and Vanzetti*, edited by Robert P. Weeks (Englewood Cliffs, NJ: Prentice-Hall, 1958). Of course, the law section of any good library abounds in case studies and trial transcripts. There are also a fair number of novels, plays, and films that are largely structured as trials in which different narrative constructions of the same evidence carry the agon. One of the most famous, and successful, of these is the film version of Judge Robert Traver's 1958 novel, *Anatomy of a Murder*, which was nominated in 1959 for numerous Academy Awards. Another is the screen adaptation of *Twelve Angry Men* (1957). Originally a television play, the narrative is largely confined to the deliberations of twelve jurors in the jury room. Two other notable film adaptations in which narrative reconstruction during a trial scene predominates are Agatha Christie's short story and 1953 play, *Witness for the Prosecution*, filmed in 1957, and Harper Lee's *To Kill a Mockingbird* (1960), which was made into a movie in 1962.

One problem with stressing the narrative use of the trial scene is that it obscures a main point in this chapter, which is that narrative contestation can be found throughout the field of life-representative texts, fictional and non-fictional (just as it can be found throughout the texture of our lives). Any well-written narrative holds us because there are a plurality of possible stories lying ahead of us as we read. In our minds, these stories jostle with each other. This is a good working definition of *suspense*. If the perennial problematic narrative, *Rashomon* (and its 1964 American adaptation, *The Outrage*), is a kind of high-water mark of unresolved narrative contestation, any complex narrative can be read, viewed, or taught as a process of narrative contestation. In this chapter, and these recommendations, I have focussed on trial literature because it so vividly anatomizes this condition of narrative.

Chapter 12

Narrative negotiation

This chapter balances the last. Both are about ways in which we think with narrative. But where in the last chapter we focussed on the chemistry of narratives in combination, here we are looking at a chemistry taking place within narratives (or, more accurately, in our interaction with them). Where in the last chapter, we looked at the ways in which narratives are used as armament in a larger contest of narratives like a trial or a political race or an intellectual controversy, here we are looking at narratives as structures made up of contests, the claims of which they may or may not negotiate successfully. In part, this chapter brings us back to the *agon* – the contest or conflict, which is so often the life of narrative. More broadly it brings us back to the observation I made in Chapter Five that larger cultural, psychological, and moral conflicts are at play in narrative, some but not all of them represented by the opponents in the agon.

Narrative without conflict

Conflict is such a powerful element in narrative that there are those who make it a necessary defining feature of the term "narrative." But given the inclusive definition of narrative that I have adopted for this book – the representation of an event or events – conflict is not a necessary component for something to qualify as a narrative. There are many short narratives, by my definition, in which conflict is nonexistent. The opening frames of Leni Riefenstahl's film documentary of the 1934 Nazi Party Conference, *The Triumph of the Will*, create a smooth narrative entirely without conflict. It opens with the sound of a plane hidden in the clouds carrying the Führer to the party conference and then moves by a series of brilliant strokes to culminate in the roar of an enormous crowd hailing Hitler's arrival. As is frequently the case in propaganda, the power of narrative in this instance, at least in the intentions of Leni Riefenstahl and in its impact on sympathetic German viewers in 1934, is exclusively *rhetorical*. In

---

fact, the kind of thinking through narrative that I will be discussing in this chapter would seriously undermine the effect Riefenstahl worked hard to create.

Narrative negotiation

Here is the well-known story illustrating the wisdom of Solomon: Two harlots appear before King Solomon with two baby boys, one dead and one living. One of the women tells what happened (in the larger story, her story is *analeptic* – it covers what happened in the story up to the point at which they come before the king). The two women had lived together in the same house and, within three days of each other, each of them gave birth. The other woman, according to the speaker, rolled over in her sleep and smothered her newborn child, killing it. She then "arose at midnight and took my son from beside me, while thine handmaid slept, and laid it in her bosom, and laid her dead child in my bosom." When she, the speaker, awoke and discovered the other's dead child in her bed, she demanded her own back, but the other claimed the living child was hers. And so they took their dispute to the king. When the woman finished speaking, King Solomon called for his sword and ordered that the living child be cut in half and the two halves be given to the two women. You know the outcome:

> Then spake the woman whose the living child was unto the king, for her bowels yearned upon her son, and she said, O my lord, give her the living child, and in no wise slay it. But the other said, Let it be neither mine nor thine, but divide it. Then the king answered and said, Give her the living child, and in no wise slay it: she is the mother thereof. And all Israel heard of the judgment which the king had judged; and they feared the king: for they saw that the wisdom of God was in him, to do judgment.
>
> (I Kings 3: 26–28)

Here is a story with an agon, a conflict between two women, and it *closes* powerfully with Solomon's brilliant ploy. Ordering one outcome to the story, the splitting of the child, he generates another, the discovery of the true mother and the reuniting of her with her child. It is a powerful story and it turns on Solomon's understanding of psychology. So, in the resolution of the agon, the story adjudicates the difference between true and false mothers. This distinction and how it is weighed rides on top of the agon involving the two women. But at the same time, the working out of the agon negotiates the claims of other opposing ideas. One is the opposing claims of possession and love. It shows through the true mother's reaction that, in the extreme case, mother-love trumps the need to possess. So this is also part of the narrative's work of negotiation. Through the action of the narrative, we are shown how these two strong human passions fall into a natural hierarchy, so that the love of a mother for her child will take precedence over the keen desire to possess the child. Another conflict in this narrative is that between harlotry and mother-hood. Both of these women are harlots, degraded figures at the bottom of ancient levantine society who make love for money. Yet the narrative implicitly works out a scheme of redemption. In the same figure, the harlot is displaced by the mother. Through her behavior in the working out of this story, the woman's harlotry is almost forgotten. She instead becomes The Mother.

How plausible must a story be?

"All Israel" was persuaded by this story. Yet when you start to think about it, how likely is it that any false mother is going to say, "All right, go ahead. Cut the child in half"? Who wants a dead half-baby? Certainly not, one would think, someone so desperate for a baby that she is willing to go to extraordinary lengths to secure a live one. There are two points to be made here. One is that there is room for further narrative discourse to fill this *gap*. Such extension of the narrative might feature the history of these two women, their intense rivalry, and the bitterness of the false mother that could lead her to make her extraordinary statement: "Let it be neither mine nor thine, but divide it." But the other point is that, even with an explanatory gap like this one, a narrative can still have immense power and do major work in the negotiation of cultural conflict, and this work can persist over the centuries, as in the case of this story.

The ostensible function of this short narrative is to show the wisdom of Solomon. This is the note that it ends on: "they saw that the wisdom of God was in him, to do judgment." Yet what gives energy to the narrative, as to all narratives, is the conflict that works itself out over the course of the story. The fuel for that energy is brought to the story in the form of our concerns as readers, concerns that are catalyzed by the conflict. In this way, narrative is a form of passionate thought. The greatest *masterplots* are narrativized over and over again because they engage conflicts that seem to be a permanent part of our circumstances as human beings. Here is a famous one:

> Laius, the king of Thebes, and his wife, Jocasta, are childless. Wanting a
> son and successor, Laius consults the Oracle at Delphi who cautions him

that should he have a son, that son will kill him. Laius heeds the warning until one night, drunk, he conceives a child with his wife, and Jocasta gives birth to a boy. Hoping to avoid his fate, Laius has the infant's feet pierced with an iron rod and orders a shepherd to abandon the child on Mount Citheron. Unknown to Laius, the shepherd takes pity on the child and through a friend delivers him to Polybus, the king of Corinth, and his wife Merope, who are themselves childless. They bring the child up as their own, naming him Oedipus, or Swellfoot, because of his wounded feet.

Later, when he is a young man, Oedipus is told by a drunken acquaintance that he is not really the son of Polybus and Merope. This and other rumors cause him to set out for the Oracle at Delphi to see what he can find out about himself. There he is told to his dismay that he is fated not only to kill his father, but also to marry his mother. Horrified, he determines to avoid this fate by never returning to Corinth. On the road, however, he encounters a traveler who is none other than Laius. In some versions, Laius is also on his way to the oracle to find out if his son had died of exposure long ago on Mount Citheron. Oedipus, as strong-willed as his father, though of course not knowing that this is his father, refuses to move out of the way for him. Laius strikes him with a whip, and Oedipus, enraged, kills Laius and all his retinue, except one who escapes.

Oedipus eventually comes to Thebes, a city in terrible straits. Not only has its king been slain (news travels fast), but it is oppressed by the Sphinx, a powerful creature, part human, part animal, who devours citizens of the city each time they fail to answer her riddle. The riddle is this: what walks on four legs in the morning, two legs at noon, and three legs in the evening, yet speaks with one voice? Creon, the brother of the widowed Jocasta, has proclaimed that whoever answers the riddle of the sphinx and frees the city from her tyranny will be made king and given his sister's hand in marriage. Oedipus, with his native brilliance, answers the riddle: it is man (who walks on all fours as an infant, then on two legs, and finally, with a cane in old age, on three). Her riddle answered, the Sphinx throws herself to her death from the walls of Thebes. Creon in gratitude unites Oedipus with his sister, Jocasta, making Oedipus king of Thebes.

As the years pass, Oedipus and Jocasta have four children: two boys, Polyneices and Eteocles, and two girls, Ismene and Antigone. But eventually a devastating plague falls on Thebes. Oedipus sends Creon to the oracle to find out what he can, and Creon returns with the news that the city is polluted because it harbors the slayer of Laius and that the plague will only lift when that man is expelled from Thebes. Oedipus now trains all his power of intellect and command on solving this mystery. Thanks to his persistence, together with the testimony of the now ancient shepherd who passed him in his infancy to Polybus and that of the servant who escaped his wrath when he killed Laius, Oedipus learns that the cause of pollution is none other than himself. In their despair, Jocasta hangs herself and Oedipus blinds himself by plunging his wife and mother's gold brooches into his eyes.

Oedipus sends himself into exile, leaving Thebes and spending many years wandering as a beggar, accompanied only by his daughter Antigone.

> At last he finds shelter at Colonus in a grove sacred to the Eumenides, remembering that long ago the oracle that had told him his fate had prophesied also that he would end his days in the safety of such a grove. Meanwhile, his sons, Polyneices and Eteocles, disputing the crown of Thebes, have gone to war. Each sends to his father for his blessing and support, but Oedipus curses them both. Oedipus then goes off to die, bidding farewell to his daughters. At the end, only King Theseus is present to see Oedipus disappear mysteriously into the earth with the assistance and the blessing of the gods.

I have cobbled together this narrative rendering of the Oedipus story out of at least nine different versions from the ancient Greek, though I have relied most heavily on Sophocles' classic treatment of the story in two plays, *Oedipus the King* and *Oedipus at Colonus* (Fifth century BC). There were surely many more than nine versions, each of them necessarily different from the others. Since that time, the story has reappeared in numerous languages throughout the world and in hundreds of analogue versions. This is clearly the signal case of a gripping masterplot, dealing with tough contradictions, that human beings have repeatedly used to think with in successive narrative renderings.

The agon at the heart of this story is most often regarded as the conflict between Oedipus and his fate. Struggle as he may to avoid the fate he learns from the oracle, he cannot escape it. Indeed, it is his very effort to escape that makes escape unavoidable. The narrative reinforces the centrality of this agon by having Oedipus's struggle with fate anticipated and doubled by the conflict between Laius and his fate that sets the story in motion. But why should such a story grip us? Few people in the West believe in the existence of a fate so particularized that it can specify that a man will kill his father and sleep with his mother. Why should we care for people in a world so governed? The easy answer is that we *suspend disbelief*. Coleridge created this phrase to account for why we allow ourselves to get wrapped up in a play even though we know it is only acted. Thus we can allow ourselves to be transported to Thebes or Colonus by a play while knowing all the time that we are seated in a theater. But why should a twentieth-century audience allow itself to go along with this Greek notion of fate?

In this case, the most likely answer is that, though we may not believe in fate the way many did in ancient Greece, we all know what it means to struggle with constraints that in one way or another govern our lives. If you are born black where black is the minority, it is a foreordained fact that you will experience racism, both directly and indirectly. The combination of your unchangeable physical features and the mindset of millions would make this an unavoidable condition of your life. This is a kind of fate. If you are deaf, or misshapen, or schizophrenic, or parentless, or in some other way deeply marked by genetics or environment, constraints are laid down ahead of you that are very much like a destiny – as unavoidable as they are deeply affecting. But there are also conditions that are as inescapable as these and that lie in wait for almost all of us. All those who survive childhood go through the changes of adolescence, most will fall in love at least once, and the majority will know what it means to lose love. If we live past our young adulthood, we will experience the loss of physical and mental power that comes with aging. And, of course, there is one fate that none of us escape. Early on, we learn the way our story in this life ends, a conclusion that we see anticipated in the deaths of others, including many whom we love.

It is the struggle between this certain knowledge of how lives are determined and the need to assert a freedom and dignity that in some way overwrites this helplessness that is the larger conflict, riding on the agon contained in the story of Oedipus. In other words, his particular struggle against his fate catalyzes the general need to control what cannot be controlled, just as his self-punishment and later wandering are a way of thinking through the effort to come to terms with the crimes he committed in spite of his best efforts. The general point is that the narrative, in negotiating Oedipus's dilemma, negotiates at the same time the general conflict between determinism and the freedom to act. An ancillary point is that different narrative renderings of this tale make for different thinking about its issues. In the version of Diodorus Siculus, for example, when Laius has his fatal encounter with Oedipus, he is seeking information about his son from the same oracle that tells Oedipus he will kill his father. This ironic coincidence heightens the sense that, in the case of both father and son, the very effort to avoid one's fate makes that fate inevitable. A bleaker reading than that of Sophocles of the whole issue of human dignity in such a world, this version has Oedipus end his days in thrall to his impious sons. Sophocles, in contrast, works the narrative differently and in the process throws the balance between fate and freedom in the other direction. In his version, Oedipus at the end of his days is presented as one whose strength of character allows him freely to reject his sons. His capacity to persevere and to grow in wisdom earns him the reverential awe of King Theseus and the chorus.

Here again, in this last chapter, I am making a "foundational" proposition about how we relate to narrative. That is, before we are Marxian or Freudian, psychoanalytic or feminist, structuralist or post-structuralist, we all share common elements in the way we relate to narrative. To make this particular case, though, it is important to stress that I am not saying that we necessarily find in narratives *successful* negotiations of differences. Far from it. But insofar as we share in our own lives the larger conflicts of which these narrative conflicts are particular examples, we are moved by the narrative, drawn into it, and become alert to how these conflicts play out. And this, I am arguing, is an important form of thinking, whether or not the negotiation of conflicts is seen to be successful. Moreover, in contrast to more abstract modes of thought, this is *passionate thinking*. That is, in narrative our thinking is intimately tied to the emotions aroused during our narrative journey.

Are narratives like arguments?

Here are two views on this question. The first comes from the eminent psychologist Jerome Bruner: "A good story and a well-formed argument are different natural kinds. Both can be used as means for convincing another. Yet what they convince *of* is fundamentally different: arguments convince one of their truth, stories of their lifelikeness. The one verifies by eventual appeal to procedures for establishing formal and empirical proof. The other establishes not truth but verisimilitude."[1]

The second comes from the American novelist and critic Ronald Sukenick: "All fiction can be profitably regarded as argument. When you define fiction by representation you end up confining it to realism at some level and arguing that fiction, as a form of make-believe, is a way of lying to get at the truth, which if not palpably stupid is certainly round-about and restrictive. My approach frees fiction from the obligations of mimesis, popularly, and most often critically, assumed to be its defining quality."[2]

Critical reading as narrative negotiation

An important qualification to this argument is that there is not necessarily any single privileged way of reading the conflict in a story, or sometimes even defining what or who it involves. This sounds extreme, but it can be especially true in longer and more complex narratives like the story of Oedipus. The reading of the Oedipus story that I proposed above, featuring the conflict between Oedipus and his fate, is only one (if the most common) among many readings of the Oedipus material. Yet – and here is the main point again – even among highly varied readings of the same story, one almost invariably finds the same underlying orientation, *an attention to conflict of some kind and how it plays out*. We can, for example, find this orientation in four famous readings of the Oedipus narrative, each of them representing a radically different take on the story from the one I chose above, yet each of them in their very different ways featuring the effort to negotiate a conflict.

Aristotle. In the *Poetics* (335–322 BC), Aristotle argued that the function of tragedy lay in its primary effect: "arousing pity and fear, whereby to accomplish its catharsis of such emotions" (631). And along the way he singled out the story of Oedipus as a masterful example of this complex emotional end:

> The tragic fear and pity may be aroused by the Spectacle; but they may also be aroused by the very structure and incidents of the play – which is the better way and shows the better poet. The Plot in fact should be so framed that, even without seeing the things take place, he who simply hears the account of them shall be filled with horror and pity at the incidents; which is just the effect that the mere recital of the story of *Oedipus* would have on one. (641)

The puzzle that the combination of pity and fear presents is that these emotions move us in opposite directions. Pity draws one toward the pitiable object in a movement of sympathy; fear drives one away in a movement of self-preservation. Yet, for Aristotle, an overbalance toward one or the other spoils the effect of tragedy. What happens in the Oedipus story is a successful transaction involving these opposed emotions whereby, despite their differences, they are both aroused and spent in a mutual catharsis. Much ink has been spilled in trying to get at the exact meaning of Aristotle's use of the word "catharsis," but it seems implicitly to refer to the arousal and purgation of powerful emotions that otherwise might control us. The point to stress here, however, is that Aristotle features as the heart of the tragic effect, epitomized by the Oedipus story, a successful negotiation of the claims of two contradictory emotions which are allowed somehow to join together. At the most fearful and repellent moment of the story – when Oedipus drives the points of Jocasta's gold brooches into his eyes – what keeps this from, as it were, "blowing us away" is that we grasp through pity the depth of despair that causes him to do this.

Freud. In *The Interpretation of Dreams* (1900), Freud situated his reading of the Oedipus story directly against the common interpretation I outlined above. For Freud, the stress on the conflict between the decree of the gods and the human desire for moral freedom is really a smokescreen: "an uncomprehending secondary elaboration of the material, which sought to make it serve a theological intention."[3] The success of the Oedipus story and the reason for its universality "does not depend upon the conflict between fate and human will, but upon the peculiar nature of the material by which this conflict is revealed" (307). In other words, it is not fate that matters in this story but the specific acts of killing the father and sleeping with the mother. And this is because these are two acts that we ("we" meaning "men") all secretly want to do. That both of these acts are treated in the same play is only fitting because, according to Freud, they are the two principal components of the same childhood yearning. Men are murderously jealous of their fathers because they want the exclusive love of their mothers. These are two yoked desires that most men successfully repress.

> King Oedipus, who slew his father Laius and wedded his mother Jocasta, is nothing more or less than a wish fulfillment – the fulfillment of the wish of our childhood. But we, more fortunate than he, in so far as we have not become psychoneurotics, have since our childhood succeeded in withdrawing our sexual impulses from our mothers, and in forgetting our jealousy of our fathers. We recoil from the person for whom this primitive wish of our childhood has been fulfilled with all the force of the repression which these wishes have undergone in our minds since childhood. As the poet brings the guilt of Oedipus to light by his investigation, he forces us to become aware of our own inner selves, in which the same impulses are still extant, even though they are suppressed.   (308)

Jocasta, trying to comfort Oedipus as he approaches the truth, unwittingly provides internal support for this reading by noting that what he fears is a dream common to men:

> For many a man hath seen himself in dreams
> His mother's mate, but he who gives no heed
> To suchlike matters bears the easier life.   (308)

In his reading, Freud has displaced one conflict with another. The conflict between fate and the free exercise of human will is displaced by the conflict between desire and conscience or, in later Freudian terms, between the urging of the libido and the tyranny of the superego. The normal price of this conflict in the everyday life of men, its negotiated condition, is repression and a kind of unlocalized malaise or free-floating guilt. In the story of Oedipus, the price of actually living the wish is self-inflicted blindness and expulsion from home. In the narrative, no compromise is possible, and expiation only ends with the death of the transgressor. For the audience, however, the transaction is more complex. Through Oedipus, the viewer is permitted the wished-for enactment of forbidden desires and at the same time allowed to separate himself (again, it must be male) by observing the punishment of his unacknowledged surrogate. The pleasures of the crime and the satisfactions of punishment are bound up in the same narrative package.

Propp. The Russian folklorist Vladimir Propp, considered by many a founder of structuralism and arguably the founder of *narratology* as well (though before the term was invented), produced a long paper on the Oedipus story in 1944. In this essay, he cast his net widely to cover a great range of variants of the story but all to the end of showing the "hybrid" character of the version Sophocles created in his two plays. Like Freud, Propp relocated the central conflict away from the ostensible struggle between Oedipus and his fate, but unlike Freud he saw the play's conflict in historical terms: "The tale does not arise as a direct reflection of a social order. It arises from a conflict, from the contradictions that occur as one order replaces another."[4] Briefly, the two orders were the older one (according to Propp's theory of social evolution) by which rule of the kingdom was determined according to matrilineal descent and the newer order by which rule of the kingdom was determined according to patrilineal descent.

In this reading of history, the older or more "primitive" fairy tales were structured to reflect a matrilineal order by which the throne passed from the father to a son-in-law. The future king is an outsider who comes in and marries the king's daughter. Along the way, however, he must conform to a number of conventional patterns: being exiled or cast adrift in infancy, losing his name and being given another, passing a number of tests, and in some versions heroically killing the old king before marrying his daughter. In Propp's reading of Sophocles's Oedipus, the skeleton of this older genre can be seen. Oedipus is cast away, and his name (which reflects the condition of his exile) is given to him later. Coming to the city, he must pass the test of overthrowing the Sphinx, and of course he kills the father. But this version of the tale has no daughter to marry. Instead, Oedipus is offered the king's widow. Moreover, the king he killed is not his father-in-law but his actual father. In this way and others, according to Propp, Sophocles synthesized a hybrid story that layers the new order over the old.

In the complex negotiation of one social order gaining ascendancy over another, Propp argues that Sophocles's sequel, *Oedipus at Colonus*, played a crucial role. This is because, in following the pattern of the old order and killing the king, even (and significantly) in doing so unconsciously, Oedipus has overlaid the heroism of regicide with the horrendous crime of patricide. He must not only pay for this crime but in the process he must also achieve some form of apotheosis that in turn validates the new order in which the son succeeds the father. This second stage is what takes place after the years of blind wandering when Oedipus arrives in Colonus at the sacred grove of the Eumenides. He is honored by king and country, his body is blessed, he is called by the gods, and he enters the earth in anticipation of rebirth as a god himself (and Oedipus did in fact have a cult following in ancient Greece). In this way, Propp argues, Sophocles anticipates the pattern of numerous retellings of the story in analogous tales such as those of Gregory and of Andrew of Crete, both of whom became saints despite their crimes of kinship and incest.

Lévi-Strauss. When the anthropologist Claude Lévi-Strauss published his classic reading of the Oedipus material in 1955, he was interested not so much in providing a reading of this specific story as in using it to show how all myths might best be read. What was revolutionary about his argument was his shift of focus from a linear reading of myth — that is, the kind of reading (like all four above) that goes from beginning to end — to a structural or "synchronic" reading that focusses on repetitions in the material. Quite literally, Lévi-Strauss spatialized the myth to get at its thinking. The repetitions within a set of mythic material like that of the Oedipus story he called "gross constituent units" or "mythemes." These operate on a "higher level" of meaning than the linguistic phenomena (phonemes, morphemes, and sememes) by which we construe them. And when they are "bundled" together, they guide us away from the myth's linear and historical content and toward its timeless content, explaining "the present and the past as well as the future."[5] Here is how Lévi-Strauss bundled the Oedipus mythemes:

Cadmus seeks his sister Europa, ravished by Zeus			
		Cadmus kills the dragon	
	The Spartoi kill one another		
			Labdacos (Laios' father) = *lame* (?)
	Oedipus kills his father, Laios		Laios (Oedipus' father) = *left-sided* (?)
		Oedipus kills the Sphinx	
			Oedipus = *Swollen-foot* (?)
Oedipus marries his mother, Jocasta			
	Eteocles kills his brother, Polyneices		
Antigone buries her brother, Polyneices, despite prohibition			
(214)			

As you can see, in order to have sufficient narrative material to develop significant bundles of these repetitions, Lévi-Strauss drew on the story of Cadmus and Europa that precedes the Oedipus material as well as the story of Oedipus's children that follows his death. This gave him enough material to reorganize the entire narrative, scoring it like music, so that the bundled repetitions stand out vertically, like chords. The result is four bundles of mythemes. Each column in the scheme above includes mythemes that share some repeated concept. In the first column, the shared concept is "blood relations that are overemphasized, that is, more intimate than they should be. . . .*the overrating of blood relations.*" In the second column, the shared concept is the "*underrating of blood relations.*" The third column features the slaying of monsters who would return us to the earth and therefore features the denial of the idea that we come from the earth (affirming that we are not "autochthonous"). And finally the fourth column features forms of lameness that are ancient signs of our having come from the earth (affirming that we are "autochthonous").

Put together, the four columns constitute a kind of thinking about ideas in conflict, for "column four is to column three as column one is to column two":

> The myth has to do with the inability, for a culture which holds the belief that man is autochthonous . . ., to find a satisfactory transition between this theory and the knowledge that human beings are actually born from the union of man and woman. Although the problem obviously cannot be solved, the Oedipus myth provides a kind of logical tool which relates the original problem – born from one or born from two? – to the derivative problem: born from different or born from same? By a correlation of this type, the overrating of blood relations is to the underrating of blood relationships as the attempt to escape autochthony is to the impossibility to succeed in it.   (216)

In other words, with the kind of knowledge that they had at their disposal, the ancient creators of these myths were thinking just as hard and just as well as we do today. Indeed, since there is no privileged version of any myth, and a myth repeats its thinking in all its versions, even Freud's interpretation of the Oedipus story, according to Lévi-Strauss, can be absorbed into this reading according to bundled mythemes:

> Although the Freudian problem has ceased to be that of autochthony *versus* bisexual reproduction, it is still the problem of understanding how *one* can be born of *two*: How is it that we do not have only one procreator, but a mother plus a father? Therefore, not only Sophocles, but Freud himself, should be included among the recorded versions of the Oedipus myth on a par with earlier or seemingly more "authentic" versions.   (217)

To return to a fundamental point in this section, Lévi-Strauss, for all his radical reorganization of the way we look at myth – to the point of turning it into something that does not look like narrative at all, but rather a much more static, spatialized entity – still finds at the heart of narrative the effort to negotiate competing claims in a major conflict of ideas. In this extreme structuralist view, then, mythic narrative is still a mode of passionate thought, seeking to negotiate some way out of the contradictions of existence. To summarize, all five of the readings of Oedipus that I have reviewed here are implicitly based on the view that people think through the agency of narrative. In the process, I hope I have shown two additional things as well: 1) how differently people can respond to the same narrative and, at the same time, 2) how persistent through all this difference is the assumption that narrative appeals through its representation of some kind of conflict.

Closure, one more time

Closure becomes important in this discussion because, at the *level of questions*, it is the end of narrative conflict. If closure of the conflict or agon coincides with closure at the level of questions, it gives the impression of resolving larger issues that are carried by the agon. Historically, there have been times when closure of this sort has been strongly advocated, at least in reference to questions of moral conduct. Early in the eighteenth century, Daniel Defoe wrote in the preface to one of his novels that "Every wicked Reader will here be encouraged to a Change, and it will appear that the best and only good End of a wicked misspent Life is Repentance; that in this, there is Comfort, Peace, and often times Hope, and that the Penitent shall be returned like the Prodigal, *and his latter End be better than his Beginning.*"[6] For Defoe, in other words, or more accurately for his authorial *persona* in this text, issues of wickedness and its consequences are closed by the end of his novel. In the nineteenth century, Anthony Trollope affirmed much the same thing about the works of his entire oeuvre when he wrote that he aimed to "teach lessons" in his novels: "I have ever thought of myself as a preacher of sermons, and my pulpit as one which I could make both salutary and agreeable to my audience."[7] And in 1929, the French novelist and playwright François Mauriac wrote that the writer "has got to reach those who are still capable of being influenced and dominated. He wants to leave his mark on this living wax and imprint all that is best in him on those who are going to survive him. . . . he wants to make them replicas of himself; he wants his own image and likeness to be resurrected in them when he himself is in the grave."[8] Each of these statements reflects a desire for clarity in the domain of morality that can coincide with narrative closure.

For others, especially over the last century, a comment like that of Mauriac would be chilling. They see authorially imposed closure as a threat to the kind of thinking that narrative can assist. D. H. Lawrence wrote that "if you try to nail anything down, in the novel, either it kills the novel, or the novel gets up and walks away with the nail." Teaching clear moral lessons, in this conception, is exactly what a novel cannot do. It cannot because "morality in the novel is the trembling instability of the balance. When the novelist puts his thumb in the scale, to pull down the balance to his own predilection, that is immorality."[9] Forty years earlier, the short story writer Anton Chekhov made the same point in a letter to a friend, but in a different way:

> You are right in demanding that an artist should take a conscious attitude to his work, but you confuse two conceptions: *the solution of a question and the correct setting of a question*. The latter alone is obligatory for the artist. In "Anna Karenin" and in "Onyeguin" not a single problem is solved, but they satisfy completely because all the problems are set correctly. It is for the judge to put the questions correctly; and the jurymen must decide, each one according to his taste.[10]

For both of these authors, narrative fits the words I. A. Richards used to describe a book: "a machine to think with." But for both, this is thinking that finds no necessary closure in the work itself. Quite the contrary, it depends on the absence of closure at the level of questions.

These two ways of approaching the negotiation of conflict in narrative – with and without closure at the level of questions – are strikingly demonstrated in rival scenarios for the conclusion of the same film, *The Jazz Singer*. The first feature-length film to use sound throughout, *The Jazz Singer* was a great hit when it came out in 1927. The conflict on which its narrative is structured is that between a son and his immigrant father. The larger question riding on this conflict is whether there can be a workable synthesis of new ways and old, or whether one of these must triumph over the other as the new generation succeeds the old. The son, Jakie Rabinowitz, played by Al Jolson, finds himself drawn to the music of Broadway and popular culture in opposition to his father's desire that his son follow in his footsteps as the sixth successive cantor in his family's male line of descent. The film opens on the eve of Yom Kippur, the Day of Atonement when devout Jews seek to atone for the sins they have committed during the year. Cantor Rabinowitz is anticipating the singing of Kol Nidre, the traditional beginning of Yom Kippur. This is music that he has carefully taught his teenage son in the expectation that tonight Jakie will sing in his place for the first time. But the wayward Jakie at that moment is singing "raggy time songs" in a beer hall. Discovered and then punished by his father with a beating, Jakie leaves home.

Throughout the film, the agon involving father and son is musically expressed by alternating renditions of the mournful yet hauntingly beautiful Kol Nidre and Al Jolson's lively renditions of "Blue Skies," "Toot, Toot, Tootsie," and other 1920s hits. The film's climax comes when Jakie, now Jack Robin, gets his big break, a starring role in a Broadway play. It brings him back to his roots in New York. But shortly after his arrival, he learns that his father is dying. To give excruciating accentuation to the conflict, the opening night of the Broadway play, *April Follies*, is scheduled to occur on the eve of Yom Kippur, the night when Kol Nidre must be sung. His father being ill, there is no one to sing Kol Nidre except Jakie. Will he sing it? Everything appears to be at stake in this decision. As the producer warns him, if Jack Robin fails to appear at the opening of the Broadway show in which he is to star, his reputation will be ruined. His girlfriend, Mary, also starring in the show and also present cries out: "you can't throw away this one great chance, Jack – the house sold out – and it will ruin me too!" Yet Cantor Rabinowitz, revived momentarily by the appearance of his son, is convinced that his prayers have been answered. The members of the synagogue have already assembled; only Jakie can usher in Yom Kippur with the singing of Kol Nidre. And if he doesn't "it will be the first time in five generations a Rabinowitz has not sung on the Day of Atonement." How will the narrative negotiate this agonizing conflict between the claims of two different cultures? How will it close?

In both the original script and the film, Jakie finds that, even as he is preparing to go on stage on opening night, he cannot abandon the old ways. But the original script ends with the cancellation of the opening night of *April Follies*, and Jakie, his prayer shawl draped over his shoulders, singing Kol Nidre in the synagogue. As he sings, his father, who recognizes his son's voice coming in through the open window, finally dies in peace. Then, in an extraordinary scene, the spirit of the father appears behind the son, and as Jakie continues singing, oblivious to his father's ghostly presence, his father places his hands on his son's shoulders in a gesture of blessing and then disappears. For all its melodrama, the scene is deeply moving. Jolson's rendering of Kol Nidre is quite beautiful and it culminates a series of fragmentary renderings of the music that we have heard throughout the film and that have prepared for this final version. The image of the father, giving his son the "laying on of hands" in a gesture of forgiveness, harmonizes with the import of Kol Nidre. In short, there is a powerful sense of closure in this final scene. The implication for the larger issue, riding on the agon, is that the old spiritual ways are irresistible, and rightly so. In them you find depth and continuity. And however joyous and alive the music of popular culture may be, and however painful its abandonment, maturity and our deeper natures require this final rite of passage.

But the film that viewers saw in 1927 did not end with Al Jolson singing Kol Nidre. "The season passes – and time heals – the show goes on," we are told, after the scene of Jakie singing Kol Nidre in the synagogue fades out. The old script is then supplemented with a new conclusion featuring Jack Robin in blackface singing "My Mammy" at the Winter Garden Theater. Both his mother and his father's friend, Moisha Yudelson, a pillar of East Side Jewish society, are seated in the front row, smiling their appreciation. The film ends with the end of the song. As the light fades out, Jakie, who is black on black, slowly disappears until all that is visible in the last second of the film is his white collar. With this addition to the film, the process of narrative negotiation is revived and appears to swing back in the other direction. But how far does it go? Does popular culture triumph and are the two beaming representatives of the old ways seated in the front row a sign of the necessary acceptance of full assimilation to American ways? After all, Jakie's mother, who "had a deeper and better understanding of life" than her husband, had already warned Cantor Rabinowitz that Kol Nidre may be in Jakie's head "but it is not in his heart. He is of America." Or is the pre-dominant note tragic or pathetic, with blackface as a sign of the inevitable annihilation of Jakie's identity? This reading would appear to be accentuated by the way he is made to disappear into blackness at the end. Or, trying again, are we meant to infer some kind of synthesis at the end, marked by the presence of both generations and keyed to the idea that the old sacred songs and the songs of the Jazz Age come out of the same impulse? It is noted on several occasions that whatever Jakie sings, he sings with "a tear in his voice." And Jakie himself in one scene quotes his father back to him on the subject of song: "You taught me to sing – and you told me that music was the voice of God – and it is just as honorable to sing in the theater as in the synagogue."

There are still other possibilities. But my own sense of the ending of this film is that closure does not occur without serious *underreading*. There are too many competing signifiers in the film's final scene to permit one of the possible readings mentioned above to prevail. In other words, the passionate thought that is aroused by this narrative is still in progress after it concludes. It is a restless film, a case of Lawrence's "trembling instability of the bal-ance." And it may be that it reflects a larger impossibility of resolution – that there is no satisfactory answer to the question the film asks. It may also be, of course, that I am finding a lack of negotiated resolution *symptomatically* where Warner Brothers had in fact intended resolution. Be that as it may, I hope the distinction of endings here makes clear how the sense of closure or its absence can impact the kind of thinking we do when we experience narrative negotiation.

The end of closure?

There are a number of viewers who would argue that, even if *The Jazz Singer* had ended with the final rendering of Kol Nidre, it would not have closed the film's dilemma as neatly as I suggested above. Both Mary, Jack Robin's co-star, and the producer of *April Follies* observe Jack singing Kol Nidre. How do we read their presence in this scene? Does it suggest an

American cultural acceptance of the triumph of the old ways in a cultural harmony in which the old and the new co-habit? Or do we see them as cultural predators from American show business, busy appreciating the potential in Jack's voice? Earlier, Yudelson, coming backstage in the theater to plead with Jakie to sing in his father's place, is embarrassed by the beautiful bare legs of a dancer from whom he cannot tear his eyes. Is this the thin edge of the wedge for this Old World innocent? After Yudelson's visit, Jack explains to Mary: "I don't really belong there [in the synagogue] – here's where I belong, on Broadway, but there's something in the blood that sort of calls you – something apart from this life." To which Mary replies: "I think I understand, Jack. But no matter how strong the call, this is your life."

More insidious perhaps is the way in which, in both conclusions, submission harbors domination. Submitting to his father, Jakie becomes the father, dominating with his voice his captive audience in the synagogue. In this way the old conclusion anticipates the same paradoxical combination that Jack Robin achieves in the film's final scene, submitting to his mother in an homage ("My Mammy!") even while he is raised above her on stage, dominating an audience of which she is a part. Finally, in 1927, it would be hard for an audience to suppress awareness that the cantor in the final scene of the original screenplay is none other than Al Jolson, and that Jolson's fame is precisely the kind that Jack Robin aspires to. Jolson's fame as a popular singer is an insistent *paratext* that would seem to give the lie to Jolson the cantor. The guise of the cantor, in other words, might well have something of the same status as the guise of blackface.

In my way, what I have been doing here by opening up these interpretative gaps is to turn the original screenplay of this film into what Roland Barthes would call a "writable" text, as opposed to a "readable" one. Instead of simply taking the concluding scene on what appears to be its own terms, I have been actively "writing" it by capitalizing on its contradictory possibilities. In the terms of this book, my interpretations are approaching *adaptation*. But I am also "deconstructing" the original conclusion: showing that what appears to be its ostensible argument contains within it the traces of an opposed reading. "Deconstruction," as I noted earlier, is grounded in the argument that uncertainty is inherent in the activity of making meaning through signs, be they written, oral, graphic, or otherwise. For Derrida, closure at the *level of questions* never arrives, regardless of the text. Moreover, since meaning is grounded not in some absolute contact with reality but in the web of differences out of which any sign acquires its signifying power, any process of narrative negotiation will never shake the differences that subvert it. Answers, in other words, that appear to emerge with closure at the level of questions will always contain traces of their opposites.

Deconstruction no longer has the cachet it had in the 1970s and 1980s, but the concept has nonetheless left a permanent mark on the way we read. Thanks to the efforts of Derrida and others, there is, among humanists across the whole range of literary approaches, a persistent suspicion of closure at the level of questions, even in the simplest, most apparently readable, texts.

How far down this road do readers of narrative wish to go? One answer, of course, is that anyone is free to go as far as she or he wants. But does the multiplicity of readings turn narrative into a kind of game, disconnected from the world of action? Does narrative then become a place where readers sport together in endless displays of ingenuity? Opponents of deconstruction were quick to charge that deconstruction was morally nihilistic and that it really meant that all readings were equal since one reading was just as good as another. But defenders were equally quick to say this was not the case. *The Jazz Singer*, they might have pointed out, does not advocate replacing American representative government with a parliamentary system, it does not comment on the digital revolution, it does not include a critique of nuclear energy. For deconstructionist critics, as for most others, the list of patently inferior interpretations is infinite. And for some, like J. Hillis Miller, in any given text the number of productive interpretations with both credibility and urgency are relatively few. But Miller and others would also argue that an awareness of the necessary openness of narrative, its lack of closure, far from being morally nihilistic, is the basis of any ethics of reading. It is ethical because it not only rests in an acknowledgment of the nature of all communication – its semantic porosity – but it also prevents the appropriation of a text to one monolithic meaning. It liberates readers to exercise their creative reading power in response to the full potentiality of narrative. In the terms of this chapter, such awareness activates the best and fullest range of passionate thinking that a narrative can catalyze in its negotiations.

This is beginning to sound good. Certainly it does to me. But in the general spirit of these comments, I would like to end this text without coming to closure on the subject of closure. I will do this by raising three questions. The first has to do with the *rhetorical* power of narrative that we discussed in earlier chapters. Allowing narrative to carry us from one point to another is one of the great pleasures it provides. But if we always require ourselves to introduce an attitude of questioning, even suspicion, into our reading, so that we have an awareness of the plurality of possibilities in any particular narrative, do we run the risk of separating ourselves from that pleasure? To put this question in another way, is the attitude of detached questioning something that functions to protect readers and viewers from the power that narrative has to move us with deep feeling?

The second question is closely allied to the first. One of the ancient functions of narrative is that it gives us sufficient understanding to make up our minds about things. It provides not only information but also values to be passed down from one generation to the next. Parents rely on stories to reinforce moral behavior in their children. More broadly, anyone's capacity to act in the moral sphere, to make tough decisions, requires what is commonly called convictions. Convictions are not necessarily absolute. They are what the word implies: something about which we are convinced. Yet without being absolutists – that is, people who feel they have found the *only* right way – we still need to dispose of ideas that are less convincing in order to arrive at our convictions. Now here is the question: if good reading depends upon maintaining in our minds opposed moral ideas in a kind of balance, does that work against the creation and maintenance of strong convictions? And by indirection does this work against the capacity for decisive moral behavior?

The third question is closely allied to the second. How true is it that narrative, by belonging to the world of language, acquires its meanings solely by the play of difference within that linguistic realm? Another way to put this question is: can we never test the truth of a narrative by reality? Derrida in a famous overstatement said that there is nothing outside the text. But many have wondered from what standpoint outside the text he made that statement. It would seem that, in order to generalize about a subject like language, one would have to have some sense of what is not language. And many scientists would argue that what they demonstrate in the narratives they tell, if they tell them well, is the "other" of language. The narratives they tell about matter and energy, or the symptomology of disease, or the growth of cells, or the movements of the earth's crust, are continually being tested by a reality outside of language. And although, in the less empirically verifiable realm of human nature and moral behavior, our thinking is saturated with language from our earliest years, is it out of the question that wisdom leaks in from the world of feelings, actions, and consequences? And do we not judge a narrative by the way this wisdom tests it?

In one form or another, these objections have followed deconstruction from its arrival on the literary scene. None of them, in my view, is a knockout blow. But I want to end with them. They are very much alive – as alive as the perception that narrative is always and forever full of gaps that we must fill and that closure, however much narrative may seem to invite it, is finally something only we can confirm, and only if we choose to do so.

Further secondary reading

The story of Solomon's wise decision can be found in the Old Testament in 1 Kings 3:16–28. The most famous version of the story of Oedipus can be found in two plays by Sophocles, *Oedipus the King* and *Oedipus at Colonus* (Fifth century BC). For many of the variants on this continually fascinating story, you can consult two good books: Lowell Edmunds and Alan Dundes (eds.), *Oedipus: a Folklore Casebook* (New York: Garland, 1983) and Lowell Edmunds, *Oedipus: The Ancient Legend and Its Later Analogues* (Baltimore: Johns Hopkins University Press, 1985).

  In thinking about narrative as thinking, it may help to consider Stanley Fish's distinction, in his *Self-Consuming Artifacts*, between a "rhetorical text" that "satisfies the needs of its readers" by mirroring "the opinions its readers already hold" and a "dialectical text" that "is disturbing, for it requires of its readers a searching and rigorous scrutiny of everything they believe in and live by."[11] Of all the works on narrative, the one that for me best features the capacity of narrative to find new understanding through the working out of the story is Paul Ricoeur's magisterial three-volume work, *Time and Narrative*. His writing can be a little dry, but it is well worth the effort.

Additional primary texts

My argument in this chapter is that most narratives of any complexity can be read as efforts to negotiate opposing psychological and cultural claims. And there are in fact some authors who have capitalized on the centrality of conflict in narrative to structure their narratives quite openly like a debate. These are perhaps worth special attention here, but only because of the way they foreground the process of narrative negotiation. Dostoevsky's longer novels almost invariably operate in this way. Among others are Shakespeare's *Hamlet* (c. 1601), both parts of Goethe's *Faust* (1808, 1831), Thomas Mann's *The Magic Mountain* (1924), André Malreaux's *Man's Fate* (1933), Georges Bernanos's *The Diary of a Country Priest* (1937), Arthur Koestler's *Darkness at Noon* (1941), John Barth's companion pieces *The Floating Opera* (1956) and *End of the Road* (1958), Nikos Kazantzakis's *The Fratricides* (1963), and Saul Bellow's *Herzog* (1964). In almost every one of these narratives, the central figure is torn by a moral dilemma and, as the narrative proceeds, is pulled back and forth between competing moral claims.

Notes

Chapter One

1. Fredric Jameson, *The Poltical Unconscious: Narrative as a Socially Symbolic Act* (Ithaca: Cornell University Press, 1981), p. 13.
2. Jean-François Lyotard, trans. Geoff Bennington and Brian Massumi, *The Postmodern Condition*, Theory and History of Literature, vol. 10 (Minneapolis: University of Minnesota Press, 1984), p. 19.
3. Roland Barthes, "Introduction to the Structural Analysis of Narratives" in Susan Sontag (ed.) *A Barthes Reader* (New York: Hill and Wang, 1982), pp. 251–2.
4. The coincidence of the onset in infancy of both autobiographical memory and narrative capability has been widely observed in psychological literature. For one discussion, see Katherine Nelson, "Finding One's Self in Time" in Joan Gay Snodgrass and Robert L. Thompson (eds.), *The Self across Psychology: Self Recognition, Self-Awareness, and the Self Concept*, Annals of the New York Academy of Sciences, vol. 818 (New York Academy of Sciences, 1997), pp. 103–16.
5. Peter Brooks, "The Law as Narrative and Rhetoric," in Peter Brooks and Paul Gewirtz (eds.), *Law's Stories: Narrative and Rhetoric in the Law* (New Haven: Yale University Press, 1996), p. 19.
6. See Oliver Sacks's discussions of Korsakov's syndrome in *The Man Who Mistook his Wife for a Hat* (New York: Simon and Schuster, 1985), pp. 23–42, 108–15; and Kay Young and Jeffrey Shaver, "The Neurology of Narrative," *SubStance* 94/95 (March 2001), 72–84.
7. Paul Auster, *The Invention of Solitude* (New York: Penguin, 1988), p. 154.
8. Paul Ricoeur, trans. Kathleen McLaughlin and David Pellauer, *Time and Narrative*, three vols. (University of Chicago Press, 1984), vol. 1: 3.
9. Brian De Palma, quoted in Eric Harrison, "De Palma," *Los Angeles Times*, Calendar Section, 2 August 1998, 30.
10. Hayden White, *The Content of the Form: Narrative Discourse and Historical Representation* (Baltimore: Johns Hopkins University Press, 1987), p. 215n.

Chapter Two

1. Barbara Herrnstein Smith, "Narrative Versions, Narrative Theories," in W. J. T. Mitchell (ed.) *On Narrative*, pp. 209–32.
2. Gerald Prince, *A Dictionary of Narratology* (Lincoln: University of Nebraska Press, 1987), p. 58. Prince goes on to give a much fuller account of narrative.
3. Seymour Chatman, *Coming to Terms: The Rhetoric of Narrative in Fiction and Film* (Ithaca: Cornell University Press, 1990), p. 9.
4. Jonathan Culler, *The Pursuit of Signs: Semiotics, Literature, Deconstruction* (Ithaca: Cornell University Press, 1981), pp. 169–87.
5. Leo Tolstoy, letter to N. N. Strakhov, 23 April 1976, in Henry Gifford (ed.), *Leo Tolstoy: A Critical Anthology* (Harmondsworth: Penguin, 1971), p. 48.
6. Claude Bremond, "Le message narratif," *Communications* 4 (1964), 4; cited and translated by Seymour Chatman, *Story and Discourse: Narrative Structure in Fiction and Film* (Ithaca: Cornell University Press, 1978), p. 20.
7. Barthes, "Introduction to the Structural Analysis of Narratives," pp. 295–6; Chatman, *Story and Discourse*, pp. 53–6.
8. Barthes, "Structural Analysis," p. 267.

Chapter Three

1. Henry James, *The Turn of the Screw* (Toronto: Dover, 1991), p. 2.
2. Manfred Jahn, "Frames, Preferences, and the reading of Third-Person Narratives: Towards a Cognitive Narratology," *Poetics Today* 18:4 (winter 1997), 441.
3. Oscar Wilde, Richard Ellmann (ed.), *The Picture of Dorian Gray and Other Writings* (New York: Bantam, 1982), p. 111.
4. Martin Amis, *Time's Arrow* (New York: Random House, 1991), p. 11.
5. Nelson Goodman, "Twisted Tales: or, Story, Study, and Symphony," in W. J. T. Mitchell, ed., *On Narrative*, pp. 99–115.
6. George P. Landow, *Hypertext 2.0: the Convergence of Contemporary Critical Theory and Technology* (Baltimore: Johns Hopkins University Press, 1997; revised), p. 215.
7. Espen J. Aarseth, *Cybertext: Perspectives on Ergodic Literature* (Baltimore: Johns Hopkins University Press, 1997), pp. 94 and 114.

Chapter Four

1. Richard Wright, *Black Boy* (New York: Harper & Row, 1966), p. 47.
2. N. Scott Momaday, *The Way to Rainy Mountain* (Albuquerque: University of New Mexico Press, 1969), p. 16.
3. E. M. Forster, *Aspects of the Novel* (New York: Harcourt, Brace & World, 1955), p. 86. Originally published in 1927.

4. Culler, *The Pursuit of Signs*, p. 183.
5. Hayden White, *The Content of the Form*, p. 6.
6. Robert Musil, trans. Sophie Wilkins, *The Man without Qualities* (New York: Knopf, 1995), p. 709.
7. Stephen Jay Gould, "Jim Bowie's Letter and Bill Buckner's Legs," *Natural History* 109:4 (May 2000): 26–40.
8. *Santa Barbara News-Press* (NY Times Service) 29 March 1986.
9. Franz Kafka, trans. Willa and Edwin Muir, "The Metamorphosis" in *The Penal Colony: Stories and Short Pieces* (New York: Schocken, 1961), p. 67.

Chapter Five

1. Enrique Anderson Imbert, "Taboo" in Philip Stevick (ed.), *Anti-Story: an Anthology of Experimental Fiction* (New York: Free Press, 1971), p. 314.
2. Jeffrey Whitmore, "Bedtime Story" in Steve Moss (ed.), *The World's Shortest Stories* (San Luis Obispo & Santa Barbara: New Times Press & John Daniel, 1995), p. 15.
3. S. S. Koteliansky (trans. and ed.), *Anton Tchekhov: Literary and Theatrical Reminiscences*, (New York: Doran, 1927), p. 23.
4. Franz Kafka, trans. Willa Muir & Edwin Muir, *The Great Wall of China: Stories and Reflections* (New York: Schocken, 1970), pp. 129–30.
5. I. A. Richards, *Principles of Literary Criticism* (New York: Harcourt Brace, 1924), p. 1.

Chapter Six

1. Henry Fielding, *Tom Jones* (New York: A. L. Burt, nd), vol. II, p. 233.
2. Gustave Flaubert, trans. Francis Steegmuller, *Madame Bovary* (New York: Modern Library, 1957), p. 153.
3. Ernest Hemingway, "The Doctor and the Doctor's Wife" in *The Short Stories of Ernest Hemingway* (New York: Scribners, 1966), p. 99.
4. Gérard Genette, trans. Jane E. Lewin, *Narrative Discourse: an Essay in Method* (Ithaca: Cornell University Press, 1980), pp. 243–5.
5. Richard Schickel, *Movies: the History of an Art and an Institution* (New York: Basic Books, 1964), p. 149.
6. Dorrit Cohn, "Discordant Narration," *Style* 34:2 (Summer 2000), 307–16.
7. Flaubert, *Madame Bovary*, p. 322.
8. James Joyce, *Ulysses* (New York: Random House, 1986), p. 609.
9. David Bordwell, *Narration in the Fiction Film* (Madison: University of Wisconsin Press, 1985), p. 62.

Chapter Seven

1. Albert Laffay, *Logique du cinéma: création et spectacle* (Paris: Masson, 1964), p. 81.
2. David Hayman, *Ulysses: the Mechanics of Meaning* (Madison: University of Wisconsin Press, 1982), p. 84. See also pages 88–104 and 122–32.
3. Umberto Eco, et al, *Interpretation and Overinterpretation* (University of Cambridge Press, 1992), pp. 25ff.
4. Gabriel García Márquez, trans. Gregory Rabassa, "A Very Old Man with Enormous Wings" in *Leaf Storm and Other Stories* (New York: Harper & Row, 1972), p. 106.
5. Robert Musil, *The Man Without Qualities*, pp. 708–9.
6. Emma Kafalenos, "Not (Yet) Knowing: Epistemological Effects of Deferred and Suppressed Information in Narrative" in David Herman (ed.), *Narratologies: Perspectives on Narrative Analysis* (Columbus: Ohio State University Press, 1999), pp. 56 60. The concept of the primacy effect comes from cognitive psychology and was first brought into the analysis of narrative by Menakhem Perry, "Literary Dynamics: How the Order of a Text Creates Its Meaning," *Poetics Today* 1 (1979), 35 64 [53ff], and Meir Steinberg, *Expositional Modes and Temporal Ordering in Fiction*, Baltimore: Johns Hopkins University Press, 1978, pp. 93ff.
7. F. Scott Fitzgerald, "The Crack-Up" in Edmund Wilson (ed.), *The Crack-Up* (New York: New Directions, 1962), p. 69.
8. Ernest Hemingway, "Now I Lay Me" in *The Short Stories of Ernest Hemingway* (New York: Scribners, 1963), p. 363.
9. Wolfgang Iser, *The Implied Reader: Patterns of Communication in Prose Fiction from Bunyan to Beckett* (Baltimore: Johns Hopkins University Press, 1974), p. 280.
10. Emily Brontë, *Wuthering Heights* (Baltimore: Penguin, 1965), p. 78.

Chapter Eight

1. Saint Augustine, trans. D. W. Robertson, Jr., *On Christian Doctrine* (New York: Liberal Arts Press, 1958), p. 102.
2. Paul Auster, *The Invention of Solitude* (New York: Penguin, 1988), p. 146.
3. *The Floating Admiral* (1931) was an authorial round robin involving thirteen separate authors, including Agatha Christie and Dorothy Sayers. *Naked Came the Stranger* (1969), by the pseudonymous Penelope Ashe, was organized by Mike McGrady, who rounded up twenty-five of his co-workers on the *Long Island Newsday* to write installments of an erotic novel. The book was a best seller even before the authorial fraud was made public, going through seven printings (90,000 copies) in four months.
4. Henry James, "Preface to the 1908 Edition," in Peter G. Beidler (ed.), *The Turn of the Screw*, (Boston: St. Martin's, 1995), p. 119.

5. Bloom developed this argument in a series of books beginning with his *The Anxiety of Influence* (Oxford University Press, 1973). See especially *A Map of Misreading* (Oxford University Press, 1975).

Chapter Nine

1. George Bluestone, *Novels into Film* (Berkeley: University of California Press, 1957), p. 62.
2. Ingmar Bergman, trans. Lars Malmstrom and David Kushner, "Introduction: Bergman Discusses Film-Making" in *Four Screenplays of Ingmar Bergman* (New York: Simon and Schuster, 1960), p. xvii.
3. Quoted by Frank Rich in "American Pseudo," *New York Times Magazine* (December 12, 1999), p. 1.
4. Sergei Eisenstein, trans. Jay Layda, "Dickens, Griffith, and the Film Today" in *Film Form: Essays in Film Theory* (Cleveland: World Publishing, 1957), pp. 195–255.
5. Dudley Andrew, *Concepts in Film Theory* (Oxford University Press, 1984), pp. 98–104.
6. Emily Brontë, *Wuthering Heights*, p. 47.
7. Leo Braudy. *The World in a Frame: What We See in Films* (University of Chicago Press, 1985), p. 196.
8. Henry James, *The Turn of the Screw* (New York: Dover, 1991), p. 14.
9. William Shakespeare, *The Tragedy of Antony and Cleopatra*, act II, scene ii, lines 196–202.
10. William Shakespeare, *The Tragedy of Romeo and Juliet*, act II, scene ii, lines 2–6.
11. Henry James, S. P. Rosenbaum (ed.), *The Ambassadors* (New York: Norton, 1964), p. 238.
12. Brontë, *Wuthering Heights*, p. 287.

Chapter Ten

1. Aristotle, trans. Ingram Bywater, "Poetics" in Richard McKeon (ed.) *Introduction to Aristotle* (New York: Random House, 1947), p. 632 (1450a).
2. Leslie Stephen, "Biography" in *Men, Books, and Mountains* (1893; London: The Hogarth Press, 1956), p. 142.
3. Henry James, "The Art of Fiction," in Leon Edel (ed.) *The Future of the Novel* (New York: Vintage, 1956), pp. 15–16.
4. E. M. Forster, *Aspects of the Novel* (New York: Harcourt Brace, 1927), pp. 67–78.
5. Ralph Ellison, *Invisible Man* (New York: Signet, 1953), p. 231.
6. Samuel Beckett, "Ping" in S. E. Gontarski (ed.), *Samuel Beckett: The Complete Short Prose, 1929–1989* (New York: Grove, 1995), p. 193.

7. Jean-Jacques Rousseau, *The Confessions of Jean-Jacques Rousseau*, n. t. (Philadelphia: Gebbie and Company, 1904), pp. 1–2.
8. Laurence Sterne, *The Life and Opinions of Tristram Shandy, Gentleman* (London & Toronto: Dent, 1912), pp. 207–8.
9. W. N. P. Barbellion [Bruce Commings], *Journal of a Disappointed Man* (London: Chatto & Windus, 1919), p. 106.

Chapter Eleven

1. Edmund Pearson (ed.), *The Trial of Lizzie Borden* (London: Heinemann, 1937), p. 232.
2. Peter Brooks, "The Law as Narrative and Rhetoric," in Peter Brooks and Paul Gewirtz (eds.), *Law's Stories*, p. 16.
3. Martha Minow, "Stories in Law," in Brooks and Gewirtz (ed.), *Law's Stories*, p. 35.

Chapter Twelve

1. Jerome Bruner, *Actual Minds, Possible Worlds* (Cambridge, MA: Harvard University Press, 1986), p. 11.
2. Ronald Sukenick, *Narralogues: Truth in Fiction* (Albany: State University of New York Press, 2000), p. 2.
3. Sigmund Freud, trans. A. A. Brill, *The Interpretation of Dreams*, in A. A. Brill (ed.), *The Basic Writings of Sigmund Freud* (New York: Random House, 1965), p. 309.
4. Vladimir Propp, "Oedipus in the Light of Folklore," in Lowell Edmunds and Alan Dundes (eds.), *Oedipus. A Folklore Casebook* (New York: Garland, 1983), p. 81.
5. Claude Lévi-Strauss, trans. Claire Jacobsen and Brooke Grundfest Schoepf, "The Structural Study of Myth," in *Structural Anthropology* (New York: Basic Books, 1963), p. 211.
6. Daniel Defoe, *The History and Remarkable Life of the Truly Honourable Colonel Jacque* (London: Oxford University Press, 1965), p. 2.
7. Anthony Trollope, *An Autobiography* (Berkeley: University of California Press, 1947), p. 124.
8. François Mauriac [no trans.], *God and Mammon* (London: Sheed and Ward, 1936), p. 85.
9. D. H. Lawrence, "Morality in the Novel" in Edward D. McDonald (ed.), *Phoenix: The Posthumous Papers of D. H. Lawrence* (London: Heinemann, 1936), p. 527.

10. Anton Chekhov, trans. S. S. Koteliansky and Philip Tomlinson, Letter to A. S. Souvorin (27 October 1888) in S. S. Koteliansky and Philip Tomlinson (eds.), *Life and Letters of Anton Tchekhov* (London: Benjamin Blom, 1925; reissued, 1965), p. 127.
11. Stanley E. Fish, *Self-Consuming Artifacts: the Experience of Seventeenth-Century Literature* (Berkeley: University of California Press, 1972), p. 1.

Bibliography

Selected foundational works on narrative

Bal, Mieke, *Narratology: Introduction to the Theory of Narrative*, University of
Toronto Press, 1985.

Barthes, Roland, "Introduction to the Structural Analysis of Narratives," in
Image-Music-Text, reprinted in Susan Sontag (ed.), *A Barthes Reader*,
New York: Hill & Wang, 1982, 251–95.

Barthes, Roland (trans. Richard Miller), *S/Z*, New York: Hill & Wang, 1974.

Chatman, Seymour, *Coming to Terms: The Rhetoric of Narrative in Fiction and Film*,
Ithaca: Cornell University Press, 1990.

Chatman, Seymour, *Story and Discourse: Narrative Structure in Fiction and Film*,
Ithaca: Cornell University Press, 1978.

Cohn, Dorrit, *Transparent Minds: Narrative Modes for Presenting Consciousness in
Fiction*, Princeton University Press, 1978.

Genette, Gèrard (trans. Jane E. Lewin), *Narrative Discourse: An Essay on Method*,
Ithaca: Cornell University Press, 1980.

Genette, Gèrard (trans. Jane E. Lewin), *Paratexts: Thresholds of Interpretation*,
Cambridge University Press, 1997.

Prince, Gerald, *A Dictionary of Narratology*, Lincoln: University of Nebraska Press,
1987.

Prince, Gerald, *Narratology: The Form and Functioning of Narrative*, Berlin: Mouton,
1982.

Rimmon-Kenan, Shlomith, *Narrative Fiction: Contemporary Poetics*, London:
Methuen, 1983.

Scholes, Robert, and Robert Kellogg, *The Nature of Narrative*, New York: Oxford
University Press, 1966.

More reading of interest

Andrew, Dudley, "Adaptation," in *Concepts in Film Theory*, Oxford University
Press, 1984, 98–104.

Aristotle (trans. Ingram Bywater), "De Poetica [Poetics]," in Richard McKeon
(ed.), *Introduction to Aristotle*, New York: Random House, 1947, 624–67.

Bhabha, Homi K. (ed.), *Nation and Narration*, London: Routledge, 1990.

Boardman, Michael M., *Narrative Innovation and Incoherence*, Durham: Duke University Press, 1992.

Booth, Alison, *Famous Last Words: Changes in Gender and Narrative Closure*, Charlottesville: University Press of Virginia, 1993.

Booth, Wayne, *The Rhetoric of Fiction*, University of Chicago Press, 1961.

Bordwell, David, *Narration in the Fiction Film*, Madison: University of Wisconsin Press, 1985.

Branigan, Edward, *Narrative Comprehension and Film*, London: Routledge, 1992.

Brooks, Peter, *Reading for the Plot*, New York: Random House, 1985.

Brooks, Peter and Paul Gewirtz (eds.), *Law's Stories: Narrative and Rhetoric in the Law*, New Haven: Yale University Press, 1996.

Bruner, Jerome, "Two Modes of Thought," in *Actual Minds, Possible Worlds*, Cambridge: Harvard University Press, 1986, 11–43.

Bruner, Jerome, "The Narrative Construction of 'Reality'," in Massimo Ammaniti and Daniel N. Stern (eds.), *Psychoanalysis and Development: Representations and Narratives*, New York University Press, 1994, 15–38.

Bruner, Jerome, "A Narrative Model of Self-Construction," in Joan Gay Snodgrass and Robert L. Thompson (eds.), *The Self Across Psychology: Self Recognition, Self-Awareness, and the Self Concept*, Annals of the New York Academy of Sciences, Volume 818, New York Academy of Sciences, 1997, 145–61.

Chambers, Ross, *Story and Situation: Narrative Seduction and the Power of Fiction* Minneapolis: University of Minnesota Press, 1984.

Chambers, Ross, *Room for Maneuver: Reading Oppositional Narrative*, University of Chicago Press, 1991.

Currie, Mark, *Postmodern Narrative Theory*, New York: St. Martin's Press, 1998.

Fehn, Ann, Ingeborg Hoesterey, and Maria Tatar (eds.), *Neverending Stories: Toward a Critical Narratology*, Princeton University Press, 1992.

Fludernick, Monica, *Towards a Natural Narratology*, London: Routledge, 1996.

Gibson, Andrew, *Towards a Postmodern Theory of Narrative*, Edinburgh University Press, 1996.

Hayles, N. Katherine (ed.), *Technocriticism and Hypernarrative*, Special Issue, *Modern Fiction Studies* 43:3 (1997).

Herman, David (ed.), *Narratologies: New Perspectives on Narrative Analysis*, Columbus: Ohio State University Press, 1999.

Iser, Wolfgang, *The Implied Reader: Patterns of Communication in Prose Fiction from Bunyan to Beckett*, Baltimore: Johns Hopkins University Press, 1974.

Jameson, Fredric, *The Political Unconscious: Narrative as a Socially Symbolic Act*, Ithaca: Cornell University Press, 1981.

Kenner, Hugh, "The Uncle Charles Principle," in *Joyce's Voices*, Berkeley: University of California Press, 1978, 15–38.

Kermode, Frank, *The Art of Telling*, Cambridge: Harvard University Press, 1983.

Kermode, Frank, *The Genesis of Secrecy: On the Interpretation of Narrative*, Cambridge: Harvard University Press, 1979.

Kermode, Frank, *The Sense of an Ending: Studies in the Theory of Fiction*, Oxford University Press, 1966.

Landow, George P., "Reconfiguring Narrative," in *Hypertext 2.0: the Convergence of Contemporary Critical Theory and Technology*, Baltimore: Johns Hopkins University Press, 1997; revised, 178–218.

Lanser, Susan Snaider, *Fictions of Authority: Women Writers and Narrative Voice*, Ithaca: Cornell University Press, 1992.

Martin, Wallace, *Recent Theories of Narrative*, Ithaca: Cornell University Press, 1986.

Mezei, Kathy (ed.), *Ambiguous Discourse: Feminist Narratology and British Women Writers*, Chapel Hill: University of North Carolina Press, 1996.

Mihailescu, Calin-Andrei, and Walid Hamarneh (eds.), *Fiction Updated: Theories of Fictionality, Narratology, and Poetics*, University of Toronto Press, 1996.

Miller, J. Hillis, *Reading Narrative Discourse*, Norman: University of Oklahoma Press, 1998.

Mitchell, W. J. T. (ed.), *On Narrative*, University of Chicago Press, 1981.

Morson, Gary Saul, *Narrative and Freedom: The Shadows of Time*, New Haven: Yale University Press, 1994.

Nichols, Bill, *Ideology and the Image: Social Representation in the Cinema and Other Media*, Bloomington: Indiana University Press, 1981.

O'Neill, Patrick, *Fictions of Discourse: Reading Narrative Theory*, University of Toronto Press, 1994.

Pascal, Roy, *The Dual Voice: Free Indirect Speech and its Functioning in the Nineteenth-Century European Novel*, Manchester University Press, 1977.

Phelan, James, *Reading People, Reading Plots: Character, Progression, and the Interpretation of Narrative*, University of Chicago Press, 1989.

Phelan, James, (ed.), *Understanding Narrative*, Columbus: Ohio State University Press, 1994.

Rabinowitz, Peter J., *Before Reading: Narrative Conventions and the Politics of Interpretation*, Ithaca: Cornell University Press, 1987.

Rabkin, Eric S., *Narrative Suspense*, Ann Arbor: University of Michigan Press, 1973.

Richardson, Brian, *Unlikely Stories: Causality and the Nature of Modern Narrative*, Newark: University of Delaware Press, 1997.

Richter, David H., *Fable's End: Completeness and Closure in Rhetorical Fiction*, University of Chicago Press, 1974.

Richter, David H., *Narrative/Theory*, New York: Longman, 1996.

Ricoeur, Paul (trans. Kathleen McLaughlin and David Pellauer), *Time and Narrative*, Volumes I, II, & III, University of Chicago Press, 1984, 1985, 1988.

Rimmon-Kenan, Shlomith, *A Glance Beyond Doubt: Narration, Representation, Subjectivity*, Columbus: Ohio State University Press, 1996.

Ryan, Marie-Laure, *Possible Worlds, Artificial Intelligence, and Narrative Theory*, Bloomington: Indiana University Press, 1991.

Schank, Roger C., *Tell Me a Story: Narrative and Intelligence*, Evanston: Northwestern University Press, 1990.

Sturgess, Philip J. M., *Narrativity: Theory and Practice*, Oxford University Press, 1992.

Torgovnick, Mariana, *Closure in the Novel*, Princeton University Press, 1981.

White, Hayden, *Metahistory: The Historical Imagination in Nineteenth-Century Europe*, Baltimore: Johns Hopkins University Press, 1973.

White, Hayden, *The Content of the Form: Narrative Discourse and Historical Representation*, Baltimore: Johns Hopkins University Press, 1987.

Whittock, Trevor, *Metaphor and Film*, Cambridge University Press, 1990.

Williams, Jeffrey, *Theory and the Novel: Narrative Reflexivity in the British Tradition*. Cambridge University Press, 1998.

Glossary and topical index

What follows are definitions of useful terms for discussing narrative. Terms in **bold face** are the terms that are essential and that have been emphasized in this book. You will also find other terms that have either proven their use or been used so often that they are now unavoidable in the discussion of narrative. This glossary also serves as a topical index for the book.

Act: Event caused by a character (as opposed to happening).

Action: The sequence of events in a story. The action and the existents are the two basic components of story. Some (including this author) prefer the term "events," since "action" can conceivably mean the collective acts in a story. 12, 16, 123–6

Adaptation: The transmutation of a narrative, usually from one medium to another. 105–22

Adaptive reading: One of three fundamental modes of interpretation (see also intentional and symptomatic readings). Adaptive readings range from interpretations freed from concerns for overreading or underreading to fresh narratives of the story either in the same medium or in a different one, as, for example, the film versions of Flaubert's *Madame Bovary* or Shakespeare's *Henry V.* 100–2, 130, 172

Agency: The capacity of an entity to cause events (that is, to engage in acts). Characters by and large are entities with agency. 124, 130

Agon or conflict: Most narratives are driven by a conflict. In Greek tragedy, the word for the conflict, or contest, is the "agon." From that word come the terms protagonist and antagonist. 51–2, 140, 153, 156–74

Analepsis: Flashback. The introduction into the narrative of material that happens earlier in the story. The opposite of prolepsis. 157

Antagonist: The opponent of the protagonist. He or she is commonly the enemy of the hero. 51, 140

Author: A real person who creates a text. The author is not to be confused with either the narrator or the implied author of a narrative. 36, 63, 77–9, 95, 97, 99

Authorial intention: The author's intended meanings or effects. The concept of authorial intention has taken a beating in this century on a variety of grounds. It has been argued that authorial intention is indeterminable; that authors are as fallible as the rest of us in reading their own work and therefore unreliable guides to reading; that the idea of an author essentializes and presumes to fix an identity that is indeterminate and fluid; and finally that seeking authorial

187

intention encourages the idea of a single privileged meaning for a <u>narrative</u> even though narratives are necessarily plural in their meanings. But don't count this concept out. We seem strongly inclined, in spite of all arguments, to read for authorial intention. Witness, for example, how authors continue to be praised or blamed for the meanings and effects readers attribute to them. An important related, but distinct, concept is that of the <u>implied author</u>. 77–9

Autobiography: A <u>narrative</u> about the <u>author</u>, purporting implicitly or explicitly to be true in the sense of non-fictional. Autobiographies come in many forms, even in <u>third-person narration</u>, as in *The Education of Henry Adams.* Autobiography is another one of those porous concepts, and the field abounds in narratives that seem to fall in a generic no-man's land between autobiography and fiction, as in James Joyce's *A Portrait of the Artist as a Young Man* or Maxine Hong Kingston's *The Woman Warrior: Memoirs of a Girlhood among Ghosts.* 49–50, 63, 131–7, 176 n.4

Beginning and *end:* Though the meanings of these concepts would seem to be obvious, their functions can be both complex and crucial. Sometimes the end can relate to a <u>narrative</u> the way a clinching point does to an argument. Bear in mind, too, that neither the beginning nor the end of the <u>narrative discourse</u> necessarily corresponds to the beginning or end of the <u>story</u>. Epic narratives, for example, traditionally begin in the middle of the <u>story</u> (*in medias res*). 52–3

Character: Human or humanlike <u>entity</u>. Sometimes the broader terms "agent" or "actor/actant" are used for character. Characters are any entities involved in the <u>action</u> that have <u>agency</u>. These would include, in addition to persons, any quasi-volitional entities like animals, robots, extraterrestrials, and animated things. E. M. Forster distinguished between "flat" and "round" characters. The former can be "summed up in a single phrase" and have no existence outside of a single dominating quality. Round characters cannot be summed up in the same way and are not predictable. In this sense, they have depth. 17, 47, 109–11, 123–37, 146–7

Closure: When a <u>narrative</u> ends in such a way as to satisfy the expectations and answer the questions that it has raised, it is said to close, or to have closure. Notice that there is a distinction here between "expectations" and "questions." By expectations are meant kinds of <u>action</u> or <u>event</u> that the narrative leads us to expect (the gun introduced in Chapter One that has to go off in Chapter Three). *King Lear,* for example, satisfies the expectations that are aroused early on when we perceive that its narrative pattern is tragedy. We expect among other things that Lear will die, and he does. But major questions are raised over the course of the play that for many viewers are not answered by the conclusion. So for many, *King Lear* has tragic closure (giving satisfaction at the "level of expectations") but not closure of understanding (giving satisfaction at the "level of questions"). 51–61, 62, 80–2, 90, 168–74

Constituent and supplementary events: Also referred to as <u>kernels</u> and <u>satellites</u> (Chatman) and <u>nuclei</u> and <u>catalyzers</u> (Barthes), these concepts distinguish two fundamental kinds of <u>events</u> in <u>narrative</u>. Constituent events are essential to the forward movement of the <u>story</u> (Barthes also called them "Cardinal functions"); they are not all necessarily "turning points," but at the least they are essential to the chain of events that make up the story. Supplementary events are not necessary to the <u>story</u>; they seem to be extra. The distinction between constituent and supplementary events is often helpful because it reminds us to ask the question: Why has this supplementary event been included in this narrative? Since it is not necessary to advance the story, why did the <u>author</u> see fit to include it? Like many of our distinctions, however, this one is not always obvious – one reader's constituent event may be another's supplementary event. 20–2, 32–3, 47–8, 55–6, 87, 89, 109, 134, 140, 145

Crux: A major point of disagreement in the interpretation of a text. Cruxes are sometimes characterized by a <u>gap</u> in the narrative, as for example the critical gap that makes us question whether or not in *Wuthering Heights* Heathcliff killed Hindley Earnshaw. This is a crux because how we fill the gap determines whether or not we see Heathcliff as a murderer. 85–8, 91

Diegesis (1): Strictly speaking, this is the telling. It goes back to Plato's distinction between two ways of presenting a story: as <u>mimesis</u> (acted) or as diegesis (told). (2): Frequently "the diegesis" is used to refer to the world created by the narration. Narratologists also speak of levels of diegesis. The "diegetic level" consists of all those <u>characters</u>, things, and <u>events</u> that are in the world of the primary <u>narrative</u> (i.e., having to do with the main story). There can be, then, other events and characters in the text that are not in the primary narrative at all but outside it in the <u>extradiegetic</u> level. The <u>narrator</u>, for example, is often found telling a story in an <u>extradiegetic</u> situation – that is, in circumstances and among people that have nothing or little to do with the story told. 68, 75,

Discordant narrator: See <u>unreliable narrator</u>. 70, 77

Distance: Used in two main senses: 1) the <u>narrator</u>'s emotional distance from the <u>characters</u> and the <u>action</u> (the degree of his or her involvement in the <u>story</u>) and 2) the distance between the narrator's moral, emotional or intellectual sensibilities and those of the <u>implied author</u>. A narrator's distance (in *both* senses) affects the extent to which we trust the information we get from the narrator, and its moral and emotional coloring. 64, 67–8, 73

Embedded narrative: Commonly, a "story within a story," or a narrative nested in a <u>framing narrative</u>). Genette calls embedded narratives the one sure sign of fictivity, since the device is shunned by historians. Its absence, however, cannot be taken as a sign of the opposite – that is, of non-fictivity or factuality. 26, 35

End: See <u>beginning and end</u>. 52–3

Entity: Also referred to as "existents" or "actors and actants," entities comprise one of the two basic components of a <u>story</u>, the other being the <u>events</u> or <u>action</u>. Humanlike entities capable of <u>agency</u> are referred to as <u>characters</u>. Most of the remaining entities in a narrative – those not capable of agency – are part of the <u>setting</u>. There is a third class of entities, however, for which neither the term "character" nor "setting" is appropriate. We can tell the story of a planet, for example, and how it was struck out of its course by an immense asteroid. As they are the subject entities, neither the planet nor the asteroid is part of the setting. Yet it would be an error to refer to them as characters, particularly if scientific objectivity is at a premium, since they are insentient objects incapable of action on their own. 17

Event: The fundamental unit of the <u>action</u>. Also called an "incident," an event can be an <u>act</u> (a kick or a kiss), or a <u>happening</u> when no <u>character</u> is causally involved (a bolt of lightening). 3–6, 12–17, 20–2, 33

Existents: See <u>entities</u>.

Extradiegetic level: See <u>diegesis</u>, <u>frame</u>, <u>metalepsis</u>.

Fabula and *sjuzet:* See <u>story</u>. 16

Fiction: Made-up, as opposed to factual. As a noun it refers to the whole range of made-up <u>narratives</u> that stand opposed to the "non-fictional" <u>genres</u> – history, biography, autobiography, reportage, etc. Like so many efforts to categorize the kinds of narrative, the distinction between fiction and non-fiction is often found to collapse, yielding troublesome hybrid classifications like the "non-fictional novel."

First–person narration: Conventionally, narration by a <u>character</u> who plays a role in the <u>story</u> narrated. Note that there are many examples of narrators who are not characters in the story but who talk in the "first person" – sometimes at length (the narrative <u>persona</u> of Henry Fielding, for example, in *Tom Jones*). These are not usually considered "first-person" narrators because they tell the story in the third person. For this reason, Gérard Genette found greater utility in the distinction between <u>homodiegetic</u> and <u>heterodiegetic</u> narration. 64–6

Flat and round characters: See <u>character</u>.

Focalization: The position or quality of consciousness through which we "*see*" <u>events</u> in the <u>narrative</u>. In English and North American criticism, the phrase <u>point of view</u> has been used for this concept, or something quite close to it, but point of view is more general and often includes the concept of <u>voice</u>. "Focalization" may be more polysyllabic, but it is more exact. Usually the narrator is our focalizer, but it is important to keep in mind that focalizing is not necessarily achieved through a single consistent narrative consciousness. Focalization can change, sometimes frequently, during the course of a <u>narrative</u>, and sometimes from sentence to sentence, as it can, for example, in <u>free indirect style</u>. In this study, I present focalization and <u>voice</u> as companion concepts. Both frequently convey a sensibility, the one through what we "see," the other through what we "hear." 64, 66–7, 70, 77, 115, 117–18

Frame and **framing narrative:** The term "frame" is used so inconsistently in discussions of <u>narrative</u> that it is important to define how you are using it. Here are two main ways in which the term is used. 1) Much recent work on narrative has drawn on cognitive theory in which frame is understood to mean a mental configuration of representative bits that stand for something in the world and that is triggered by cues that we sense, allowing us to understand what we are seeing or hearing. 2) A more informal use of "frame" refers to any <u>extradiegetic</u> preliminary and/or concluding material in a narrative not essential to the <u>story</u>. Sometimes the frame in this sense is a *framing narrative*, a narrative within which a narrative is embedded. Conversely, one can speak of an <u>embedded narrative</u>. 25–6, 34–5, 143

Free indirect style: <u>Narrative</u> representation of a <u>character</u>'s thoughts and expressions without quotation marks or the usual addition of phrases like "he thought" or "she said" and without some of the grammatical markers. Take the following example: "It was a hot day. Elspeth wondered to herself: 'What on earth am I doing lugging stones on a day like this?'" In free *direct* style, it becomes: "It was a hot day. What on earth am I doing lugging stones on a day like this?" This is *free* because the attributing phrase "Elspeth wondered to herself" has been dropped. In free *indirect* discourse, the passage becomes: "It was a hot day. What on earth was she doing lugging stones on a day like this?" Here, the key second sentence is still marked by Elspeth's intonations, but it is cast in the <u>third person</u> and in the past tense, neither of which she would use. In other words, the third-person narration *freely* adapts itself for the temporary *indirect* expression of a character's words or thoughts. 70–2, 74

Gaps: Wolfgang Iser's term for the inevitable voids in any <u>narrative</u> that the reader is called upon to fill from his or her experience or imagination. Gaps are everywhere in narratives, many of them quite small. But there are also major gaps in narratives, some of which, over the years, have become interpretive <u>cruxes</u>. 83–7, 100, 114–15, 125–7, 146–7, 158, 172, 174

Genre: A recurrent literary form. There are <u>narrative</u> and non-narrative genres. The novel, the epic, the short story, the ballad, are all examples of narrative genres. Genres can be highly specialized. The Bildungsroman, for example, tells the <u>story</u> of its hero's coming of age. It is a genre that fits within the larger genre of the novel. Sometimes, genres can be so discrete and specialized that scholars use the term "sub-genre" to describe them. 2, 45–6, 54, 57

Gutter: The space between frames in a cartoon comic sequence. The gutter is a form of narrative <u>gap</u> that is built into the medium of the comic strip. It is the space in which the reader imagines <u>events</u> unfolding in time. 115–16

Happening: One of the two kinds of <u>event</u> in a <u>narrative</u>. Unlike <u>actions</u>, happenings occur without the specific <u>agency</u> of a <u>character</u>.

Heterodiegetic narration: Narration from a <u>narrator</u> situated outside of the <u>diegesis</u> or world of the <u>story</u>. Opposed to <u>homodiegetic narration</u>. 68, 75

Homodiegetic narration: Narration from a <u>narrator</u> situated within the diegesis – that is, a <u>character</u> in the <u>story</u>. Opposed to <u>heterodiegetic narration</u>. 68

Hypertext narrative: <u>Narrative</u> conveyed in electronic media (on CD or the Web) that capitalizes on hypertext capability to permit (or require) the reader to switch attention instantly to other <u>lexia</u> – texts or graphics, which may (but not necessarily) be different segments of the narrative discourse. 28–30

Implied author: Neither the real <u>author</u> nor the <u>narrator</u>, the implied author is the image of the author constructed by the reader as she or he reads the <u>narrative</u>. In an <u>intentional reading</u>, the implied author is that sensibility and moral intelligence that the reader gradually constructs to infer the intended meanings and effects of the narrative. The implied author might as easily (and with greater justice) be called the "inferred author." 61, 69, 77–9, 80, 83, 86, 87, 90, 91, 95–9, 128

Implied reader (<u>implied audience</u>): As the <u>implied author</u> should be kept distinct from the actual <u>author</u>, so the implied reader should be kept distinct from the actual reader. The implied reader is not necessarily you or I but the reader we infer to be an intended recipient of the <u>narrative</u>. Some argue that the implied reader is the reader the implied author writes for. My own view is that implied authors and implied readers are not neatly symmetrical concepts. There are any number of implied readers that an implied author may well scorn, even as he or she creates them. This is the case in much satirical narrative.

Intentional reading: An interpretation that seeks to understand a text in terms of the intended meanings of its <u>implied author</u>. 83, 95–7, 98–104, 128, 135

Interior monologue: The thinking and feeling of a <u>character</u> conveyed without the usual grammatical signs of narrational mediation (e.g., quotation marks or the phrases "he said, she said"). "Interior monologue" is sometimes used interchangeably with the phrase "stream of consciousness." My preference is to use the latter to describe how thinking and feeling occur (or might be conceived as occurring) in human beings, and the former for representational modes used to convey that stream of thinking/feeling. In short passages, interior monologue is often indistinguishable from <u>free indirect discourse</u>. 71–2

Interpretation: The act of conveying in one's own way the meanings – including ideas, values, and feelings – communicated by a text. Interpretation can take a number of forms. Commonly it is found in critical or hermeneutic writing. But the production of a play is often referred to as an "interpretation" of the play or script, and even a narrative can be seen as an interpretation of a <u>story</u> that has been told before. In this book, I distinguish three kinds of interpretation: <u>intentional readings</u>, <u>symptomatic readings</u>, and <u>adaptive readings</u>. 21, 25, 36, 62–3, 71, 73, 76–104, 128, 135

Intertextuality: The condition of all texts, including <u>narratives</u>, as comprised of preexisting texts. Intertextuality can be distinguished from "allusion" and "imitation" as an inevitable, rather than a necessarily selective, condition of texts. It is based on the assumption that we can only express ourselves through words and forms that are already available to us. In this view, the work of even the most original of artists draws in all its parts on the work of predecessors. The power of such work must lie in the way it recontextualizes the multitude of bits that have been cannibalized in this way. 94, 106

Kernels & satellites: See <u>constituent</u> and <u>supplementary events</u>.

Lexia: Roland Barthes in *S/Z* called lexia the "units of meaning" in a text, "blocks of signification" which amount to anywhere from a few words to several sentences. The term has since been adapted in discourse on electronic <u>narrative</u> to refer to passages of varying length triggered by hypertext linking. 28–31

Masterplot: Recurrent skeletal <u>stories</u>, belonging to cultures and individuals that play a powerful role in questions of identity, values, and the understanding of life. Masterplots can also exert an influence on the way we take in new information, causing us to <u>overread</u> or <u>underread</u> narratives in an often unconscious effort to bring them into conformity with a masterplot. As masterplots, by their nature, recur in many different <u>narrative</u> versions, it is an obvious mistake to employ the often misused term "master narrative" for this concept. 16, 42–6, 47–8, 49–50, 54, 57, 59, 88, 119, 120, 132, 148–52, 158, 160

Medium: The vehicle conveying a <u>narrative</u> – written language, film, oil paint, lithe bodies moving silently on a stage. Some of these media would be considered unfit for narrative by the first set of scholars referred to in the definition of narrative below. 72–3, 105–22

Melodrama: Sensational narratives deploying flat characters who are either very good or very bad and who often speak in overwrought language. Originally used to describe plays, the term is frequently used in a derogatory way to describe narratives in other media. 51

Metalepsis: A violation of narrative norms, usually in which the diegesis, or world of the story, is invaded by an extradiegetic entity or entities, as for example when a "spectator" leaps on stage and becomes a part of the action, or the "author" appears and starts quarrelling with one of the characters.

Mimesis: The imitation of an action by performance. According to Plato, mimesis is one of the two major ways to convey a narrative, the other being diegesis or the representation of an action by telling. By this distinction, plays are mimetic, epic poems are diegetic. Aristotle (Plato's student) used the term "mimesis" as simply the imitation of an action and included in it both modes of narrative representation.

Montage: Literally, in French, "assembly." The art of editing film by connecting disparate shots one after another. 114–16, 117

Motif: Prince defines motif as a "minimal thematic unit." This works well. A motif is a discrete thing, image, or phrase that is repeated in a narrative. Theme, by contrast, is a more generalized or abstract concept that is suggested by, among other things, motifs. A coin can be a motif, greed is a theme. 88–90

Narration: The *telling* of a story or part of a story. Often used indistinguishably from narrative, narration as it is used here refers to the activity of a narrator. 60, 62–75

Narrative: Commonly, the telling of a story. I prefer to call it the representation of a story. Some scholars have argued that there cannot be a narrative without someone to tell it (a narrator), but this view would exclude most drama and film, which though they present stories, usually do so without a narrator.

Narrative discourse: The story as narrated – that is, the story as rendered in a particular narrative. Some narratologists use the term plot for this concept, but this can be confusing because in English we commonly use "plot" and "story" interchangeably. Note that the distinction between "story" and "story as narrated" can be taken to imply that stories exist independently of narrative presentation – in other words, the same story can be narrated in more than one way. This distinction raises a number of ontological (perhaps even metaphysical) questions. If a story does not exist in its narrative presentation, where does it exist? If the same story can be presented in different ways, how do we recognize it as the story that it is? What is necessary for us to see that it is this story and not another? And can a story ever be fully told? 13–22, 28, 29–34, 43

Narrativity: A disputed term, used here to mean the degree to which one feels a story is being told or performed. 22–3, 38, 40–2

Narratology: The descriptive field devoted to the systematic study of narrative. Some narratologists see their field as a science analogous to linguistics. Many of the terms in this glossary come from the work of narratologists. In the first section of the Bibliography ("Foundational Works") are entries squarely in the field of narratology by Bal, Barthes, Chatman, Cohn, Genette, Prince, and Rimmon-Kenan.

Narrator: One who tells a story. The narrator is not necessarily the author. Some narratologists assert that the narrator can never be the author, even if the narrative is an autobiography. Others (a bit more moderate) say that, since at the least we can never know for sure if the narrator is the same as the author, it is senseless to speak of the author as if he or she were necessarily implicated in the views of the narrator. This is an interesting philosophical question involving the relation of voice, character, and identity (whose voice is this you are reading now? Is it my voice or is it the voice of a character-like entity I created to present these ideas – a mask that I wear in print, my persona?). 13, 17, 47, 69–75, 76

Omniscient narration: Narration by a narrator assumed to know everything connected with the story narrated. Though it is widely used, this is a troublesome term that is finally more confusing than helpful. There are, it is true, narrators who seem to know everything, but no narration was ever omniscient (literally "all-knowing"). All narration is riddled with blind spots – gaps – which we must fill from our limited knowledge. 66

Overreading and **underreading:** The activity of importing into the text material that is not signified within it (overreading) or of neglecting material that is signified within it (underreading). Both would appear to be inevitable to some degree. Reducing them to a minimum could be said to be the object of an intentional reading. 79–83, 87, 88, 90, 91, 94, 100, 127, 133, 171

Paratext: Genette's term for material outside the narrative that is in some way connected to it. Paratexts can be physically attached to the narrative vehicle (book, magazine): prefaces, tables of contents, title pages, blurbs on the jacket, illustrations. They can also be separated from the vehicle but nonetheless connected by association: comments by the author, reviews, other works by the same author. Paratexts have the capacity to inflect the way we read and interpret a narrative, sometimes powerfully. Genette did not include plays and movies in his discussion, but here, too, we can see paratextual material in the form of playbills, previews, marquees, public disclaimers, etc. 26–7, 34, 35, 99, 101, 144, 172

Performative: A term widely and diversely used in a variety of fields (linguistics, philosophy, dramatic art, feminist theory). In this book, the term has been used to stress not what a narrative is about, or what its story is, but how it functions in the world, with the implicit or explicit object of achieving certain ends. 134–6

Persona: Literally "mask," persona is used most commonly to refer to the personality constructed by an author to narrate or, at the least, speak in his or her name. See first-person narration. 66, 168

Plot: A vexed term. Commonly in English plot is used to mean story. Another (generally European) tradition equates plot with the order in which the story-events are arranged in the narrative. Plot has also been used to mean the chain of *causally* connected events in a story. But if it is used in this way, then the common phrase "episodic plot" would be a contradiction in terms, since in this context "episodic" usually means "causally *dis*connected" events. 14, 16, 43

Point of view: Prince distinguishes point of view from <u>focalization</u> as being the *perceptual or conceptual position* as opposed to the *perspective* "in terms of which the narrated situations and events are presented." But in practice, perceptual/conceptual position and perspective are often difficult to discriminate. I recommend using the term <u>focalization</u> for that complex of perspective, position, feeling, and sensibility (or the lack of these) that characterize specifically our *visual* purchase on the narrative, even if it may fluctuate from moment to moment. And I recommend the use of the term <u>voice</u> for the same complex as it is achieved through the language we imagine ourselves hearing. 66, 73

Prolepsis: Flashforward. Introduction into the <u>narrative</u> of material that comes later in the <u>story</u>. The opposite of <u>analepsis</u>.

Protagonist: In an <u>agon</u>, the hero (though not necessarily a "good guy"). Opposed by an <u>antagonist</u> (who is not necessarily a "bad guy"). 51, 57, 140

Récit: Sometimes used in French narratology for <u>narrative discourse</u> and opposed to "histoire" (*story*). See *narrative discourse* and *story*.

Reflexivity/reflexive narrative: A reflexive or self-reflexive (or self-conscious) narrative is one that, either by formal or thematic means, calls attention to its condition as constructed art. Reflexivity is a condition that can be found in non-narrative as well as narrative texts. 144

Repetition: The recurrence in <u>narrative</u> of images, ideas, situations, kinds of <u>characters</u>. Repetition is one of the surest signs of the <u>meaningful</u>. If you are stuck trying to interpret a text, one good question to ask yourself is: What is repeated in this narrative? <u>Theme</u> and <u>motif</u> are terms commonly used for kinds of repetition in narrative. 88–90, 91, 99, 166

Retardation: The slowing down of the <u>narrative discourse</u>. Often, but not always, a way of increasing <u>suspense</u>. 109

Setting: All those elements within which the <u>entities</u> of a <u>story</u> take part in the story's events. 17, 48, 55

Sjuzet: See <u>story</u>. 16

Stereotype: See <u>type</u>. 45, 137

Story: With <u>narrative discourse</u>, one of the two basic dimensions of <u>narrative</u>. Conveyed through the narrative discourse, story is a sequence of <u>events</u> involving <u>entities</u>. Slightly adapting Chatman, events in a story are of two kinds, <u>acts</u> and <u>happenings</u>. Entities are also of two basic kinds: <u>characters</u> (who can engage in <u>acts</u>) and <u>settings</u> (in which <u>happenings</u> occur). Story should not be confused with narrative discourse, which is the telling or presenting of a story. A story is bound by the laws of time; it goes in one direction, starting at the <u>beginning</u>, moving through the middle, and arriving at the <u>end</u>. <u>Narrative discourse</u> does not have to follow that order. The distinction between story and narrative discourse was first anticipated early in this century by Russian structuralists. The terms they used for this distinction – <u>fabula</u> (for story) and <u>sjuzet</u> (for the order of events in the narrative) – are still widely employed in the discourse on narrative. 13–22, 29–34, 55

Stream of consciousness: See <u>interior monologue</u>. 71–2

Suspense: Uncertainty (together with the desire to diminish it) about how the narrative will develop. Suspense can vary from mild to acute, but it is possible to argue that suspense is always present to some degree in those texts that keep us from putting them down or from walking out of the theater. 53–7, 59, 109, 155

Suture: In film, the point at which one fragment or sequence or shot is connected with another. The term connotes the invisibility of these connections.

Symptomatic reading: Decoding a text as symptomatic of the author's unconscious or unacknowledged state of mind, or of unacknowledged cultural conditions. Generally opposed to intentional reading. 97–100, 101–4, 135, 171

Temporal structure: How the time of the narrative discourse relates to the time of the story. There are two major ways in which the time of the narrative discourse can depart from that of the story: 1) by rearranging the order in which events are revealed to us (see prolepsis and analepsis), 2) by expanding or contracting the time devoted to individual events (see retardation).

Text: Used broadly in much, though not all, narrative theory to mean the physical embodiment of the narrative, as book, short story, performed play, film, and so on. Texts, of course, are thought of in common discourse as things composed of words. The broader meaning of the term invoked here rests on the idea that, regardless of the vehicle, narratives are always "read" in the sense that we grasp them through a process of decipherment. Without some understanding of the symbolic code in which the narrative is told, we cannot know what happened.

Theme: A subject (issue, question) that recurs in a narrative through implicit or explicit reference. With motif, theme is one of the two commonest forms of narrative repetition. Where motifs tend to be concrete, themes are abstract. 88–90, 99

Third–person narration: Conventionally, narrative in which the narrator is not a character in the story, and the characters are referred to in the third person ("He did this"; "She says that"). Like first-person narration, the term is not a satisfactory generic classification since third-person narrators can refer to themselves in the first person, and first-person narratives almost invariably abound in stretches of third-person narration. Genette features the cleaner distinction between homo- and heterodiegetic narration. 64–6

Type: A kind of character that recurs in different specific renderings across a range of narrative texts. Oedipus, Othello, and Willy Loman all fit within types of the tragic hero. But characters in narratives are almost invariably compounds of various types. Othello is a compound of the types of the tragic hero, the jealous husband, the outsider, the military hero, the man of eloquence, and the Moor. Willy Loman is a compound of the types of the tragic hero, the optimist, the dreamer, and the salesman. When a character is composed without invention, adhering too closely to type, it is considered a stereotype. Stereotype can also be used more broadly to refer to any literary cliché. 45, 48, 109, 119, 129–33, 136–7, 148–52

Underreading: See overreading.

Unreliable narrator: A narrator whose perceptions and moral sensibilities differ from those of the implied author. There can be degrees of reliability and unreliability among narrators. It is useful to follow Dorrit Cohn in distinguishing between those narrators who are <u>unreliable</u> in their rendering of the facts and those who are reliable in rendering the facts but unreliable in their views. The latter she designates as *discordant narrators*. 63, 69–70, 71–2, 73–4, 77, 109–10, 143

Voice: The sensibility through which we *hear* the <u>narrative</u>, even when we are reading silently. Voice is very closely associated with <u>focalization</u>, the sensibility through which we *see* the characters and events in the story, and sometimes hard to distinguish from it. 64–6, 68, 70–1, 86

Index of authors and narratives